THE TEVIS CUP

THE TEVIS CUP

To Finish is to Win

Marnye Langer

THE LYONS PRESS
Guilford, Connecticut

An imprint of The Globe Pequot Press

The Lyons Press is an imprint of The Globe Pequot Press

10 9 8 7 6 5 4 3 2 1

Printed in the United States of America

Designed by Stephanie Doyle

Map by Stefanie Ward

Library of Congress Cataloging-in-Publication Data

Langer, Marnye.
  The Tevis Cup : to finish is to win / by Marnye Langer.
     p. cm.
  ISBN 1-59228-148-6 (trade cloth)
  1. Tevis Cup Ride. I. Title.
SF296.E5L25 2004
798.2'4—dc22
                                        2003023647

❧ DEDICATION ❧

To my childhood friends from Squaw Valley. How I treasure the hours and days we spent riding in the meadow and in the mountains. Thank you to my one friend, Patty Fox Nuccio, who got this sissy show-ring rider out of the arena and onto the mountain trails. I am forever grateful. And to all my wonderful horses who have carried me into the mountains.

❧ CONTENTS ❧

❧ ACKNOWLEDGMENTS ❧

A project of this nature is only accomplished with the assistance and support of a number of people. While many Tevis Cup ride competitors, veterinarians, volunteers, and ride officials patiently answered my questions, and enthusiastically told me their stories and experiences, a few went the extra mile. Thank you to all of those who shared their stories with me. I wish I could have included them all. Several people were instrumental in the comprehensive nature of this story:

Shannon Weil, of the Western States Trail Foundation office—thank you for providing so much data, pointing me toward interesting people, and proofing this entire book for factual errors. You helped me preserve the spirit of both the ride and the run.

Hal Hall—thank you to you, and your family, for giving me access to your archives, telling me stories, and allowing me to sit on your living room floor by the hour taking notes.

Larry Suddjian—thank you for letting me spend an entire Tevis Cup weekend riding around with you in your blue Blazer we dubbed "Tevis 1." What a great perspective you gave me on the ride.

Mitch Benson and all of the great Tevis Cup vets—thank you for letting me spend so much time with you during the Tevis Cup rides. I recognize the trust you have bestowed in me over the years. I was the journalist in this story who was escorted off the grounds in 1991 during the Haggin Cup judging, prompting Mitch to lobby for a change in its judging presentation. I smile every year when I walk into McCann Stadium on Sunday morning for the Haggin Cup judging.

To John Strassburger, my long-suffering editor at *The Chronicle of the Horse*—over the years I have regularly tried your patience with my Tevis Cup articles that exceeded my assigned maximum word length. One year, when you received a five-thousand-word article instead of the expected two thousand words, you said in exasperation, "Why don't you just write a book?"—You planted the seed.

To Steve Price, the editor of this work—thank you for your patience and insights. You knew when to pat me on the head and say, "Relax, you are doing fine," and you knew when to kick me in the behind.

Finally, to my family—Thanks, Mom, for giving me the best education you could so that I learned how to express myself, and letting me grow up in Squaw Valley during the '70s. Those experiences served as the foundation for this book. Thank you to my husband, Larry, and my son, Ian, for living through the creation of this book. One night as I sat down to write, nine-year-old Ian said, "I will be glad when you get this stupid book done so I can get my mom back," and then in the next sentence asked when the Tevis Cup ride was going to be that year. He looks forward to joining me each year when I go to the ride to gather my stories and write my articles. A dedicated hunter/jumper professional, Larry never knew anything about endurance riding and now speaks authoritatively about the Tevis Cup! Thank you, Larry and Ian, for your patience and your encouragement.

❊ Introduction ❊

Several years ago while riding an elevator in New York, a middle-aged gentleman in a finely tailored three-piece suit boarded with me. As we ascended and people got off and on, he shifted his jacket and I noticed a familiar silver glint. I stared for a moment and then caught his eye and asked quizzically, "Is that a Tevis belt buckle?" Grinning like a little kid who has lost his first tooth, the man parted his jacket to show the entire buckle and said with amazement, "You know what this is?" I nodded. During our short elevator ride (that seemed to last for an hour), he told me about his Tevis Cup ride during the 1970s. He only rode the ride once but he earned a belt buckle which he often wore, especially for important meetings.

For a moment, two complete strangers in the midst of New York City were linked by a silver belt buckle and all that it represents. I don't have one of those belt buckles, but I know what they mean.

I first learned about the Tevis Cup ride when my mom, my brother, and I moved to Squaw Valley in 1975. My horse came with me, and during my first summer I rode in the arena in the Squaw Valley meadow. One of my newfound friends, Patty, invited me to go on a trail ride with her. I was intimidated about riding outside of the arena and I thought Patty wasn't a very good rider because she did not ride with show-ring style; however, I did go trail riding with her that one day, and quickly learned to love it. Her mother, Pat Fox, often took us up to the high country and taught us how to read trail markers, determine direction, and about general trail safety. I don't remember Pat without her Tevis Cup belt buckle, and we often prompted her for stories. Every year we looked forward to the start of the ride and one time we even camped overnight in the high country just so we could cheer for the riders as they passed by Watson's Monument.

∾   ∾   ∾

Over the years Patty and I explored miles of trails. Whenever we got lost we took her mom's advice and just let our horses pick their way. We always made it home. My friend Patty taught me to love riding in the backcountry, and I taught her about the fun of competing in horse shows. To this day, I trail ride my show horses in Griffith Park, near my home in Burbank, California, and Patty still enters an occasional horse show.

The Tevis Cup ride first caught my interest as a child, and when I got the opportunity to write about it for *The Chronicle of the Horse* in 1991, I jumped at the chance. Over the years I grew to love the event. Although I am not an endurance rider, I love the Tevis Cup ride: its history, the trail, and all the people who make it happen. Every year I show up at the ride and like many others, the Tevis Cup is in my blood. The purpose of this book is to tell this event's story, to celebrate the many horses and riders, and so that if you ever see a Tevis Cup belt buckle, you will have an idea of its significance.

➤ FOREWORD ◄

Matthew Mackay-Smith, DVM

This is a book that reaches way beyond its title. Marnye Langer shocks the reader's senses and credulity in the first paragraph, suggesting that persons apparently sane annually repeat an undertaking so quixotically improbable that a passing madness must guide them. As things unfold, three centuries are involved in the conception, gestation, and birth of an equestrian challenge which begat a growing international sport. The author uses didactics, homiletics, and old-fashioned storytelling to engage, inform, and secure our attendance on this remarkable journey.

So much is remarkable here that we first must ground our understanding in the context of the Tevis Cup: its geographic and geologic features, its climatic extremes, the colorful history of its founders, the culture of the horse, and horsemanship in the pioneer West.

The Sierra Nevada is large, young, and rugged, a poster child for the awesome concept of tectonic plate movement. It seems as much perched as planted. Even today the geography rebuffs familiarity, with large expanses rightly reserved as wilderness in perpetuity. Airline travelers feel dwarfed by its topographic dimensions.

The pioneers of the early-twentieth century described here—who both loved these mountains and lusted for their bounty in timber and minerals—were undaunted, visionary, and indomitable. Others' obstacles became their opportunities. Born in the nineteenth century, they were centaurs—wed in mind, heart, and body to the back of a horse, unconscious geniuses in the prudent use of their indispensable four-legged partners. Though riding was a pleasure, they did not ride merely as a pastime. They could not have foreseen the late-twentieth century explosion in riders who don't know horses.

In these pages we meet Wendell Robie, who wanted others to experience the mountains as he knew them—and 100 miles at a time! Already into his late middle age, and accustomed to command, he wanted everyone to go down the trail as fast as they could, but behind him. Since he always went as fast as he prudently could, that was standard enough. But just the mention of one person leading the others was the germ that generated a competition, where at first he saw only participation.

The stories of the yearly rides set a framework in which the reader can see the evolution of the sport of endurance riding that thousands now love and millions know about, an evolution which seeks this grail: how to display the quality of a horse's endurance performance without using up its capacity to endure.

I presume to comment on the context and effect of the Tevis Cup and its kin because of my long and varied experience. I began with the Tevis Cup in 1964. That was the first time I paid money to ride a horse on *any* trail, which I did to accompany my wife. I rode a borrowed horse, Copper Moyle, conditioned for only a few weeks. I came in fifth or sixth with a fresh horse, riding in my pointy-toed spider-killers, jeans, and a ten-gallon straw. Piece of cake! The infection has not lessened in eight or nine subsequent trips—not all finishes, with one first-to-finish—yet all winners, irrespective of my luck on the day.

I presume to add some of my own observations because I am renowned for doing so.

Despite the unique all-around athleticism of the horse, "keeping on keeping on" is what most horses do best. This has been true over the whole ten thousand plus years that man and horse have cooperated to shape human destiny and global change. But this gift of wings to the rider obliges mankind, in return, to be stewards of the horse, to respect and meet his needs from birth through death, at work and rest, in health and decline.

The exhilaration of riding a willing horse in any of its chosen tasks confers a power that seems limitless, but which is ultimately finite, and surprisingly frail.

The three pillars of equine athleticism are speed, strength, and stamina. Racing, pulling a load, and endurance riding each test one of these pillars. While the first two risk mechanical injury, the subtle cumulative effects of long, steady exertion tax basic bodily functions to an extent that can be more threatening. This threat, recognized and avoided by the founders of endurance riding, is now the object of renewed concern among endurance riders.

This book unselfconsciously chronicles a cultural shift in the equestrian world across the second half of the twentieth century. Today, the care of one's horse is rarely driven by practical and commercial necessity. Calling ourselves civilized, we are incorporating horses into a whole culture of caring which dignifies the life of all sentient beings.

Endurance riding, we see in this book, is at the cutting edge of reconciling the exhilarating use of our horses with the obligation to minimize their risks.

This is a book that reaches way beyond its title.

PART ONE

✳ 1 ✳

IN THE BEGINNING . . .

California's Sierra Nevada mountains soar suddenly out of the Nevada desert toward the deep blue sky before beginning their tumultuous descent toward the fertile Sacramento Valley. At their peak, the granite escarpments of the mountains climb above the tree line and then plunge precipitously into canyons and gorges thousands of feet deep and seemingly impenetrable. In this setting riders from all over the world gather annually to test their mettle and that of their horses in the Western States Trail Foundation's famous Western States Trail Ride, Tevis Cup 100 Miles— One Day endurance ride, commonly referred to as the Tevis Cup ride.

What started as a dare in 1954 has evolved into an organized international sport. There was no such thing as "endurance riding" back then, but Wendell Robie and the world-famous Tevis Cup changed all that. Endurance riding is now one of the fastest-growing equestrian sports, and is practiced by many people in all walks of life. The goal is simple: ride your horse along a designated trail or route and complete the distance within a certain amount of time. Along the way, horses are examined by veterinarians to make sure they are not becoming too fatigued. The vets also check for soundness to make sure the horse is not lame or developing an injury that could be detrimental in some manner. These "vet checks" ensure the safety and health of the horses.

Endurance riders like the challenge of conditioning themselves and their horses for distances of fifty, sixty, seventy, and even one hundred miles. With the rise of so many extreme sports in the past twenty years, many can trace their roots back to the very first extreme test of endurance and stamina. Before the Iron Man; before the ultramarathon; before the many other endurance rides featuring horses, there was one event: the Western States Trail Ride, Tevis Cup 100 Miles—One Day.

At the beginning of each year, riders from all over the world send in their applications in the hope of a chance to compete for a Tevis Cup belt buckle given to those who complete the route within the allotted time. Only 250 entrants are allowed on the ride, which is held each year during the summer full moon, in mid-July to early August. Because the horses and riders must travel at night, the schedule of the ride follows the full moon, rather than a set date in the calendar.

However, the Tevis Cup is much more than a single event, and much more than just an endurance ride. The Tevis Cup transcends ordinary status, and has grown into something very special. If there was a medal for endurance riding, undoubtedly it would be awarded to the winner of the Tevis Cup, for a Tevis Cup belt buckle is like an Olympic gold, or a Super Bowl ring, or a World Series title. However, the Tevis Cup is about much more than being the first to ride across the finish line—it is an adventure and a pilgrimage. The Tevis Cup is a journey of the mind, the body, and the spirit through a remote wilderness bisected by an arduous trail that remains much as immigrants in the mid-1800s experienced it. Many come to the Tevis Cup not for the result, but for the journey and the experiences it reveals.

My alarm beeps at 4:15 A.M. and for a moment I am tempted to roll over and go back to sleep, but then I remember what lies ahead of me. Today, this special day, I am going to ride my horse one hundred miles over some of the most rigorous trail in the world, and I have twenty-four hours to accomplish the task. I crawl from my sleeping bag and peer out of my tent. The stars still pepper the sky and at this high elevation they shine like a million diamonds scattered across the inky black of the galaxy. The air is crisp and cold, filled with the aroma of the fragrant pines surrounding me. I hear other riders begin to move around, horses stamp their hooves, and gradually this little section of the forest comes alive.

My horse has been munching on hay all night and will need every ounce of energy the feed will provide, for in the day to come there will be little time to eat and rest. Today, I am going to ask him to climb mountain peaks where the air is thin and few plants grow, then descend into canyons along trails etched into the walls, wending their way down more than two thousand feet. Gradually we will make our way through the mountains, to the foothills, and will emerge one hundred miles later with stories that will last a lifetime, as they have for so many others.

Two hundred forty-nine other riders and their horses will be undertaking the same path, but each will tell a different story. Only half of us will make it to the finish and earn a coveted Tevis Cup buckle, our public badge in an elite fraternity of riders.

It is now 4:45. I climb on my horse for the short walk to the starting line set in the forest. Other riders are congregating, and there are low murmurs as people make that last check for a sponge, a water bottle, horse treats, and energy bars. Occasionally a horse nickers, and many play with their bits, creating a clanking symphony of excited horses. Some prance to the start, eager to attack the mountains that lie before them and to face the challenges this historic trail presents. Others are more reserved, perhaps understanding that they must conserve every ounce of energy for the upcoming test.

Our various crews, the family members and friends who volunteered to help us in our quest, shout words of encouragement, last minute reminders, and a "See you down the trail!" They will be waiting for us throughout the day at designated spots along the trail, but for most of the time we will be traveling through remote wilderness.

We mill toward the starting line, becoming more compressed and anxious. I want to get out of this mass of horseflesh, for it reminds me of the busy freeways of the cities. I yearn for the backcountry solitude where I will spend much of my next twenty-four hours. I will ride with groups of other riders for a while, and then spend time with just myself and my horse, deep in the Sierra Nevada mountain range. Every thirty miles or so I will come to a rest stop, where I will briefly rejoin humanity, and my crew, before heading out on my trek again. Ultimately I hope to ride into Auburn, California, at the end of my journey with a sound horse and a lifetime's worth of memories and experiences from this ride through the mountains.

Darkness still permeates the sky although sunrise will greet us within the hour. Already the dark of the night is giving way to a faint glow in the east, but we are too deep in the forest to see the coming of dawn. Five o'clock and we are off. Some gallop ahead, eager to get a good start. Like many others, I settle into an easy pace, for I must help my horse find his stride. Although he has been trained and prepared for long distances, I am his guardian and I have a responsibility to make this passage safely. In the first few miles the riders spread out and ride in small clumps. Once I cross the Truckee River just a few miles ahead, I will enter into Squaw Valley, site of the 1960 Winter Olympics. Once riders negotiated the valley floor, passing houses in the early morning hours as they headed toward the first of the mighty mountain faces. Now we traverse the southern edge of the valley along a small ridge that divides Squaw Valley and Alpine Valley. Riding through the trees, I glimpse the large mountain meadow below me. Squaw Creek wends it way along the valley floor on its journey to join with the Truckee River. In these early hours, I cannot see the creek, but only its misty shroud snaking its way through the lush summer grasses.

The trail leads me out to the rocky slopes of KT-22, one of three major peaks comprising the world-famous slopes of Squaw Valley. In the winter the area is buried in more than ten feet of snow, and is among some of the most difficult skiing terrain in the United States—some say the world. The summer terrain is no easier. Instead of snow, my horse and I pick our way through rocks, and for the next several hours we will concentrate on every footstep, ensuring we are on solid footing. For at least an hour I ride across these slopes—Olympic Lady, KT-22, the 75 Chute—and then begin a more noticeable ascent. Although the trail has been gradually rising across the mountain face, my climb now begins in earnest. On my left is Squaw Peak and on my right, Granite Chief. I am heading for the gap, the saddle between the two peaks, known as Emigrant Pass. Watson's Monument greets me at the top, a large tower of rocks commemorating the man who rediscovered this historic trail.

Atop the divide of the mighty Sierra Nevada, for a moment my horse and I will pause on the precarious ridge before beginning our long descent. Behind me lies Squaw Valley, further off Lake Tahoe sparkles in the early morning sun, and further still are the sheer eastern slopes of these majestic mountains. Before me unfolds the entirety of the Sierra, and for a moment I feel as if I am perched on the summit of the world.

Throughout, I am confronted by the wonders and unique attributes of the Sierra Nevada, and I wonder how they came to be.

❋ 2 ❋

THE SIERRA NEVADA MOUNTAINS

In the late nineteenth century John Muir, who made the mountains his second home, wrote, "It seemed to me that the Sierra should be called, not the Nevada or Snowy Range, but the Range of Light." These mountains have challenged and inspired many. The early Spaniards who came to California in the late sixteenth century dubbed this impressive range Sierra Nevada, or "snowy mountains." Yosemite and Sequoia National Parks are both found here. The Sierra Club, founded by Muir, derives its name from these mountains as well. In its almost five-hundred-mile length, the Sierra Nevada is a study in geologic diversity, boasting eight national parks, a multitude of federally designated wilderness areas, and enough history to comprise a college course.

This is the largest single mountain range in the contiguous United States. Although the Rocky Mountains and the Appalachians may seem larger, they are actually considered mountain systems, chains of smaller mountain ranges linked together over long distances. In fact, the Sierras comprise an area that equals the Swiss, French, and Italian Alps combined. Located along the eastern border of California, the range is fifty to eighty miles wide, and features the tallest peak in the continental United States, Mount Whitney. At 14,496 feet, this mountain is home to the world's tallest trees—the Giant Sequoia—and the world's oldest trees—the last great stands of bristlecone pine. This imposing range presented a barrier to California for many years, and once immigrants began their trek to the Golden State, many veered north through Oregon to avoid the perilous range. Even the native tribes found travel daunting, and often deadly in winter.

California's agricultural breadbasket, the Sacramento and San Joaquin Valleys owe their existence to the great mountain range to the east. An enviable combination of rich soil carried from mountain streams and ample rain, as Pacific storms are stopped by the mountains, make this area the country's leading agricultural producer.

The Sierra Nevada is a geologic wonder, exhibiting both stunning beauty and treacherous terrain. The oldest rock found in the Sierra Nevada dates back five hundred million years, to a time when the area was under a huge sea, its coastline far to the east. About two hundred million years ago, the Sierra Nevada range as we now know it began to take shape. Once home to an inland sea, today geologists and hikers on the eastern slope find many fossil remains as proof of its oceanic roots.

Underwater vents and volcanoes created the range's bedrock, adding material, layer upon layer, from deep within the earth to the forming mountain range. Heat and pressure slowly changed the underlying bedrock to a form referred to as hornfels, an even, fine-grained metamorphic rock characteristic of the Sierras, which includes quartzite, schist, and slate.

Tremendous geologic forces heaved the rock upwards, bending and sheering rock as if it were as soft as dough. Hikers and horseback riders will attest to the amazing vertical rock faces and sudden changes in terrain.

Veins of gold, silver, and quartz formed. These served as a siren, calling men to mine the riches buried within the mountain range. The mountains would tempt these "Forty-Niners" with bits of gold lying in stream beds. However, the richest veins still lay deep beneath the surface.

During this same time period, the mountain range's enormous granitic spine was forming. Huge masses of granite pushed up from deep within the earth and then cooled above the older metamorphic rock of earlier eras. The Sierra Nevada is a virtual exhibit of many types of granitic rock, pieced together by thousands of plutons that formed huge conglomerates of varying types of volcanic rock known as batholiths, shaping the backbone of the splintery high sierra peaks. Yosemite's spectacular Half Dome is an example of such a granite intrusion. Granite gives the Sierra Nevada its grandeur, the extremes of its terrains, and magnificence of its vistas. As this type of rock cools, it forms sharp joints, yielding the steep, splintered rock faces found in the high country. Huge faces of protruding granite will also sheet, like a large, rocky onion, peeling away layer upon layer of its rocky face.

By sixty-five million years ago, while the rock continued solidifying in the heart of the range, clay and silt formed layer upon layer along the marshy western slopes. As the surrounding forests grew and died, they combined with the underlying greenstone and serpentine to create the red clay and soil so characteristic of the western foothills of the Sierra Nevada. Many an early settler bemoaned the fine red dirt that permeated everything, and quickly turned whites to a shade of pink.

Thirty million years ago when the mountains erupted, they began to grow to their majestic heights of today. Hot ash exploded from fissures and was carried on air currents where it settled hundreds of miles away. Heavier material formed the striking high-altitude plateaus commonly found in the northern end of the range, producing cinder cones, domes, and calderas that one can still see today—testament to the Sierra Nevada's volcanic growth.

Much of the chaotic terrain found throughout the descent from the high country is cooled mudflow, devoid of much plant life. Rocks are a common obstacle on the Western States Trail, and many riders have bemoaned the rock that bruises a horse's hoof and eliminates their Tevis Cup dreams, veterans often reminiscing about the "rock with their name on it," somewhere up in the high country.

A little over one million years ago, ice crept in and permeated the mountain range; like a many-tentacled beast, it made its way into crevices, canyons, and valleys. All but the highest of the Sierra peaks were covered in ice and snow; whipped by the wind, and polished clean, the result is the spectacular gleaming of these peaks today, as the sun catches them.

The largest of glaciers formed in these high mountain valleys, where the cool temperatures allowed snow to accumulate for hundreds of years. In their path these immense glaciers remodeled the mountain landscape, carving out valleys with walls as smooth as glass, and resulting in the spectacular canyons seen today. Tevis Cup riders spend hours traversing the American River Canyon, first descending to its depths and then climbing back up to wind along a ridge, only to drop down to the bottom again. All the while, the river loosely guides them on their long downward journey; the riders face the geologic history of the Sierra Nevada up close and personally.

The Sierra Nevada reach heights of up to nine thousand feet in the Lake Tahoe and Donner areas. The main ridge is known as the Crystal

Range, for the white peaks that remain well into the summer months. Even when the snow eventually melts, its polished granite face shines almost as bright. Through these massive, sheer, granite mountains wends the Western States Trail, a route traveled by Indians, miners, immigrants, and now, modern-day horses and their riders, on a quest made all the more challenging by the mountains they seek to cross.

❧ 3 ❧

HISTORY OF THE TRAIL

Throughout the entire westward movement, the Sierra Nevada's high peaks, rugged terrain, and deep snowpack made entering California from the east an almost insurmountable task. In fact, Sierra Nevada routes into California were the last major routes traversed by immigrants.

Prior to the 1849 gold rush, the Sierra Nevada mountains, especially around Lake Tahoe, were inhabited primarily by the Washoe tribe. As settlers moved westward, crossing the Sierra Nevada created even more challenges than did the Rocky Mountains. The high elevation combined with steep canyons made the mountain range seem impenetrable. Because of their close proximity to the Pacific Ocean, the Sierra Nevada had a much deeper and wetter snowpack, and frequently snow remains in the high country well into June, or even July. Because of the early winters and the late snowmelt, there are only several months when the Sierra Nevada are free of snow. Because of these conditions, the few non-Mexican settlers arrived either by an arduous ocean voyage, or overland through Oregon.

Two intrepid mountain men opened up routes for the stream of immigrants who came following the cry of "Gold!", or seeking a new life. In 1826, California was finally entered via a land route when Jedediah Smith took a southern route skirting the Sierra Nevada range, and came into the Los Angeles basin across the Mojave Desert. After almost losing a large number of his party, he reasoned that the desert route was not viable.

Joseph Walker set out upon a quest for new routes into California while in the employ of Benjamin Bonneville, a captain in the U.S. Army. Although records are hazy, the story goes that Bonneville took leave of the Army to pursue the lucrative fur trade in the northwest territories of the

United States. However, there is also solid evidence that this was a cover for his more important mission: to spy on the Mexican government based in Monterey. Bonneville needed to get to California, and in 1832 sent Walker to make the first foray. Walker was considered one of the greatest of the mountain men and explorers, and Bonneville asked him to find a mountain route into California. Instead of heading south, as Smith did, Walker headed west across Nevada, and followed what is now known as the Humboldt River.

Walker and his men scaled Tioga Pass, and became the first white men to set eyes on the Yosemite Valley. While the ascent of the great mountain range proved very difficult, the descent was even more perilous. The crossing took longer than Walker anticipated, and the party ran low on provisions. Starving and trudging through deep snow, Walker's party came upon a precipice. The great San Joaquin Valley spread below them, but they were faced with a two-thousand-foot drop. Native Americans had warned Walker of the difficulty in crossing the range: "Rock on rock, snow on snow, and even if you get over the snow you will not be able to get down from the mountain." Walker and his party backtracked, and eventually descended the steep canyon to make their way down out of the mountain range. The Sierra Nevada had finally been crossed, and Walker did not lose a single man.

The next year when Walker led his party out of California to report back to Bonneville, he attempted a more southerly route outside of Bakersfield. Walker's Pass, as it came to be known, proved completely unsuitable for wagon trains.

By the 1840s another route north of Walker's first crossing was developed. It diverged from Walker's Pass around Reno, followed the Truckee River, and then traversed the infamous Donner Pass. In the winter of 1846–47, members of the ill-fated Donner party, against the advice of the more experienced members of the group, began the Sierra crossing with the approach of autumn. Snow came early that winter, and the group was trapped on the summit near a small mountain lake that would later come to bear their name, Donner Lake. Out of food, the party resorted to cannibalism during one of the worst winters on record for that region. Although most of the women and children survived, the Donner party's tragedy made the route famous and proved to the world the difficulty in crossing the Sierra Nevada.

The lure of great profits from gold and silver in both the Sierra Nevada gold fields and the silver mines in Nevada drove men to find a way through the mountain range. Miners sought reliable links between the silver lodes in Nevada and Sacramento in order to test their assays and ship their precious metals. In 1849 this link was a rarely used Native American trail. At its eastern edge, the trail emanated from Carson City and ascended the Carson Pass before dropping down into the Lake Tahoe Basin. From there the trail followed the lake northward to the natural outlet for the Truckee River, at its northwest corner where modern-day Tahoe City, California, is based. The trail then meandered northward along the Truckee River for about five miles until it reached the intersection with Squaw Creek. Heading west, the trail followed the creek into a large, high mountain valley of over five hundred acres into what became known as Squaw Valley. After passing through the large meadow, the trail made its way up to Emigrant Pass along the ridge of the east–west divide of the Sierras. The trail then began a long descent west toward Sacramento. Following the general direction of the Middle Fork of the American River, the trail reached Michigan Bluff, a small mining town nestled in the foothills of the Sierra Nevada before reaching Sacramento some sixty miles further west. Scott's Route, as the trail was known, provided the shortest crossing of the Sierra Nevada. The Tevis Cup follows this route from Squaw Valley westward.

With the advent of the gold rush, leaders in Placer County wanted to make Scott's Route a major thoroughfare. The area encompassed a major portion of the gold-filled Sierra Nevada foothills, up into the Donner and Truckee area, and south to Squaw Valley. By improving Scott's Route, Placer County would attract the new immigrants and the money they would generate.

Placer County spent $20,000 to improve the trail and called it the Placer County Emigrant Route. For three years traffic increased, then declined. Although the shortest of the trans–Sierra routes, Scott's Route was simply too difficult. The steep climbs, loose shale, and granite escarpments were daunting to all but the most intrepid of men and surefooted horses. In many places it was not possible to maintain a track wide enough for a wagon, even if it could be hauled up the steep passes and down the near-vertical drops. Although travel across the Sierra Nevada was difficult at best, immigrants found Carson, Donner, and Johnson passes more inviting. Once again, Scott's Route languished.

∾   ∾   ∾

Fame almost struck the area again. On November 22, 1857, two miners, Ethan Allen Grosch and Richard M. Bucke, carried the secrets to the Comstock Silver Mine. Their claims, assays, specimens, and charts would reveal one of the largest silver mines in the United States, which would be theirs if they could only get to Sacramento to file the necessary documents. With winter setting in they did not have time to take the Donner Pass, so they decided to take the formidable Scott's Route through Squaw Valley. The two men faced a fresh snowstorm as they made the ascent, and were repelled several times by the extreme weather. The deep snow made travel impossible. Although low on supplies, the men had to get across the Sierra Nevada to ensure their claim to the Comstock lode. When the weather relented, they crossed Emigrant Pass and for a moment stood on the crest of the Sierra Nevada. However, the pair were too weak—and too desperate—to notice or care. They began their way west only to become hopelessly lost and bogged down in the deep snow. When another blizzard set in, Grosch and Bucke decided to bury their evidence to lighten their load and improve their chances of surviving the journey.

On December 5, nearly fifteen days later, a party of Mexican miners found the two nearly dead men and took them to Last Chance, a small mining enclave. Grosch died and Bucke had part of his leg amputated to save his life. Once recovered, he returned home to Canada and made no attempt to go back and find his buried treasure. Grosch and Bucke were the first true discoverers of the Comstock Lode, but their secret remained trapped in the high country, undiscovered for almost another year.

In the late 1860s Placer County again attempted to improve the route to lure travelers. This effort at revitalization was thwarted by the completion of the transcontinental railroad in 1869, and never again was a serious attempt made to promote the route as a main thoroughfare into California. The route would become famous—but not in ways historians would have imagined.

The crossing through Squaw Valley remained in use over the decades. In 1863, a rumor of gold and other valuable ores in diminutive Squaw Creek and the nearby Truckee River brought a flurry of activity. Land prices were greatly inflated. Once assays proved the rush was phony, Squaw Valley and the surrounding area were abandoned just as quickly as they had been populated. Many other "mini" rushes were fueled by rumors that led to hastily built towns. Most fell into disuse, but a few became established. One short-lived rush did lead to the establishment of Tahoe City, which became a cornerstone of the development and expansion of the entire Tahoe-Truckee region.

Aerial view of Squaw Valley from the north near Emigrant Pass (Watson's Monument), looking south; Lake Tahoe in the background, circa 1960. [Courtesy of Western SkiSport Museum]

By 1872 Squaw Valley was bustling with activity, at least in the summer, and by the standards of the time. The valley floor, lush with native grasses, yielded several tons of hay by the end of summer. A water-powered shingle mill produced 275,000 cedar shingles. Quality timber surrounded the high mountain meadow, and there was plenty of fish and wildlife available.

As the valuable ores died out, many men found other and greater riches within the vast Sierra Nevada. Timber became a major industry.

Once the easy timber along flatter areas at the bases of canyons had been cleared, lumberjacks headed up the steep canyon sides. They constructed timber chutes made of felled trees and greased them slick. Logs falling into the chutes would hurtle down the mountainsides at upwards of seventy miles per hour, plunging into a river or pool below. Some of the hardier lumberjacks rode the logs down the chutes and then jumped off before the log free-fell into the pool of water. If the log rider's timing was off, he would be crushed by the other logs floating in the holding pond before they were rafted to the sawmill further downstream.

Tourism arrived with the dawn of the new century, and the region attracted several hotels and spas for city dwellers from San Francisco and other urban areas who made their way to the high mountain retreats to enjoy the crisp air, crystal blue skies, and incredible vistas. Although primitive, the lodges were considered exclusive retreats, but it took the most hardy and intrepid travelers to make the difficult mountain trek. A primitive road existed for those lucky enough to own a car and handy enough to keep it repaired and running. Cars traveled what became Highway 40, and eventually U.S. Interstate 80, roughly parallel in route to the Central Pacific Railroad. Once travelers passed through the logging and railroad town of Truckee—which long claimed to have a higher elevation than it had population—they headed south along the narrow-gauge railway running along the Truckee River to Tahoe City. One of the most notable retreats was the Deer Park Springs Inn located in what became known as Alpine Meadows, just south of Squaw Valley.

With the increase in automobile traffic, many of the old foot and wagon trails began to disappear back into the wilderness. Road builders chose the easiest of the rigorous mountain passes, many of which paralleled established rail lines. Often these routes followed old trails, but some of the more difficult trails receded back into the wilderness.

The Tahoe region in the 1920s and 1930s was a rough-and-tumble lot of frontier individuals. Robert Montgomery Watson, a prominent citizen of the area, served as sheriff of Tahoe City and the surrounding enclaves for many years. Watson also served as a guide for the burgeoning tourism industry. The hardy souls who made the trek often engaged Watson to guide them into the surrounding mountains, high-country meadows, and crystalline lakes.

Watson was one of the few men in the area who could recognize and follow the old trails. He noted that all that remained of some sections of trails were the blazes in the trees. Early mountain men carved large square "eights" deep into the bark of pine trees to mark their routes. The sap would bleed into the cuts and form a prominent signature for all to see. Trailblazers also built cairns—piles of rock that formed a small pyramid about two feet tall—but cairns were not a reliable trail marker, as the deep winter snows obliterated all signs of a route. The tree blazes served as the most reliable year-round signposts for those who dared travel the remote trails.

Concerned at the loss of the trails, Watson rallied his peers in Parlor 59 of the Native Sons of the Golden West to join him in the task of identifying the old immigrant route that once linked the silver mines of Nevada's Carson Valley to the many gold camps of the Sierra Nevada foothills. This was a fraternal organization dedicated to preserving the history and legacy of western Americana. The men of Parlor 59 began their task in September of 1931, and succeeded in marking the entire length of the route, from Auburn to Tahoe City. The Western States Trail, as it was renamed—one of the few remaining historic trails that bisects the Sierra Nevada—continues to offer a route largely untouched by civilization. Those negotiating the trail today face many of the same challenges, perils, and difficulties encountered by those who crossed more than 150 years ago.

In the winter of 1850–51, Scandinavian sailors who had jumped ship to become miners introduced the first skis to the west. These skis, up to fourteen feet long, provided an effective means of travel, so that for the first time the impenetrable Sierra Nevada became accessible even in the winter.

With little work activity in the winter, skiing flourished. Ski clubs formed and competition followed. John A. "Snowshoe" Thompson is regarded as the most notable skier and outdoorsman of the era. In addition to rarely losing a race, he could cover distances of up to ninety miles carrying packs weighing as much as one hundred pounds. Thompson regularly crossed treacherous passes in the dead of winter that few dared traverse even in the snowless summer, delivering much of the winter mail throughout the region. He and his kind contributed to year-round civilization in the heart of the Sierra Nevada.

Ladies preparing for a ski race, circa 1880. [Courtesy of Western SkiSport Museum]

Although Squaw Valley and the surrounding areas are considered by many as the birthplace of skiing in North America, for several decades this area and the sport languished. Except for the mountain men, skiing had not yet become known on the west coast. But in 1934, the fortune of the valley changed when a young man named Wayne Poulson bought most of the valley floor and its environs, convincing investors to purchase much of the surrounding mountainous land. They began building a few ski lifts, and in 1949 Squaw Valley was on its way to becoming one of the country's premier ski resorts. Alex Cushing, one of the main investors in the ski resort, put together a bid for Squaw Valley to host the 1960 Winter Olympics. The International Olympic Committee accepted the bid, and Squaw Valley was thrust into the international spotlight.

For twenty years Tevis Cup riders started their travels in the meadow of this world-famous ski area. And it was skiing, a winter sport, that was the precursor to a brand-new sport based on an age-old challenge: endurance riding.

*Putting snow on the ski jump for the 1933 Berkeley competition.
More than 75,000 spectators attended the event.* [Courtesy of
Western SkiSport Museum]

❧ 4 ❧

WENDELL ROBIE:
A MAN OF VISION AND DETERMINATION

Many great things begin with an idea, often the vision of an individual. If the idea is truly great, it can transcend even its founders and take on a life of its own. Wendell Robie germinated the seed of an idea that would become Western States Trail, Tevis Cup 100 Miles—One Day Ride; more commonly referred to as the Tevis Cup.

Robie was a colorful and very influential character in his hometown area of Auburn, California, but his influence extends throughout the Lake Tahoe area. He was opinionated, strong-willed, even domineering, but he also had a passion for life. He was not afraid of a challenge, preferably met from the back of a good horse.

Robie's parents lived in the Auburn area, a small town in the foothills of the Sierra Nevada about thirty miles east of Sacramento. Robie's father, E.T., ran a lumber mill. Wendell was born in 1895, and grew up playing in the woods, hanging around the local town, and just being a kid. Although his parents were not interested in horses, Robie was fascinated by the creatures. In the fall of 1902 a couple of cowboys drove some scraggly mustangs through Auburn with the goal of selling them to the area folk. Mesmerized, seven-year-old Robie followed the three cowboys and their little herd. When they stopped just outside town, Robie hung out and watched as they settled the horses. Impulsively, the little boy dashed home, broke open his piggy bank, and returned with his fortune of twenty dollars, which he handed over in exchange for a rank, unbroke little mare.

Robie knew nothing about horses or horsemanship, let alone training a wild horse, but he was tough, and persevered. Every time the horse flung Robie to the ground, he got up, dusted himself off, and climbed back on, never thinking he could fail. Although his father was not happy about Robie's purchase, other family members convinced him that having a horse would teach the young boy responsibility and a work ethic. A small business owner, E.T. Robie prized those attributes and wanted to instill them in his son. Robie spent a lot of time on the ground during the first few months he owned the little mare that he fondly referred to as a pony, both as an endearment and because of her small size. Gradually, however, she became accustomed to the little kid who wouldn't let her alone. Soon Robie could sit on the mare, and before long he was riding her through town.

E.T. insisted that his son take part in the family business. Although Robie's entrance into the business world wasn't exactly what his father imagined, Robie showed great imagination and tenacity. He got off to an early start by helping deliver bills aboard his pony. He could pretend to be a Pony Express rider delivering the latest news to eagerly waiting Californians, as well as letters from loved ones and news of the nation's capital. Robie also became a self-appointed bill collector. If someone was a slow pay, young Robie would badger him to the point where it was easier to pay up rather than than face the boy on his pony. During Robie's childhood, his father also received a charter to open a savings and loan. Unbeknown to Robie, his father was leaving him a legacy of viable businesses that would support his family and allow him to pursue his passions. Using his own business acumen, creativity, and tenacity, he was able to grow the two companies into dominant businesses known throughout Placer County.

In keeping with his father's vision, Robie headed off to the University of California at Berkeley to study forestry. Robie had difficulty in the confines of academia, and returned home a year later after pulling one too many pranks at the university. A friend once described Robie's time at Berkeley rather ironically: "The world was young and delightfully encouraged new ideas."

Shortly afterwards, Robie attended the University of Arizona. His father wanted his son to complete his education, and he had interest in a lumberyard in nearby Benson, so Robie lived and worked in Benson and commuted to Tucson for classes. One day Robie spotted a lovely girl named Inez on the arm of a prominent football player, and was totally smitten. Throughout life Robie pursued his desires with a single-minded devotion. When he saw something he wanted, he went after it with fierce determination; "can't" was not a word in his vocabulary.

Although Robie knew little of football and cared even less for the game, he tried out for the cheerleading team so that he could be close to Inez and get to know her. As with almost anything he attempted, Robie succeeded, and was soon a member of the cheerleading squad. Robie was relentless in his pursuit of Inez, but she remained merely cordial.

For a second time Robie's strong personality and temper got him in trouble at school, and once again he was expelled for unruly behavior. Even so, Robie remained determined to catch Inez's attentions. He learned that she sang in a church choir and, though he was not a religious man, he joined the parish and was soon a member of the choir. Finally Inez agreed to go out with Robie, mostly in hopes of getting rid of him. She was taken by his strong personality and charm, however, and on September 6, 1916, they were married. While Robie worked at the lumberyard in Benson, Inez finished her degree at the university. The young couple settled in Benson, Arizona, where Robie continued his forestry work. In 1917 Inez gave birth to their only child, John.

Robie's larger-than-life personality led to many stories and legends about the man. One of the earliest showcases his determination and heroic nature. The story goes that a young boy in Robie's town became quite ill and desperately needed medicine from Tucson, forty miles away. The roads were impassable due to floods and night was setting in, so Robie saddled up his horse and headed out. All night he pushed through the high desert landscape, and arrived in Tucson in the morning. He covered the rugged countryside and the eighty-mile round trip in less than twenty-four hours. He delivered the medicine, the boy was saved, and the story became legend. The fact frequently omitted from this Robie story is that the ailing boy was Robie's own son, John. He rode for the life of his son and the heart of his wife. In addition, the impact of his eighty-mile ride planted a seed that germinated and grew years later.

With the timber industry in a slump, E.T. decided that divesting himself of the Arizona-based business was best. Besides, he wanted Wendell and his new family closer to home. Robie joined his father at the Auburn Lumber Company and eventually at the savings and loan. Both were good businesses, and Robie threw himself into their operations. At that time, railroad lines were expanding in the area, and the Robies' lumberyard supplied much of the timber needed for the railroad ties. Robie also continued his passion with horses. He spent hours and hours timber cruising, which exposed him to much of the backcountry of the Sierra Nevada. He enjoyed both the solitude and the magnificence of the area. At that time some of the old-growth Douglas fir, their girths exceeding twenty feet across, still existed in some of the most remote areas. Much of the old-growth was harvested during the nineteenth century, but the extremes of this rugged terrain kept early timber harvesters from some of its deepest canyons. Improved technology allowed the men of Robie's era to harvest some of these huge trees, though some very large specimens remain to this day.

Robie came to know many of the prominent and interesting characters throughout Placer County, from Auburn to the Lake Tahoe region. Robert Montgomery Watson became a fixture in Robie's life, and an integral part of the creation of the ride known as the Tevis Cup. Watson spent time in the territory of Alaska in the final decade of the 1800s, mining, trapping, and trailblazing. He returned to the Tahoe area in 1900, and became a noted guide for the fledgling tourism business involving hunting, fishing, and hiking. Watson also became the constable of Tahoe City, still a rugged, frontier-like area. The Placer County seat was a hundred miles and a mountain range away; local law enforcement was needed, and Watson was the man. One of his passions was identifying and preserving old immigrant routes through the Sierra Nevada. Because of their shared interests, it was only a matter of time before Robie and Watson met. The bond between the two individuals was immediate.

Living in Auburn, on the edge of civilization and a distance from cultural events, Robie was drawn to the winter pastimes of dogsledding and skiing. In early 1929, Robie, Watson, and several others were recounting their adventures in the recently completed three-day, ninety-six-mile Lake Tahoe–Truckee Dog Sled Derby. As the liquor flowed, their tales turned to the heady days of the gold rush and the many different routes through the mountains used by the intrepid men of that era. Watson lamented that the old Emigrant Road passing through Squaw Valley had all but vanished. The men, all avid outdoorsmen who appreciated and valued the history of the area, vowed to meet in September of the next year when cattle and sheep were driven from the high mountain pastures down into the Sacramento area. They would spend several days riding the old route and marking it to preserve its illustrious history.

Although Watson spent much of the next summer identifying the high-country sections of the old trail, the September meeting did not happen. Again in 1930 the men failed to meet. In the meantime, Robie's interest in the history of the area led him to join the Native Sons of the Golden West; he was drawn to the older members who remembered times when the west was still wild and a man had to live by his wits.

Encountering others who shared his passion, Robie decided to make sure the September meeting happened. The party consisted of Robie, Watson, Earl Lukens, Doc Briner, Bill Patrick, and Jack Shields. Lukens ran the hardware store in Auburn and was well respected as a packer. Shields was the son of John Shields, a Placer County surveyor. Robie assumed the role of photographer and recording historian. Doc Briner lugged along a 16-mm camera to record the group's adventures.

Despite an early winter storm that dropped a few inches of snow on the high country, Robie and his group set off and, after a day's ride, they arrived at Robinson Flat. Fortunately the weather warmed and much of the snow melted, thus making the thirty-mile trek to the crest of the Sierra range a bit easier. The group followed the route rediscovered by Watson, and alongside some of the old tree blazes, made a century earlier, they nailed new, modern metal signs emblazoned with "Tahoe–Auburn Trail—NSGW." A few of the old metal signs placed by these Native Sons of the Golden West can still be found more than eighty years later, though many have been taken as souvenirs.

When they reached the Sierra's great crest, on the granite ridge looking east into Squaw Valley and west toward the vast Sacramento Valley, the men paused to celebrate. Using granite rocks and quartz Watson had gathered below, the group built a large rock monument on the crest of Emigrant Pass. Named Watson's Monument, it commemorates the many immigrants and miners who dared test this most difficult route.

At the end of their three-day ride through the backcountry, the men returned home and went their separate ways. Where the others put the adventure in the back of their minds, Robie could not forget his experience. He remained fascinated with the area's rugged terrain, and the idea of traveling in the footsteps of early explorers.

With the trail rediscovered and identified, none of the men realized the significance of their actions. Even Robie did not envision that the Lake Tahoe–Auburn Trail would become world-famous and host to two groundbreaking events. As the deep snow piled up on the Sierra Nevada's brilliant granite crest during the short winter days, business throughout the area slowed. Stories of old-time skiers intrigued Robie and his peers. They wanted to try skiing, but there were no skis available. One day while looking through a catalog at the lumber company, Robie came across some skis carried by a company based in Chicago. He ordered a few pairs and they flew off the rack. He ordered a few more, and then a few more. After selling more than forty pairs, Robie decided it was time to organize, so he and several other enthusiasts formed the Auburn Ski Club. Years later, lessons learned organizing the sport of skiing on the west coast served him well when it came time to put his vision of a one-hundred-mile trail ride into place.

The newly formed club convinced Placer County supervisors to allow them to use land above the two-lane Highway 40. Using mules and plows, club members built the first ski jump in California. When Pacific Gas & Electric informed the Auburn Ski Club that they were using land owned by the utility, Robie used his creative problem-solving talents when he countered with a proposal to PG&E: that the club would take the PG&E linemen who were assigned to the mountain areas and train them to ski. If the linemen could traverse their mountain routes throughout the winter, PG&E could keep the power on, thus building business for the utility. In exchange, the Auburn Ski Club leased the land for their skiing activities for one dollar per year.

In the 1930s skiers had to be hardy. Equipment was primitive, the ski hills were rough, and roads were not plowed after the first big storm of the winter. Locals along Highway 40 hand-shoveled the routes because they wanted tourists and their dollars.

Auburn Ski Club member Senator Cassidy submitted a bill to his colleagues in the state legislature that proposed plowing Highway 40 throughout the winter and to offset the cost with a gas tax. His fellow legislators were skeptical. Robie got involved. To make their point, club members convened at the state capitol in Sacramento, and ferried the legislators up Highway 40 to the ski club. Word got out, and more than one thousand cars followed the caravan up the mountain, where they were embraced by a glorious, sunny, crisp winter's day. Guests were awed by the spectacular setting; the Auburn Ski Club could not have scripted a more perfect day. Spectators enjoyed skiing demonstrations, and sipped on "mountain dew," a rare treat in the era of Prohibition. Inhibitions relaxed to the point where several legislators even strapped on a pair of skis and tried the fledgling sport.

Traffic was heavy returning along the two-lane road, which encouraged Senator Cassidy's bill to pass unanimously. Highway 40 and subsequent trans–Sierra routes have been kept clear ever since. No longer was rail the only way to ship goods across California's rocky eastern barrier.

With increased traffic, Highway 40 expanded and became what is known today as Interstate 80. With the expansion of the highway, once again the ski club had to relocate to property they found near Cisco Grove, higher up the mountains at about five thousand feet. Robie and key club members oversaw construction of the first championship ski jump in California. As interest in skiing grew, the California Ski Association was formed. Robie, a member of the largest club in California, was elected CSA's first president. In 1932 the West Coast hosted the 1932 National Ski Championships, and Robie's club hosted the first slalom and giant slalom events held there. They even revived the gold-mining era downhill events and races. To help train future skiing stars, in 1932 Robie enticed Roy Mikkelson of Minnesota to come to California. The Swedish native split time between work at Robie's lumberyard and the steep Sierra slopes. Mikkelson represented the Auburn Ski Club twice at the U.S. Ski Jumping Championships, and he even skied on the U.S. ski team at the Olympics. Other members of the club participated in the 1932 and 1936 Olympics and won several national titles. Under Robie's direction, the Auburn Ski Club formed a rescue patrol, a group of men trained to deal with accidents and other emergencies. This elite group eventually became part of the well-respected National Ski Patrol.

Ever the visionary, Robie was not content with the relatively small number of people enjoying winter sports. His lumberyard remained the exclusive seller of skis for many years. Robie figured that if he couldn't get more people to come to the snow, he would take the snow to the people. After much research and correspondence, Robie ascertained that weather conditions in Berkeley, near San Francisco on the east side of the bay, were ideal for maintaining snow even though the city was at sea level. U.C.

Berkeley donated a steep hill above the campus to the cause, and members of the Auburn Ski Club built a ski jump. Robie arranged for a trainload of snow to be shipped down from the Sierra Nevada high country. Volunteers hand-shoveled the snow from the train cars to the ski jump. People in San Francisco could see the ski jump and the snow-covered hill from their homes across the bay.

In 1934 the lowlands of the San Francisco Bay area, not the regal peaks of the Sierra Nevada, served as the location for the San Francisco Bay Area Ski Jump Championship. Some jumpers attained distances of 153 feet, competitive distances that would have held up in any top competition. Robie amassed the largest audience in the world to ever witness ski jumping, but it was definitely not a financial success. Nonetheless, Robie had brought skiing to the public with his 11,000 cubic feet of snow on a hill above Berkeley. Robie re-created snow in San Francisco when the organizers of the 1939 World's Fair asked the Auburn Ski Club to organize skiing's World Championships. Skiers from all over the world participated in skiing events at the World's Fair on Treasure Island, a man-made island in San Francisco Bay, and up in the Sierras at the Auburn Ski Club.

As the 1940s approached and war loomed, attention turned from the fun of skiing to more serious matters. Winter sports waned, but not Robie's imagination. The idea planted years ago during his long horseback ride to save his son's life had germinated in his mind. Each step, from accompanying Watson on the marking of the rediscovered Emigrant Trail to the creation of winter sport in the Sierra Nevada, led him on toward the Tevis Cup ride.

In response to the war, the Auburn Ski Club formed a team of skiing riflemen modeled after the Finnish team that served as a branch of the Finnish military, and several members of the Auburn Ski Club joined the Tenth Mountain Division. Skiing, as a sport, languished, and Robie concentrated on his businesses. Once the war concluded, America rebounded with more energy than ever. In the early 1950s the multi-lane Interstate 80 replaced Highway 40. The expansion of I-80 forced the Auburn Ski Club to relocate again, for the final time. The club moved all the way to the highest ridge of the Sierra Nevada, onto 244 acres located at Donner Summit, where the Boreal Ski Resort now operates.

In keeping with Robie's belief in recording and keeping the history of the area alive, the Auburn Ski Club was instrumental in forming the

Western SkiSport Museum, dedicated to the history of skiing. A huge bronze of Snowshoe Thompson towers over the entrance. Robie had ensured a legacy of skiing to enthusiasts in the Tahoe area, and beyond.

By the early 1950s, with winter sports firmly established, Robie turned his sights on a comparable summertime activity. He and his friend, Jack Shields, organized a three-day ride along the trail they helped Watson find and mark in the early 1930s for the purpose of fun and camaraderie, and to make others more aware of the history of the region. The handful of men had a great time riding the trail, telling stories, and camping under the stars. The three-day ride became a fun annual event, though not a competitive one unless one counted the volume of alcohol consumed and number of tall tales told. However, Robie still longed for competition.

A letter written by Bill Stewart of Miles City, Montana, in the February 1950 issue of *Western Horseman* provided Robie's final catalyst. Stewart had responded to an article by John Richards Young contending that the Arabian horse holds all the world's records for distance. Stewart took exception to this claim, and in his letter stated that he rode his Thoroughbred gelding, Drifter, eighty-one miles in seven hours, ten minutes, and twenty-seven seconds. He continued, "A year later I rode the same horse 127 miles (from Hill Creek to Miles City, Montana) in 12 hours and 10 minutes and 36 seconds. These times were officially clocked by three judges and I haven't heard of any other horse accomplishing the same distance or even 50 miles at that speed an hour. I also challenge Dr. Conn, Carl Raswan or any other Arab enthusiast to an endurance race any distance from 50 to 200 miles for money, marbles or chalk."

That was all Robie needed. He quickly penned:

> In your February issue, the first item in your Letters from Riders department is a 50- to 200-mile endurance race challenge to any Arabian horse owner for money, marbles or chalk by one Bill Stewart. I accept this challenge and being the challenged party, I select the Auburn–Lake Tahoe horse trail in California for the race at any date during the next summer which will be to Mr. Stewart's convenience. The distance is 90 miles and, in

view of Mr. Stewart's astonishing records over long distances, it is hoped that he will not consider this too short.

However, since the 90 miles of horse trail climbs and crosses the crest of the Sierra Nevada, he may find it ride enough. This is a direct west to east trail starting at elevation 1400, crosses the Sierra in Squaw Pass at 8600 feet, and drops to Lake Tahoe at 6225. From Auburn to Lake Tahoe this trail is on a natural footing of dirt and mountain rock. It is selected by reason of being a California trail—removed and free from oil surfaced automobile road travel. I will bet $250 on my horse Bandos AHRC 1785 by Nasr from Baida, against the chalk, marbles or equal money on Stewart's horse Drifter. Each horse shall carry equal weight and I would like a minimum of 165 pounds.

While calling this gentleman on his challenge, I do not want to be considered as using it to name my horse a champion to represent Arabian horses. There are so many good horses, but Stewart wanted an endurance race of distance he named from any Arab owner, and so he can have it.

In the October 1950 issue of *Western Horseman,* the magazine editors wrote:

Our readers will remember the letter from Bill Stewart which appeared in the February 1950 issue in this section in which he challenged ". . . any Arab enthusiast to an endurance race, the distance from 50 to 200 miles for money, marbles or chalk." In the March issue this challenge was accepted by [Wendell] Robie, and, so we thought, the race was on. Since the letter carried in the June issue, we have heard nothing from either party. *Western Horseman* sent the following letter to Mr. Stewart with a copy to Mr. Robie, and we are quoting—

Dear Mr. Stewart,

Quite a few of our readers have been inquiring as to the status of the race on which Mr. Robie accepted your challenge. Since the acceptance of the challenge carried in this magazine, we would like to keep our readers posted on it and would appreciate any information you have. We would like to know the place the race will take place, the start date, ending, and other details. We are sending a copy of this letter to Mr. Robie and sincerely hope that you will give us the information at an early date.

The magazine and Robie waited and waited for a reply from Bill Stewart. Finally, on March 14, 1951, *Western Horseman* received a note from Robie and a copy of the letter he sent in reply to Bill Stewart. Although no record exists of the letter Robie received from Stewart, his response made the content of Stewart's letter quite clear:

Dear Mr. Stewart:

I just came in this morning from the redwood country up on the northwest coast and hasten to answer your letter which arrived here yesterday. In it is a note that you want to place the endurance race of your horse with mine at Miles City or Colorado or Idaho and you suggest the purse should be $1500. In another place, you might consider the race in California over the Auburn–Lake Tahoe horse trail if 10 Arabian horses are entered to make a purse of $1500. Why do you want to change your proposal now? This doesn't read like your challenge spread far and wide by *Western Horseman.* Then you challenged any Arab owner "to an endurance race for money, marbles or chalk." From the words you bloomed in print with, you would let the world believe you are raring to go anyplace for a race with an Arab horse, and you don't care what there is for it, but you want a race.

I am a challenged party and have the right to call the turn on your play in keeping with the condition you named. I can't go to Miles City, Montana, Julesburg, Colo., or someplace else, and with that in mind, I have bet $250 my horse will beat yours. That, likewise, is my choice from your challenge, and I have told you that you can put up the same or run without it. My money stays offered to go to the winning horse.

As far as I am concerned, this is a race between your horse and mine, called from your challenge and on a first-class route for it, over the Sierra Nevada on a horse trail with an Arab horse, and you don't care what there is for it, but you want a race. Auburn to Lake Tahoe. If you want to enlarge the field, that suits me too, but not with a limit on only one or two breeds of horses. I do not care how many are the entries or what kind of horses. Also, I am not interested in raising the ante or entry fee above $250 to keep anybody out. Neither do I have time to monkey with the promotion of entries from others.

If you want to play it open for everybody who may want in, I am for it on the basis they pay their entry to the bank, and the winner take it all. I would like to see anyone else in and welcome. Plenty of good men can be counted on here for starting, finish, trail judges and timers.

You asked if the Auburn–Tahoe horse trail can be followed by an automobile? This is a horse trail and cannot be followed by car, although cars can meet the trail and view portions at some scattered points. I will expect you here on any day you select then. Stable accommodations are easily available in Auburn, and I will help any way I can to make this pleasant for you, up to race time.

(s) Wendell Robie

Their correspondence fizzled, but an idea that had slowly been growing in Robie's head began to develop.

During this letter-writing campaign, a young woman in the Los Angeles area followed the exchanges. Betty Veal had gone through nursing training during World War II, and after the war she and three girlfriends decided they wanted to leave the city to enjoy a more rural life. "One of the girl's parents had a farm in Auburn," Veal said. "We planned to go to Oregon and thought we would stay over in Auburn for a while." They didn't even know where Auburn was, but they loaded up a car, horse trailer, and their few belongings, and arrived in Auburn in 1950. Veal had always loved horses but never had one as a child. "When I got my first paycheck,

I bought my first horse. I had 'horse disease' and I rode cavalry horses at the different bases and forts." Veal bought a pinto gelding named Spunky, and the two settled in Auburn. Over fifty years later Veal still called Auburn home, and two of her girlfriends in Los Angeles also remained in the foothill town. "We all married local fellows and became part of the area," said Veal, noting that she married a local man, Jack, who had also served his country during World War II.

"I kept my horse at the Auburn Fairgrounds," explained Veal, "and I would run into Wendell on the trails." Although their paths often crossed, Veal and Robie didn't strike up their friendship for several more years. In 1951 Robie came to speak to the Sierra Rangers, a local horse club where the Veals were members. "I didn't associate the man in front of the room with the one who wrote those letters in *Western Horseman*," recalled Veal. "As he talked, he suggested the possibility of riding a horse one hundred miles in one day. I looked around the room, and I was the only one who didn't think he was crazy."

Veal was among the first to embrace his vision, though nothing daunted Robie. He was determined to see it become reality. At that time many people were afraid that harm would come to the horses. "It was very hard for Wendell to get accepted by the horse community," explained Veal, "but he wouldn't quit." As Wendell continued to share his thoughts with various riding clubs and horse groups, his ideas began to take shape, and his vision became clearer. Many people became aware of the man with the preposterous idea. Most just laughed to themselves; a few wondered if there was some merit to Robie's claims; and a handful began to believe. The Veals became close friends with the Robies. "When Wendell told you what to do," recounted Jack Veal, "there was only one answer: Yes, Sir!"

In succeeding years, Robie organized several three-day treks along the trail which became both social outings and a precursor to the actual one-day competition. "Wendell would have me bring supplies up to Todd Valley to meet the riders for the final night. There were some rip-snorting parties," laughed Veal. Robie welcomed female participants; however, following the thinking of the times, he did request that they not ride stallions. He recognized that women were part of the historic western movement and had contributed greatly to its expansion. The second year of what was to become the Western States Trail 100 Miles—

One Day Ride, three intrepid women joined in, and women have participated ever since.

Although Robie's three-day rides got people into the backcountry on the back of a horse, Robie still longed for a competitive activity. He wanted an ultimate test, and a three-day ride was not the formula he was seeking. While the trail was difficult, most competent horsemen and reasonably fit horses could make it within three days. The trail ride was a great outing and an excuse for carousing, but it was not a true test of ability and spirit.

In the fall of 1954 while riding with members of the Sacramento sheriff's posse, Robie postulated that horses and men of their era were every bit as good as those of the Pony Express, the Texas Rangers, and the cattle drivers. Of the many interesting aspects of the westward movement, Robie was particularly fascinated by the Pony Express. He admired the lithe, young boys who courageously galloped their mounts day and night in all kinds of weather to move their precious cargo west, step by step, and mile by mile. He was amazed by the horses that had galloped for miles across flat plains, and through steep mountain passes.

The men of the posse laughed at Robie and told him that twentieth-century horses and riders were in no way as tough and hardy as their forebears. Their disbelief only encouraged Robie even more. Besides, with skiing now established and growing, he needed a new outlet for his energies and visions. Robie's ability to promote an idea had already put snow sports and Squaw Valley on the map in perpetuity—and he was on the verge of creating another worldwide phenomenon that would transcend all of his other accomplishments.

✤ 5 ✦

AN IDEA TAKES SEED

Summertime activities now dominated Robie's thoughts. He loved the region and wanted to get more people into the mountains year-round. Robie also loved his horses and sought a way to combine his two passions. What better way to get people into the mountains on horses than with an event? Despite the success of his three-day trail rides, the naysayers were convinced that a modern-day horse and rider could not cover the one hundred miles in one day. He set out to prove his point that a horse and rider *could* accomplish the feat. When Robie set his mind to something, no one could stop him, even with few supporters.

Over five years, Betty Veal had come to know Robie well. As he spoke more of his vision, he found in her a stalwart supporter. The young nurse was detailed, meticulous, and willing to let Robie have the limelight. These traits proved critical for Robie throughout his life. While he had grand visions and the guts to tackle the most daunting of projects, Robie needed a lieutenant who was willing to quietly follow behind him and help make his visions reality. Veal was the first person to do so when it came to the creation of a one-hundred-mile contest on horseback.

Veal began the detail work that would transform Robie's ideas into something concrete. On March 1, 1955, she announced the first organizational meeting to plan a one-day ride, in addition to the already popular three-day ride Robie organized. Jack Shields was appointed president of the fledgling group, Robie was treasurer, and Veal logically became the secretary.

On this same day, a baby boy named Hal Hall was born. Hall's future and the announcement of the one-day ride would become inextricably linked. Their paths would cross and later merge for a lifelong journey.

When the letter of invitation was published, the group selected August 7 as the date for the historic inaugural one-day ride along the Auburn–Lake Tahoe Trail, now called the Western States Trail. Initially the group called itself the Lake Tahoe–Auburn Trail Ride Committee, and eventually became the Western States Trail Foundation (WSTF), which oversees the ride to this day.

Robie, ever the promoter, began heralding the great benefits of trail riding to Auburn. Real estate values would rise and Auburn would move from being a sleepy little town in the Sierra Nevada foothills to a well-recognized locale. Robie explained that several families from Sacramento, just down the hill on the flat plains of the Sacramento Valley and only about thirty miles away, had purchased property in Auburn to pursue their love of trail riding. Before the term was invented, Robie understood the concept of "bedroom community." Fifty years later Auburn is a booming town with many people commuting down to the Sacramento metropolis. In 2003, a year shy of the fiftieth anniversary of the Tevis Cup ride, the city of Auburn fittingly adopted the title of the Endurance Capital of the World. The Chamber of Commerce estimates that annually, the endurance ride and the endurance run bring in over three million dollars of revenue to the community.

While Robie was out in the field promoting his event, Veal was writing letters. One was spotted by Norene Mansfield as she sat reading the Reno *Gazette Journal.* Her husband, Lincoln "Nick" Mansfield, was instantly intrigued. Mansfield worked at the casinos in the Reno area and dabbled with horses. He kept a string of ponies at his 102 Ranch and brought them into downtown Reno. Mansfield collected dimes from parents so their eager children could take a pony ride. Like the Pied Piper, Mansfield would lead his string of ponies through the streets with children excitedly waving at their parents. He started with a couple of mustangs bought on their way to the slaughterhouse. He broke and trained them, selling them as working ranch horses. Although he did not know a lot about horses when he first started, many people claimed that he had "horse sense." Ultimately horses became his mainstay. Like Robie, Mansfield was interested in the Old West, and enjoyed riding his horses long distances.

Over the years Mansfield trained many endurance horses, both for himself and for others. However, on that day in 1955 he had just one horse that might be able to cover a long distance. Buffalo Bill was a scrappy Morgan crossbred Mansfield used for ranch work and distance riding. When Mansfield asked his wife when the ride would be, she told him it was on Sunday, just two days away. Mansfield knew he had to be part of the ride.

In preparation for this great adventure, Robie and his small group first decided on a route, and then on the rules. Although few, they were strict, and Robie was unwavering. He proclaimed that riders had to obey the trail boss, Robie himself; they had to follow trail etiquette; junior riders and women could not ride stallions; and any junior between twelve and seventeen years old had to be accompanied by an adult. The group also asked veterinarians from the University of California at Davis Veterinary School to examine the horses prior to the start, to check the horses at designated points during the ride, and then to perform a final examination at the conclusion of the journey. Robie did not want complaints that horses were being abused by this one-day trans–Sierra crossing. While the U.C. Davis vets oversaw the horses, Robie also appointed a physician to oversee the veterinary commission. Dr. Tom Schulte presided at the inaugural event and for several years thereafter. Dr. Wheat headed up the team of vets from U.C. Davis and remained associated with the ride for many years.

The committee decided to follow the early route up and over Squaw Valley's Emigrant Pass and then along the ridges of the highest Sierra Nevada crest before dropping down to follow the Middle Fork of the American River. The route had to be marked. Tree blazes still existed along parts of the trail, but Robie realized that something more obvious was needed.

There are different stories about Robie's marking of the trail, but some consistent facts emerge. Since that first ride in 1955, the route is always marked in yellow surveyor's tape. Why yellow? Foresters traditionally steer away from yellow ribbons as they are not very visible in forest areas, but despite his forestry training, Robie chose yellow because it reminded him of the bold yellow stripe running down the breeches of U.S. Cavalry riders. Legend has it Robie asked his granddaughter, Marion, who was then nine years old, to get a yellow sheet out of her grandmother's linen closet. Marion chose the finest sheets, which her grandfather promptly tore into strips in order to mark the route. His wife was undoubtedly furious, but she also recognized her husband's single-minded nature.

Robie decided to begin his quest in Tahoe City in honor of his friend Robert Montgomery Watson, who had served as its first sheriff. The route from Tahoe City along the Truckee River was relatively flat and easy. At the junction of Squaw Creek with the larger Truckee River, the trail turned west and headed into the valley. Riders then crossed the meadow along Squaw Creek. Unlike many mountain valleys, Squaw Valley is quite large and spacious: The valley floor is over a mile wide and several miles long, encompassing several hundred acres. At the time, a small enclave of people lived there year-round, with other families maintaining second homes. Today Squaw Valley is a thriving resort community

While the surrounding terrain was steep and rocky, the meadow could be quite boggy, and riders had to be careful not to get their horses in deep, dangerous footing. Coming out of the meadow, riders were faced with their first serious mountain climb, ascending the rock-strewn slopes toward Emigrant Pass. To the northeast is Granite Chief, at 9,006 feet, and to the southwest is Squaw Peak, at 8,886 feet. Emigrant Pass, marked by Watson's Monument, is a rocky, barren ridge at 8,774 feet, not much lower than the two peaks anchored at either end of the shallow saddle.

Many ridges unfold in both directions, but at this point there are no more mountains obstructing the view, in front or behind. Halting here, riders have crested the magnificent Sierra Nevada range—a last opportunity for wide, panoramic views in all directions. Looking southeast to KT-22, the third of the major peaks surrounding the valley, riders can see most of Lake Tahoe sparkling sapphire-blue in the distance. This is a moment to savor, for it is akin to standing on top of the world; and how better to view it than from the back of a good horse? Robie felt that hard work should go hand-in-hand with rigorous outdoor recreation, and wanted to share his passion and experiences with others.

Once Robie had marked the trail leading up to the highest point riders would cross, he began the slow descent. Marking the trail here became more difficult, for riders would reenter the tree line where visibility was limited. In many places the trail might be barely discernible among the rocks, granite slabs, and forest debris. (Riders can ill afford to become complacent as they ride the Western States Trail. Even today it is very easy to get lost, and ride organizers love saying that no horse and rider has ever been lost . . . for more than three days!)

From here, Robie chose a northwesterly route along the southern slope of Granite Chief and Needle Peak. Below these towering granite peaks scraping the cold, blue sky, riders must carefully guide their horses across sheer faces of granite; a treacherous route, but the alternative is a small valley route marking the headwaters of the river, often impassable due to late snowmelt.

Leaving the area, Robie crested Picayune Bluff overlooking Picayune Valley and Mt. Mildred from the rimrock. Standing on the rim, riders are treated to one of many spectacular Sierra views. Early travelers relied on this visual landmark to ensure they were heading in the correct direction and used this spot to get their bearings before heading down to the canyons. Getting lost here, deep in the heart of the Sierra Nevada— where even summer weather can be unpredictable—could mean death for travelers.

As Granite Chief melts away, Lyons Peak emerges to take front view. The trail slowly wends it way along and it eventually carried Robie along a privately owned logging campsite known as Hodgson's Cabin. There were many such sites throughout the Sierra Nevada, but over the years time and the elements have slowly eroded early landmarks of man's ventures into the very heart of this range. Next Robie contended with the ridges that lead down to the great Sacramento Valley, and the trail to the top of Foresthill Divide, separating the Middle Fork and North Fork of the American River. These ridges run perpendicular to the crest of the Sierras, like ribs from the spine. Here Robie paused to look north, down into Royal Gorge, named for the incredible two-thousand-foot-deep crevice where this section of the American River begins its journey down to Sacramento. Surrounding canyons and meadows reflect names given by early miners and loggers such as Sailor Meadow, Lost Emigrant Mine, and Wildcat Canyon.

Traversing this ridge, the trail rises and falls with the terrain. Along the ridge, Robie was treated to incredible vistas on either side. If there is a single aspect of the route that people have heard of, it is Cougar Rock, a daunting, volcanic outcropping which horses and riders must scale in order to continue down the trail. In fact, Cougar Rock makes one pause and wonder how early immigrants tackled this narrow, steep passage. Horses must scramble up and over the outcropping, and a picture crossing Cougar Rock is almost as prized as the coveted Tevis Cup belt buckle.

Experienced horses have little trouble navigating Cougar Rock, but many a rider has worked himself into a complete state of panic in nervous anticipation. Cougar Rock is a Tevis Cup ride rite of passage and veterans enjoy telling wild stories to first-time riders.

After putting Cougar Rock behind him, Robie continued down the Foresthill Divide to Elephant's Trunk, so named for its profile. Further down the trail he saw the first evidence of civilization since leaving Squaw Valley at Soda Springs Road, a dusty, single-lane track. Robie then followed a U.S. Forest Service dirt road along Red Star Ridge where he rode among the old-growth forest of Duncan Canyon. At this location, some of the Douglas fir can be up to ten feet in diameter or more, while one hundred fifty years ago some of the trees were up to twenty feet across. Few people ever see these mighty giants, but horseback riders are cooled by their shade, and dwarfed by their size.

Traveling the old Emigrant Road, Robie chose Robinson Flat as the first official rest stop, or "gate-hold," as it would later be named. Robinson Flat became a "crossroads of the Sierra" with its beautiful, high-country meadow and freshwater spring where sheepherders, loggers, immigrants, miners, and travelers could stop to refresh themselves. When he reached this point, Robie had traveled the first third of the trail and survived the high country's rocks, rubble, and shale. From the highest ascent at Emigrant Pass of 8,774 feet, Robie had lost two thousand feet in elevation, the last gradual descent he would face. While the rocks were behind him, the steep climbs and drops of the canyons were in front of him with sixty-four miles yet to travel.

Hitting the trail again, Robie split from the old immigrant road, and headed southwest along a dirt road that served as an old wagon road in the late 1800s. This route carried him along to Barney Cavanaugh Ridge. Robie descended the first of the canyons, to Deep Canyon Creek, then began a short climb up to Dusty Corners, not much more than an old, unpaved road atop a promontory, with a breathtaking, precipitous drop. Dusty Corners is at mile 45, and he enjoyed a relatively flat ride five more miles down to Last Chance, another of the ubiquitously named abandoned mines.

On June 25, 1992, in recognition of the historic nature of this entire route, ride organizers were instrumental in getting the section of the trail from Last Chance to Michigan Bluff designated in the National Register of Historic Places. If Robie had been traveling a hundred and fifty years ago, he would have crossed paths with a rugged Scottish couple, Duncan and Jessie Ferguson. Ferguson maintained and improved the trail from Last Chance to Michigan Bluff from his hotel and bar in Deadwood. He charged a toll to anyone using the route whether they were on foot, horseback, driving cattle, or a mule train. This was California's first toll road, and the only passable route in the area. Pacific Slab Mine lies along an offshoot of the old toll trail, and was the longest-operating hydraulic mine. The descent down the canyon to the first crossing of the North Fork of the American River is so steep that many riders dismount and lead their horses down the two-thousand-foot drop. At the bottom they can either ford the river or ride across "Swinging Bridge," a narrow suspension bridge. Some horses refuse to cross the swaying, bouncing bridge, but most traipse across it as just another of the many challenges faced on this trail. Since most riders enter this phase of the one-hundred-mile journey at midday, temperatures can soar to above 100 degrees in the canyons, so letting horses drink their fill whenever water is available is mandatory. Horses normally lose over two hundred pounds of water weight during their twenty-four-hour, hundred-mile trek, and riders cannot let them become dehydrated.

Climbing out of the canyon while marking the trail, Robie traversed its short, steep switchbacks. Here, riders may feel as if they have emerged from hell, a feeling validated by Devil's Thumb, a large, volcanic outcropping nearly fifty feet high named for the hellish conditions existing in the area. Devil's Basin Hydraulic Sourdough and Basin mining pits have left telltale signs of the feverish search for gold of one hundred and fifty years ago.

The former town of Deadwood is a little over a mile from Devil's Thumb, perched along the ridge separated by El Dorado Canyon and the North Fork of the Middle Fork of the American River. Little remains of Deadwood, named by the prospectors who claimed the area with the idea of "easy pickings," though it existed long enough to have a cemetery. Robie passed by the silent markers as he headed into the chasm of El Dorado Canyon. At Deadwood riders are at 4,365 feet; at the canyon's bottom, three miles along, they've descended to 1,700 feet, the most extreme drop of the entire route. Climbing out of the steep gorge, Robie arrived at Michigan Bluff, another old mining camp. Going through the canyons is like riding on hot pavement. The canyon's exiting face is almost devoid of trees and plants, and the rock absorbs the direct heat of the sun beating down. Heat is the enemy at this point, and each rider must ensure that he and his mount are well hydrated in these torturous canyons.

Michigan Bluff was the exit point for over $100,000 worth of golden ore each month during the heyday of the gold rush. Many made their fortunes in the town, which had a population of three thousand at its peak. Leland Stanford, founder of the university bearing his name and one of the Big Four—the men who helped build California and this country's transcontinental railroad—made his early fortune from ore pulled out of mines around Michigan Bluff.

While environmentalists bemoan the fate of the landscape in this area, the fact remains that man exposed more rock and ore in a few years than nature could have done in centuries. Miners washed away more than one hundred fifty feet of soil to expose the underlying bedrock where the ore ran in thin, but steady, veins. However, these actions had their repercussions. The denuding of the landscape caused massive erosion and landslides. The entire town of Michigan Bluff began to slide down the steep, exposed rock face to the canyon below. Between 1858 and 1859, the entire town drifted to its present location. In fact, the original locale was known as Michigan City, but when it was relocated to higher ground it became known as Michigan Bluff.

At sixty-three miles, Robie had marked two-thirds of the trail. The town provided a rider's first entry back into civilization. They could sleep under the stars or in a hotel bed. As the ride grew over the years, the town of Michigan Bluff enthusiastically supported the riders who rested in the shade along the main street, barely more than a paved strip lined by a few houses and shops for the length of two city blocks. However, the sleepy little enclave became quite festive one day a year for the Western States Ride. People sat on their porch stoops watching the hot, dusty horses and riders emerge from the trail. The local guild fired up their barbecues and used the funds for local activities. Many of the riders enjoyed the stop here, and the crowds bolstered many a flagging spirit.

Robie headed up the main street where the trail beckons again, and headed down into the final major canyon, Volcano Creek at its bottom. At this point manzanita replaces the high-country chaparral, and the canyon walls are the distinct red of their embedded ores. In two miles

Robie dropped over one thousand feet via switchbacks, dropping deeper and deeper into the final major canyon, then climbed another one thousand feet out of the rocky abyss.

After climbing out of the final canyon, Robie arrived at Foresthill, with two-thirds of his trail-marking journey complete. Robie had survived the rocks and difficult terrain of the high country, then the arduous ascents and descents in the furnace-like canyons. Although he had ridden sixty-nine miles, thirty-one more remained.

When Robie left the plateau above Foresthill he trotted alongside Foresthill Road right down Main Street. Leaving the historic town, Robie turned away, and was slowly carried back to the solitude of the Sierra Nevada. Traveling along Mosquito Ridge, then Baltimore Mine Ridge, the trail steadily loses elevation, dropping from 3,225 feet at Foresthill to 800 feet in just over ten miles. Along the way Robie crossed several creeks and rode parallel to a ditch, running from Dardanelles Creek, like those used to carry water to provide electricity for small towns and camps over a century ago.

At this juncture Robie traveled along a wide canyon rim offering a spectacular panorama before dropping down to the river below via well-traveled switchbacks. Ford's Bar, Poverty Bar, Rattlesnake Bar, and Granite Bar reflect the descriptive names given to many of the old mining camps along the deep, swift-moving river. Leaving the canyons behind and with the sun now setting, Robie reached Ford's Bar, having traveled eighty-one miles. On the other side of the river he came to Francisco's, a former homestead nestled in a picturesque little meadow.

The next significant challenge Robie faced was crossing the American River at Poverty Bar. Depending on the amount of snow in the Sierra and the rate of snowmelt, the river can flow fast and deep. In those early years, riders had to be prepared to swim with their horses across this stretch of river. More recently, ride officials have worked with various local, state, and federal water agencies to control the river flow.

Once safely across the river, Robie passed Maine Bar and Murderer's Bar on his way to Lower Quarry and the little town of Cool. Leaving this spot, he crossed Highway 49 and traveled along an old wagon trail that carried him back to the river. Upon reaching No Hands Bridge, Robie was in the last stretch to the finish. The bridge was completed in 1912, and at that time was the longest concrete-arch railroad bridge in the world. The narrow-gauge steam engines that ran on the route carried limestone from the nearby quarry to Auburn where it linked up with the famed Central Pacific. The bridge is considered an engineering marvel and survived the devastating flood of 1964 when Hell Hole Reservoir gave way. The Highway 49 bridge, less than half a mile upstream, was built much later and was destroyed by the flood, but stalwart No Hands Bridge survived the torrent of water, debris, and boulders. In the Valentine Flood of 1984, the bridge was submerged, but it was still standing when the waters receded. However, the years and the unrelenting river wore at the footings of the bridge. In 1996 the U.S. Bureau of Reclamation threatened to close access to the bridge because they claimed it was in danger of collapsing. Western States Trail Foundation leaders combined forces with the Western States Endurance Run Foundation and other recreational user groups to fight the closure. Since the cessation of the trains in the 1940s, the bridge was used solely for recreational purposes.

Flood of December 24, 1964, that washed out Highway 49 bridge less than one-half mile above No Hands Bridge. [Courtesy of Western States Trail Foundation]

After crossing No Hands Bridge, Robie traveled alongside the river before climbing up to what is now Robie Point, where his home overlooked the spectacular canyons and high mountain peaks of the Sierra Nevada. When he wasn't riding in the mountains, he was able to gaze out upon them from his home. The mountains were in the man.

Passing Robie Point, he was once again near civilization. The lights of Auburn dim the stars, and the sounds of the mountains fade. For a short distance the trail entered a dense, forested area and then, leading up a short rise, to the present Western States Trail Staging Area, the official one-hundred-mile mark with the Placer County Fairgrounds below.

Today, horses finishing the ride can take a deep drink from a well erected by the WSTF, then head down to the crowd waiting to cheer their arrival. Riders take a victory lap in McCann Stadium in front of the waiting crowd. It is a long journey not only of distance, but of eras as well.

☞ 6 ☜

1955: THE INAUGURAL RIDE

With a marked trail, invitations sent, and inches of press in the Sacramento and San Francisco newspapers, Robie just had to cross the Sierra Nevada on horseback from Tahoe City to Auburn in under 24 hours. Five riders gathered outside the Tahoe City post office at 5:00 A.M. on August 7, 1955: Robie, Nick Mansfield, Pat Sewell, William "Billy" Patrick, and Richard Highfill. To make the proceedings even more official, Robie arranged for the postmaster to swear in all five riders as official postal carriers. Each man carried a piece of postmarked mail to signify the start of his journey; the mail would be cancelled upon their arrival in Auburn to designate the official completion. (For the first six years, cancelled mail served as the official timing mechanism for the ride.)

This first ride began a long friendship between Robie and Mansfield, both rugged, outspoken, passionate individuals. They rode together throughout the many miles, often providing encouragement to the three younger men accompanying them.

The five men began their journey and headed north along the Truckee River toward Squaw Valley following the same route Indians, emigrants, and miners had followed over one hundred years before. Crossing sheer granite faces along Red Star Ridge, Highfill's horse had slipped. Although these were experienced horsemen with surefooted horses, the route was not easy. At Robinson Flat, only a third of the way into the journey, the vets who examined Highfill's horse suggested he retire from the ride. Disappointed, Highfill agreed. The other four continued on with Robie in the lead, based on an unspoken understanding that Robie should lead this first journey.

Descending into the canyons after leaving Robinson Flat, the riders experienced the heat of the midday sun and the unrelenting red dust of the ore-rich soil. Although the trail is rocky, the accompanying red dirt is so fine that a single horse kicks up a cloud of dust that hangs lazily in the sultry, hot air. Four horses created an almost impenetrable cloud. Although at times they were scattered down the trail, they were never separated by more than about thirty minutes. Fifty years later endurance riders employ an impressive array of equipment, technology, and knowledge about distance riding, but not these first riders. What these riders lacked in sophisticated knowledge and high-tech tools, they made up for with tenacity and ruggedness. Robie and Mansfield could live in the backcountry for days. Nick Mansfield even carried a small anvil and shoeing equipment, just in case. Mansfield estimated that his additional gear probably weighed almost sixty pounds, and he was a stout man himself. However, none of the men gave a second thought to the weight the horses were carrying. Most were working ranch horses, used to carrying weight and being out all day, and carried well over two hundred fifty pounds on such a ride. Modern-day endurance riders who try to keep their tack and equipment below thirty pounds in addition to their own body weight would be aghast at the weights these early endurance horses carried.

At 4:21 A.M. the next day, the four riders reached Auburn. Mansfield, Sewell, and Patrick hung back to let Robie cancel his mail first and then lead the parade to the Auburn Fairgrounds, the symbolic finish line to their journey.

Robie had proved what he long believed, that modern-day horses and men were every bit as tough as their counterparts of a century ago. Just like the early mountain men and the fabled Pony Express riders, Robie and his compatriots covered a long distance over rigorous terrain in a fast time. Robie was thrilled with the results, and reveled in the many accolades and resulting press coverage following this first test in the *Auburn Journal,* the *Sacramento Bee,* and *The San Francisco Chronicle.*

The riders were honored at a reception in Auburn. That evening Dr. Wheat announced that he was happy with the outcome of the ride; he did not find that any of the horses had been harmed, and the four completing horses did not suffer any undue stress. To commemorate their triumph, Robie unveiled a plaque he called the "Real Horseman's Trophy." In talking about the inaugural ride, Robie was quoted as referring to, "our little ride over the mountains." At times arrogant, Robie could also be quite charming and self-deprecating.

Wendell Robie at finish line of inaugural ride, giving his horse a drink from a canteen. [Photo provided by Western States Trail Foundation]

Robie left that first year convinced that Arabian horses were the ideal long-distance mount, while Mansfield left believing that any good, hardy horse was fine, but that his own Buffalo Bill was equal to none. Over the years many different breeds and types of horses have finished the ride, but it is Arabians that dominate. Of the ride's winners since 1955, all but three were either full or part Arabian.

Word spread about Robie's amazing accomplishment, and in 1956 twenty riders signed up for the adventure. Although women had not participated in the three-day rides and the inaugural Western States Trail 100 Miles—One Day Ride, three signed up in 1956. Wendell's niece, Ina Drake; Nick Mansfield's daughter, Nancy; and Brenda Ratcliff rode alongside the men. They faced the rigors of the wilderness and all three completed the ride. Crossing the old narrow-gauge train trestle after leaving the quarry, Ina Drake dubbed it, "No Hands Bridge," since in those early days there was no railing where the span crossed the North Fork of the American River churning below. She loved making the crossing with her horse's reins looped over his neck, spreading her arms out wide, and cantering across. To this day it is still known as No Hands Bridge.

Another young woman watched the ride set off in 1956, and she vowed to be part of it some day. Patricia Fox's family moved to Tahoe City in 1918 five years before she was born. Her family lived next door to the Watsons, and Fox often listened to the elder Watson regaling his listeners with his stories and adventures. "When I was only six a group of us walked up to Emigrant Pass to see the monument built in honor of Watson," she remembered. Fourteen years earlier, in 1941, when Fox was in her teens, she joined a group of men driving cattle from Tahoe to Yosemite in search of high mountain meadows for summer grazing. "The war was on and there weren't as many men around. I think that is one of the reasons they let a girl join them on a seventeen-day cattle drive," recalled Fox decades later of her early memories associated with riding in the mountains and the Tevis Cup ride.

Fox, twenty-eight years old in 1956, remembers watching the riders start in front of the Tahoe City post office. Again Robie rode his Arabian stallion Bandos, or Smokey, as he called him. To mark their official start, each rider postmarked his or her mail with 5:00 A.M., August 18, 1956, before following Robie into the early morning darkness. Betty Veal again served as ride secretary, a position she continues to this day, and Dr. Wheat again headed up the veterinary committee.

The twenty riders did not all stay together, but spread out along the trail. Jack Veal was among them. "Wendell wanted me to go," said Veal of his first of two one-hundred-mile journeys. "He told me to go get this horse out of his pasture. His name was Colonel. I don't think he was hardly broke, but by the end of the ride I could steer him and stop him!"

Amazingly, no horses were eliminated or pulled until Michigan Bluff, more than sixty miles into the ride. Four riders retired at this point, one was pulled at Francisco's near the final river crossing, and the sixth was pulled at the finish line. Robie was emphatic that a horse had to maintain its soundness and well-being throughout the ride and at the finish. He wanted to recognize superior individuals and Robie knew that he would face intense criticism if the ride allowed lame or overly stressed horses a "completion" designation.

Bill Hussey from Carmichael, California, led the pack of riders into the night. Although he was the first to reach Auburn, he got lost on the way to the post office to have his letter cancelled. Robie was a short distance behind Hussey, and while Hussey wandered around the streets of Auburn at one in the morning, Robie and his niece rode directly to the Auburn post office and had their letters cancelled at 2:22 A.M., August 19. Robie went into the record book as the official winner of the second Western States 100 Miles—One Day Ride.

In addition to Robie on his Arabian stallion Bandos, Mansfield rode Buffalo Bill, a horse of uncertain origin, but often credited as part American Thoroughbred, although Mansfield claimed he was part Morgan. Besides these two horses, other breeds included Morgans, Quarter Horses, and a variety of crossbreds.

For the third start in 1957, nineteen riders gathered at Tahoe City. Once again Robie led them, this time riding an Arabian mare named Molla. Sixteen riders completed the journey. In promoting the 1957 ride, Wendell claimed that it was the "only organized One Hundred Miles—One Day Ride in America." Although a one-hundred-mile ride had been held in Vermont since the 1930s, this event took place over several days. Only after the implementation of the Western States 100 Mile Ride did the Vermont organizers hold a similar ride to be completed in twenty-four hours. However, Robie never saw this as competition, but proof of his belief that there were plenty of people who shared his passion and love for the outdoors, horses, and challenges.

A critical tenet of Robie's ride became a foundation not only for the Western States Ride, but for the entire sport of endurance riding. Despite Robie's competitive nature, he remained adamant that the Western States was a ride, not a race. It was the ultimate demonstration of horsemanship, not simply a race to the finish, and so began the motto, "To finish is to win." Whether Robie was the first to utter the words is unknown, but he did articulate the concept.

As the ride grew in popularity, Robie remained convinced that every contest needed a winner. He explained that while all the finishers were recorded, there was only one winner. "There are no place points," said Robie in his no-nonsense manner. At this point riders still participated for the honor of saying they had accomplished the challenge and to have their names inscribed on Robie's horsemanship plaque. In 1958 Robie began making a few changes.

One of the biggest and most significant changes to Robie's life was the arrival of a woman named Drucilla Barner, or "Dru" to her friends. A San Francisco socialite, she was fed up with her marriage and with life in the city. She moved to Auburn while her husband remained in the San Francisco area, although they never officially divorced. While Inez was a loyal wife and provided him with a stable home and a child, she never matched Robie's intellectual prowess or his driving ambition. Perhaps she never fully recovered from the difficulty of their son's birth. Although Robie loved his wife and was loyal to her, he was not faithful, nor was Barner, who remained married to an abusive husband, but for all intents and purposes, lived as a single woman. She and Robie hit it off. "Dru was such a lady," recalled Jack Veal. "She was like a big sister to me. She was from San Francisco society and she brought finesse, poise, and class to all of us."

Barner was an accomplished horsewoman and ably kept up with Robie and his friends on rides throughout the American River Canyons and beyond. Soon Barner joined Robie at the bank and worked as his personal assistant until his death many years later. Barner also replaced Betty Veal in many ways. Veal had been instrumental in helping Robie start his one-hundred-mile ride, but she and Jack had their own lives. While committed to Robie's vision, she didn't share the personal dedication Barner placed in the event and in Robie personally. Veal remained the ride secretary, but Barner took over much of the organization work and was the recipient of Robie's musings, brainstorms, and ideas. While Robie spun complex visions, Barner quietly worked behind him and helped ensure that his ideas came to fruition.

In 1958, almost twice as many riders registered for the one-hundred-mile ride as in the previous year. Thirty-five riders gathered at the Tahoe City post office on August 1 where they again had their mail postmarked to authenticate their start time. Again Robie rode Molla, and again he finished in first place. This time he rode with Barner right by his side. By now his closest friends and associates had figured out the unspoken aspects of the relationship. Robie's wife became aware of Barner's existence, and while she undoubtedly did not like the relationship, neither did she choose to leave her husband. This tacit arrangement continued throughout the remainder of their lives.

Crossing the finish line in Auburn and taking the required victory lap at McCann Stadium at the Placer County Fairgrounds, Robie was reminded of the importance of formally acknowledging a winner. An event as significant as this one needed a special trophy.

In part due to his larger-than-life persona, Robie was known by a lot of people and often rubbed elbows with state politicians, movie stars, and other public figures. Robie knew of a man named Will Tevis who set his own long-distance riding record and was dubbed the "Iron Man of the Age." In July 1923 Tevis took on the challenge of riding 257.5 miles from the California-Nevada border to San Mateo, south of San Francisco, against nine of the best U.S. Cavalry officers. Riding Pony Express–style, switching horses every few miles, Tevis bested the nine men who spelled one another through the Sierra Nevada, following the old Pony Express route to Sacramento, continuing on toward San Francisco, and eventually finishing at the San Mateo County Fairgrounds. Tevis, who took no rest stops, was a superb horseman and outrode the officers to finish in the amazing time of eleven and a half hours. Robie was impressed. Who better to approach about an award for his one-hundred-mile ride?

Will Tevis met with Robie and the two discussed horses, Robie's one-hundred-mile ride, and contests in general. Robie knew that Tevis's grandfather, Lloyd, had taken over Wells, Fargo & Company in 1872, and although the Pony Express had ceased to operate, it was Wells Fargo that ran the overland mail service. Robie had long admired the Pony Express riders, and they were part of the inspiration that led to the creation of the Western States One Hundred Miles—One Day Ride. In honor of his grandfather, Will Tevis and his brothers, Lloyd and Gordon, offered a Lloyd Tevis Cup to the first horse to finish. Robie saw the award as one of distinguished merit for outstanding horsemanship in completing the ride in the fastest time. Lloyd Tevis was a most appropriate honoree, and since that day the ride has been more commonly known as the Tevis Cup.

❋ 7 ❋

LLOYD TEVIS:
CAPITALIST AND ENTREPRENEUR

Lloyd Tevis was born to a prominent family in Shelbyville, Kentucky, and after receiving his college degree, followed his father's footsteps into the field of law. As much as he enjoyed practicing law, Tevis was even more intrigued by business. He went to work for a dry goods wholesaler, and soon found himself working on the financial side of the business; when the company later failed, Tevis handled the receivership. Thanks to Tevis's business acumen, negotiating skills, and tenacity, he managed to get all the liabilities paid and thus satisfy all the parties involved. His actions caught the attention of leaders of The Bank of Kentucky. They offered Tevis a position which he accepted. Once again his skills drew recognition, and a St. Louis, Missouri, insurance company hired him. This position was short-lived, however, as a devastating fire in May 1849 ruined much of the city, and the insurance company was overwhelmed by the claims.

Temporarily jobless, Lloyd answered the call of gold and silver from the west that had lured many young men before him. The journey west was difficult, and Tevis found that the work in the gold fields was laborious. He was further discouraged by the element of luck gold mining required. Reevaluating his goals, Tevis decided that perhaps he was more suited to business, civilization, and the company of men, preferring to rely on his skills rather than luck. He headed to Sacramento and combined his knowledge of the law with great business skills, to become one of the richest and most successful men in California.

In April 1850, Lewis Birdsall, M.D. was selected as the first county clerk of the city. For $300 a month, Tevis joined three other clerks in recording the many documents in the legal ledgers. In this position, Tevis demonstrated his ability to analyze a situation, come up with a plan, and then implement the plan, even if it took months or years. He saw that his fellow clerks were lazy and that much work in the quickly growing city of Sacramento was not getting completed. He approached Birdsall, offering to come in two hours early every day to catch up on the work at no extra expense. Some time later Tevis made Birdsall an offer he couldn't refuse: to do the work of all the clerks on his single salary. Birdsall took him up on the offer.

Oscar T. Shuck, a chronicler of the California bar, recorded some of Tevis's early thoughts. "When I came to Sacramento, young, poor, and ambitious, I had to decide whether I would strike for political fame or for money. I concluded to go for money. I owe my fortune in life to my good penmanship."

Living frugally allowed Tevis to save $250, which he used to purchase his first piece of real estate. Because of his position, Tevis knew land values, who owned what property, and the financial situations of many of the purchasers, and leveraged this knowledge into savvy land investments. Developing insider insights and knowledge were skills Tevis would continue to employ, especially for his lifetime coup of orchestrating one of the first corporate raids in United States history.

In October 1851, Birdsall's term in office ended, and Tevis moved on. By then James Ben Ali Haggin, a fellow Kentuckian and college friend, had also come to California. The two formed a loose partnership and began practicing law, although Tevis remained an entrepreneur as well. He leveraged every dollar he could by loaning money to various associates for interest and continuing to purchase real estate. As their fortunes slowly grew and the two men felt more secure and established, Haggin sent for his wife, Eliza Sanders. Accompanied by her sister, Susan, the two arrived in California. Tevis was attracted to Susan and shortly after her arrival they married, thus furthering the bond between the two men.

Personable and outgoing, Tevis socialized with many prominent people and was included in many social functions. Heinrich Schliemann, a financier from St. Petersburg, Russia, came to Sacramento to handle some family business. While setting up a bank affiliated with the House of Rothschild, Schliemann became acquainted with Tevis. The two men shared similar outlooks and continued their friendship after Schliemann left Sacramento. A few years later Schliemann was pursuing his personal passion for archaeology and had uncovered the ancient cities of Troy and Mycenae. Tevis was captivated and inspired by Schliemann's worldwide adventures and discoveries, believing that there were no fetters except those one put on oneself.

Lloyd Tevis. [Courtesy of Wells Fargo Bank History Room]

As California grew, so did Tevis's fortunes and his involvement in the ever-expanding state. In documents from the time, Tevis listed himself variously as "Capitalist" and "Money Lender." By 1854, both Haggin and

Tevis were looking for greater opportunities than Sacramento offered. Although they both held quite a bit of land in the area, they moved their office to Clay Street in the heart of downtown San Francisco. The two men shared office space and often invested in each other's ventures, but they did not set up a formal partnership, operating instead on a handshake and their spoken word.

Opportunities in California abounded, and Tevis was involved in many different business deals. He served as President of Pacific Ice Company, and was a director for Spring Valley Water Company, Riston Iron Works, and State Telegraph Company. He eventually sold the latter to Western Union. He invested in a venture to drain the Tule swamp land in central California, thus opening up tremendous amounts of agricultural property. In creating fertile land that could be used throughout the year, California became and remains one of the largest agricultural producers in the world.

In many of his deals Tevis affiliated with some of the biggest names of that time. He was among the principal investors in the California Dry Dock Company, and a syndicate member of the North Pacific Fur Trade to bring furs from Alaska. Tevis also invested in transportation and owned many miles of stagecoach routes, interest in the California Steam Navigation Company, and a local railroad that eventually became the Southern Pacific, of which Tevis served as a director. Through his railroad contacts, Tevis got to know many of the promoters of the Central Pacific Railroad, and he participated with Charles Crocker (one of the Big Four in the transcontinental railroad) in the Oakland Water Front Company. Although Tevis never held any ownership in the Central Pacific Railroad, he loaned money to its principals. It took years for the railroads to turn profits for their investors, but Tevis was a patient man and knew he would reap not only money, but valuable connections and allies from these relationships. Although men of Tevis's time and ilk are often referred to as "robber barons," they are the men who built California and helped connect it to the rest of the country via the Pony Express, stagecoach routes, the transcontinental railroad, and the telegraph. These men were producers and visionaries and bettered the lives of all who came to the region.

During this time, Tevis pursued transportation and infrastructure projects, and Haggin invested their money in a number of highly profitable mines, including the Anaconda in Montana. When John D. Rockefeller bought out the various partners, Tevis pocketed eight million dollars.

While Tevis was solidifying his place in California's history, the various express companies formed as a result of the gold rush were battling one another for survival. Delivery service to the West had begun earlier on, and with the cry of "Gold!", reliable and timely service became more necessary than ever. These services were provided by private companies. The U.S. Post Office did not have the scope or infrastructure at the time to undertake mail service to the western territories, much of which was not yet part of the union; however, none of the express companies had achieved dominance and consistent profitability. The market needed thinning and a number of express companies sought domination. Adams & Company was the preeminent company, and various upstarts, including Wells, Fargo & Company, took a run at them. One by one other companies folded, leaving just Adams and Wells Fargo. Both companies slashed rates and vied to be faster and better. The fierce competition combined with the financial panic of 1855 ruined Adams & Company, which left Wells Fargo as the only major express service to the west. However, dominance did not come without a significant price. The value of Wells Fargo stock plummeted from $100 to $13 per share. In addition, the danger of Indian attacks on stagecoaches was increasing. Wells Fargo now owned the market, but it was questionable whether the company would survive the battle it fought so hard to win.

At this juncture the paths of Wells, Fargo & Company and Lloyd Tevis met, and ultimately merged. In keeping with his interest in promoting the development of the West and reaping the rewards of expansion and improvements, Tevis wanted a piece of the express business. During the competition between Wells Fargo and Adams, Tevis was readying himself to move in. When Wells Fargo stock dropped precipitously, Tevis bought up large amounts. With the blessing of Governor Leland Stanford, whom Tevis had often provided with much-needed financing for his Central Pacific Railroad, Tevis formed the Pacific Express. The company existed only on paper, but Tevis included several prominent California businessmen on its board of directors: D. O. Mills, a Sacramento banker; Henry D. Mann, a mining agent; Josiah Stanford, Leland Stanford's brother; and Lewis Cunningham, another capitalist.

When Tevis filed the articles of incorporation for the new venture, he had more in mind than just an express company. Tevis was orchestrating one of America's first corporate takeovers. Included in its purpose, the Pacific Express's articles of incorporation stated, ". . . for said purposes or any other purpose, to lease, buy or sell all or any part of the Capital Stock of any other Company or Companies and to make any contract whatever relating thereto."

On May 10, 1869, directors of the Union Pacific and the Central Pacific met in Promontory Point, Utah, drove the golden spike linking the two rail lines, and opened America's transcontinental railroad. In the case of Lloyd Tevis, driving the golden spike was one of the last elements in his quest to own the dominant express company in the United States.

Wells, Fargo & Company directors saw the transcontinental railroad as their ticket to putting the company back on a profitable path. They could now ship by rail, which was faster, more reliable, and could carry a much greater volume of goods. Wells Fargo had achieved dominance and was now moving toward profitability—until September 15, 1869. On that day, the Central Pacific Railroad informed Wells Fargo that it had signed an exclusive, ten-year-long shipping agreement with Pacific Express. They further informed Wells Fargo that the agreement would go into effect two weeks later. Suddenly the company was facing yet another competitor—one that was not even in business. To clinch his position, Tevis took out an ad in the *Sacramento Union* announcing that Pacific Express leased the Masonic Hall on J Street and was looking for a larger, more permanent site.

On October 4, 1869, Tevis, Mills, and Bacon met with founders William G. Wells and Charles Fargo, and A. H. Berry, president of Wells Fargo, in Omaha. In what has come to be known as the Omaha Conference (and is still used as a case study in corporate raids), Tevis and his associates set the terms between Wells Fargo and Pacific Express. Pacific Express would grant its railroad contract to Wells Fargo and would not go into business. However, Wells Fargo had to increase its capital stock by a third, from $10 million to $15 million. With Pacific Express holding the much-needed railroad contract and Tevis holding huge amounts of Wells Fargo stock, Pacific Express received $5 million of the newly expanded stock. In order to meet the terms set by Tevis and his group, Wells Fargo had to distribute its surplus assets to the existing stockholders and sell them in order to increase its capital stock.

Wells Fargo had little choice; however, Tevis was not done. Given the increased stock, Tevis asked for three additional board seats and that Wells Fargo's principal office be moved from New York to San Francisco. This would be the first major corporation to operate from the West Coast.

Will Tevis, grandson of Lloyd Tevis, and his granddaughter Sandra Tevis. [Courtesy of Western States Trail Foundation]

Wells Fargo directors could have litigated, but the time it would take to go through a protracted lawsuit would have driven them out of business. In order for the company to survive, it had to bow to a tougher adversary, even if that adversary existed only on paper.

On February 8, 1872, Lloyd Tevis became President of Wells, Fargo & Company. He served for twenty years, the longest-serving president in the history of the corporation. Under his leadership and vision, Tevis expanded express service throughout the United States, and then across the Atlantic to England and the rest of Europe. Tevis also oversaw the development and growth of the company's banking arm, now the dominant aspect of one of America's oldest corporations. Of all his accomplishments throughout his life, Tevis, who died in his home in San Francisco on July 24, 1899, valued his Wells Fargo coup as the finest and most gratifying.

Lloyd, Will, and Gordon Tevis, grandsons of Lloyd Tevis. [Courtesy of Western States Trail Foundation]

❈ PART TWO ❈

❯ 8 ❮

1959: Awarding the First Tevis Cup

As the 1950s drew to a close, Robie's ride took yet another step in developing its own identity and autonomy. In 1959, for the first time, the Western States 100 Miles—One Day Ride had a prize for the first horse and rider to finish the event. Robie wanted to be the first winner of the Tevis Cup, but it wasn't meant to be. In fact, after 1958 Robie never again led a band of horses and riders across the finish line to win first place.

However, Robie and the other Western States Trail Foundation directors wanted to ensure that the one-hundred-mile *ride* did not turn into a one-hundred-mile *race*. To remain true to their original vision, they developed a completion award that has become a badge of honor for all who have earned it during the past fifty years. The Western States belt buckle would be awarded to every rider who completed the journey in less than twenty-four hours on a fit, sound horse. Harking back to the horsemen whom Robie so admired, the silver belt buckle features a medallion of a galloping Pony Express rider modeled after Herman Hansen's painting, *Indian Gauntlet*. Inscribed on the buckle are the words, "100 Miles—One Day." For many recipients, their Tevis Cup belt buckle is their Olympic medal, a badge of honor proudly worn by an elite fraternity; a symbol of horsemanship, tenacity, and courage.

Thirty-six riders gathered at the Tahoe City post office on the morning of August 15, 1959. For her first and only time Betty Veal joined with her husband, on his second and final ride. She had a wonderful Appaloosa stallion named Crow, and Robie encouraged her participation. She knew much of the route, for prior to the ride she worked alongside the men performing trail maintenance and repair. The long, heavy winters in the

Sierra Nevada constantly take their toll on the trail, and every spring volunteers work many hours to repair damage caused by erosion, snowmelt, fallen trees, and shifted boulders. Veal routinely joined her husband, Jack, Robie, and others in preparing the trail for the annual event. That year she actually participated.

"The experience was exhilarating," said Veal, reflecting back over the decades. "I finished fourth, and I was thrilled. I felt like I had really accomplished something. I helped build the trail, and then I rode the trail. When we got to the river crossing the horses just took off, but they never ran themselves out." Veal earned one of the inaugural Tevis Cup belt buckles, a treasure she cherishes to this day. "I only rode the ride once. It was too much. Besides," she added with a sly smile, "Wendell wanted me to be the ride secretary." Every year Veal checks the riders in at the start, seeing them off on a journey where about half of them will realize the sense of accomplishment that Veal did on that August day in 1959.

At the awards ceremony that same year, Nick Mansfield was the one who stood up to accept the very first presentation of the Tevis Cup. His is the first name inscribed on the cup bearing the words, "Horses and men are equal, some excel in performance." Mansfield was also vindicated by his win, having long felt that his horse, Buffalo Bill, was superior; this honor only confirmed it. Mansfield never won the Tevis Cup again, but almost twenty years later, Buffalo Bill was one of the first horses inducted into the Endurance Hall of Fame.

The rules for the ride remained straightforward and simple. Riders had to stick to the marked trail, and they had to complete the distance in twenty-four hours or less. The veterinarians had the final say regarding the welfare of any horse, and could pull a horse at any point during the ride. With the awarding of the Tevis Cup, Robie also stated that horses had to carry a minimum of 165 pounds, based on the early letters Robie wrote to *Western Horseman* that led to the creation of the ride. Initially this policy was easy to abide by. Riders rode in heavy western saddles and traditional western garb like jeans and chaps. With this kind of gear, even a 125-pound woman could make the weight limit without having to add lead weights. As the ride became more sophisticated, the weight limit came under great discussion. (In the late 1960s the weight requirement was changed to apply only to those competing for either of the two special awards, the Tevis Cup and the Haggin Cup;

those riders seeking a belt buckle for completion did not have to maintain a minimum weight.)

Nick Mansfield on Buffalo Bill. [Courtesy of Western States Trail Foundation]

As testament to the interest the Tevis Cup ride generated, long-distance rides began springing up. Most were unofficial gatherings, but as they grew in number they were modeled after the Tevis ride by having a set distance, a time limit, and veterinary examinations to ensure horses were not overridden. A fifty-six-mile ride from Reno, Nevada, to Tahoe City was held, and many of the Tevis riders brought a second horse. They completed the shorter ride, then tackled the Tevis Cup the next day.

The 1960s began, and change was everywhere. President Kennedy announced that the United States would put a man on the moon by the end of the decade, the Vietnam War would divide the country, and children would look at their parents and rebel like no generation ever had before. The Tevis Cup was not immune to the changes going on everywhere else. Fortunately, many of these tensions and challenges would only further inspire the event and set the foundation for the emergence of a sport that would spread across the world.

The date of the annual ride is set to coincide most closely with the second full moon of the summer, to maximize the amount of daylight. In 1960 forty riders gathered on August 6. Nick Mansfield was once again in the field, as were Robie and Barner, but none of them was first to cross the finish line. Ernie Sanchez, a horse trader of dubious character and a jockey at the smaller tracks, rode his mustang, Marko B, ahead of the field. Among some of the other interesting participants in the 1960 ride was a mother-and-daughter team, Margaret and Charlotte Williams, from Los Angeles. More and more people were traveling long distances to take part; riders representing forty-one states, as well as Austria and Mexico, had made the journey. The interest shown in the 1960 ride hinted at the international stature it would eventually claim.

Following the completion of that year's ride, the *Auburn Journal* proclaimed, "The Tevis Cup is fast becoming the outstanding event of its kind throughout the world." Although the praise was well-deserved, there were few rides of its kind anywhere else in the world.

Robie helped publicize the ride by inviting various celebrities and VIPs to be involved. Robie discovered that Clark Gable was filming a movie in the area and promptly invited him to be an honorary judge. The movie star was accompanied by an Austrian count, Frederick von Lederber, and Milt Smith, who played football for UCLA in the Rose Bowl before going on to play for the Philadelphia Eagles. Although celebrity figures were a fun touch, the ride didn't need them, and marched steadily forward on its own merits.

As the 1961 ride approached, the United States was no longer big enough for Robie. In the announcement letter Robie extended an invitation to "riders of all nations," proclaiming, "The ride proves good horses. It tests good horsemanship."

That year saw three major changes. The first was the implementation of official timekeeping. Until then, riders started at the Tahoe City post office and then rode to Auburn. Now that the Tevis Cup trophy was in place and interest in the ride was growing, the time had come to more officially record the times of all the finishers.

The second change involved the start of the ride. The number of riders had grown over the years and the trailhead was often congested, so Robie implemented a controlled start. Ride officers, Robie among them, set a pace for several miles after leaving Tahoe City. From Bear Creek (now commonly recognized as the entrance to the ski resort Alpine Meadows, south of Squaw Valley), riders set off in two-minute intervals, in groups of ten. This system spread the riders out along the trail, and allowed the faster riders to take the lead. Though only one rider could earn the honor of having his name inscribed on the Tevis Cup, the basic tenet of the ride—completion—remained.

The third change ensured the longevity of the ride, when Dr. Richard Barsaleau joined the veterinary panel. Barsaleau, who became an integral part of the ride and its success, brought an aura of professionalism that helped the ride through some of its more stormy times, especially later, when animal welfare groups questioned the health and welfare of the horses.

Barsaleau was heavily influenced by the U.S. Cavalry methods throughout his childhood on the East Coast. During World War II, Barsaleau joined the Marines and afterwards headed to college in Colorado, where he developed a reputation for breaking and training problem horses. There was no magic in his methods, just solid, consistent horsemanship based on Gordon Wright's Cavalry Manual and writings from the French Cavalry School at Saumur and other European classical horsemen. "I guess you could say I'm a bibliophile," chuckles Barsaleau, who is still a voracious reader. "I consider myself a student of the horse, and my early teachers, like my father, did things by the book."

Barsaleau received his veterinary degree from Colorado State University, settling in Southern California with his wife, Maggie. He worked at various ranches and farms for private individuals, and became familiar with area horsemen, several of whom became icons in equestrian sport. "I really admired Jimmy Williams and Clyde Kennedy. One of my greatest moments was beating both of them and Barbara Worth in a stock horse class." (Williams, Kennedy, and Worth were prominent horsemen in California during the 1950s and 1960s, winning most of the major awards presented at that time.)

While working at a Thoroughbred farm in the San Fernando Valley, Dr. Barsaleau was asked to do something unethical. As a man of unswerving principles, he promptly resigned his position. Moving to San Luis Obispo, he did veterinary work at the Hearst Ranch, and he and his family then settled in Visalia, a small farming community in the heart of the San Joaquin Valley. He got more and more involved in horse showing, obtaining his American Horse Shows Association judge's license for hunters, jumpers, hunt-seat and stock-seat equitation, and Arabian horse divisions. He also actively showed his own horses in the western divisions. Regardless of what he was training a horse to do, Barsaleau remained dedicated to the principles his father imbued in him. "My father preached lateral work, balance, and lightness. If a horse can feel a fly, what are we doing with whips, spurs, bits, et cetera?" His favorite saying, from the British sportsman Robert Smith Surtes, sums up much of his philosophy about horses, "There is no secret so close, as that between a rider and his horse."

In the spring of 1961 Barsaleau received a phone call that would forever change his life. "Wendell Robie called and asked me to be part of the ride. I had heard he was a horseman. I told him that I was working on it," said Barsaleau with a twinkle in his eye, as he recounted his first conversation with Robie. Initially Barsaleau was reluctant to join, but Robie was persistent, and after several conversations he convinced Barsaleau to join the veterinary panel examining the horses. Robie had no idea he had just found a man as stubborn and as much a visionary as himself.

One of the vet checks that Barsaleau manned was the one-hour hold, then at Michigan Bluff, which for many years served as the second, and final, mandatory rest stop. That day in 1961, Robie rode in on his mare, Spica. After the initial examination Barsaleau proclaimed the mare lame. Robie was incredulous, and the other vets and ride officials looked at Barsaleau as if he was crazy. Robie argued; Barsaleau stood firm. Finally Robie walked off for his one-hour wait. During that hour, many of the other vets and officials told Barsaleau it would be his first and last time at the Tevis Cup ride, but Barsaleau did not care. He knew a lame horse when he saw one, and he said he "didn't care if God was riding it. "An hour later I saw Wendell walking toward me. He stuck out his hand to shake mine and said that he accepted my decision. Once he cooled off, he too could see that the mare was lame. We became friends at that moment."

Although Robie was eliminated (or pulled) at Michigan Bluff, Dru Barner continued on with her Arabian-cross gelding, Chagitai. Forty-five riders started that year, and Barner crossed the finish line first. Not only was her name inscribed on the trophy as the first woman to win, she also logged the first official time for the event, finishing in thirteen hours and two minutes. (The husband-and-wife team of Ralph and Betty Deever served as the first timers for the Tevis ride, a post they held for years. Poring through old records, one can find the number of starters, the number of pulled riders and where they were pulled, and the number of finishers.)

After the 1961 Tevis Cup ride, Dr. Jasper, who had served as head vet for several years, told Robie he felt it necessary to step down. There was no doubt in Robie's mind who he wanted for the post; however, Barsaleau was not as enthusiastic. "Wendell didn't even have a vet in charge of the veterinary panel, just a friend of his who was a medical doctor. I didn't think that was right, and I told Wendell so." By now Robie was realizing that Barsaleau would "tell him so" whenever he felt adamant about an issue. Although Barsaleau didn't prevail on every point, he did on most because he picked his battles, and stood up only for issues he felt were integral to the ride and the good of the horses. Barsaleau also told Robie that not paying the ride veterinarians was very unpopular. Robie stood firm that the entire ride should be a volunteer effort. But Barsaleau was a patient man, and in 1963 the vets began receiving a $50 honorarium, a policy that continues to this day (although the amount has increased).

In these early days, there was no existing research about the effects of long-distance riding, preparing horses, or nutritional guidelines. "In those days," said Barsaleau with disgust, "endurance riders would call just in time to say a prayer over the horse." Barsaleau was determined to change that approach.

"The early days were rough," recalled Jack Veal. "Doc Barsaleau brought care and finesse to the horses. He is a pillar of the ride."

"When I took over, I insisted on professional status," said Barsaleau. "We were at the ride to render protection to the horse. Some vets tried to play favorites, but I insisted on objective criteria. One policy I put in place was that unless impossible, it took two vets to eliminate a horse," explained Barsaleau. He made the vets wear ties, in order to present a more professional image, but allowed them to dispense with coats. Barsaleau is very proud of the number of veterinarians who have been associated with the Tevis Cup ride over the years. "We've had many prominent vets like Charlie Reed, Scott Jackson, president of the American Association of Equine Practitioners, and R. M. Miller." To this day the panel of Tevis Cup vets comprises some of the best veterinarians in the endurance riding community, and they help set the worldwide standard for veterinary procedures in the sport.

❧   ❧   ❧

In 1962 Paige Harper, a colorful character and close associate of Robie, earned his place on the Tevis Cup riding one of Robie's horses. Thirty-one riders started that year, and twenty-five finished. One of the most notable was Alexander Mackay-Smith, a noted horseman, editor, and author from Virginia. Mackay-Smith, who had heard of Robie's incredible ride, made the journey to California to discover its allure for himself. Mackay-Smith further cemented the Tevis Cup's growing stature when he wrote about his experiences on the ride in *The Chronicle of the Horse*, a prominent weekly equestrian magazine. Before endurance was even recognized as a sport, Mackay-Smith, who served as *The Chronicle's* editor-in-chief for many years, realized the specialness of the event. "The Tevis Cup is a graduate course in horsemanship," he wrote. "[The Tevis Cup] requires a degree of courage and fitness and an effort on the part of both horse and rider, which is fully comparable to the Speed and Endurance Test of the Olympic Three-Day Event." Although some would argue that the Tevis test is even more demanding and difficult, the point was made.

Mackay-Smith was impressed by the terrain, the horses, the riders, and the veterinary review, but most of all by the scientific research. He wrote, "The data thus collected is of twofold significance. In the first place it reveals a technique for protecting the horse, not only in this particular competition, but also in others calling for maximum effort, such as the Speed and Endurance test of the Olympic Three-Day Event." Over thirty years later, data carefully collected during the annual Tevis Cup ride would be used to help prepare and care for the Olympic horses at the 1996 Games.

Mackay-Smith rode a Thoroughbred gelding named Banner, loaned to him by Will Tevis, Lloyd's grandson. Mackay-Smith, more familiar with Thoroughbreds than Arabians, was impressed by the latter's superiority over the length of the trail. Of the two Thoroughbred horses on the ride that year, Mackay-Smith wrote, "Undoubtedly the Thoroughbred blood induced these horses to perform partly on their courage, thus conveying a partly inaccurate impression of stamina to their riders." Toward the end of the ride Banner needed to ease up as his pulse and respiration recovery rate was slow coming out of a mandatory rest stop. Although Mackay-Smith had ridden at a brisk trot with Pat Fitzgerald, Robie,

Barner, and Harper for much of the ride, he now held his horse back to a walk. Banner perked up at the more leisurely pace, and Mackay-Smith found himself riding with Robie's son, John. John, who earned a buckle more to please his father than for himself, felt duty-bound to attempt the ride, and fortunately had a good enough horse to reach the finish line. Although John Robie never amounted to much in his father's eyes, he did marry, and his daughter, Marion, received the doting attention Robie never gave to his son.

In 1962 the first mule completed the ride. Mules were long recognized as steady, hard-working animals. Despite their stamina, mules can be truly stubborn and will typically quit when tired or stressed. Where a horse can be ridden to utter exhaustion, it is almost impossible to make a mule work beyond its inclination or capabilities. Joanne Harris and her mule, Chongo, earned the first Tevis belt buckle presented to a finisher on a mule; but Chongo wouldn't be the last mule to receive honors.

That same year, George O'Brien, a buckle recipient the year before, created a profile map of the Tevis Cup route that showed the cumulative elevation changes. He computed that horses and riders ascend over 22,000 feet and descend more than 19,000 feet, a total matched by no other one-hundred-mile endurance ride in the world.

Although the Veals eventually divorced, Jack and Betty remained intimately involved with Robie and the Tevis Cup ride for years to come. "Wendell wouldn't let me ride, he wanted me to help down in the canyons," said Jack Veal. "I was a 'canyon keeper' and would ride down in the canyons to help any of the riders." As more riders came to test themselves against the trail, Robie and the WSTF Board of Governors recognized the need for mounted assistance. Drag riders were assigned specific segments of the trail, and they would ride behind the last riders and sweep the trail to make sure no one was left in the wilderness needing assistance. Like many other aspects of the Western States Ride, the drag rider format was copied at other rides. Today, Sweep Riders of the Sierra, or S.O.S., encompasses the drag riders, ham radio operators, and other efforts to deal with various types of emergencies. In the early days, it was just Jack Veal and a few other dedicated men on horseback.

One year in the late 1960s, Veal and his drag riders found themselves in a predicament. "I was riding drag in El Dorado Canyon near Kaput Springs. This big, old, hammer-headed horse out of Nevada had gone off the cliff," recalled Veal. "The rider was okay, but the horse was stuck down in the bottom of the canyon." In the past, injured horses that fell down the canyons were generally shot and left for the scavengers. That year *Sports Illustrated* was covering the ride and the magazine's photographer hiked down to the location after hearing about some kind of excitement brewing. Robie had also arrived, as he made his way along the trail. Realizing he was facing a serious public relations situation, Robie brazenly announced that they were in the process of staging a rescue right at that moment and that they would get the horse out with a helicopter.

Veal immediately turned his attention to finding a helicopter. "Dr. Hank Cook had shown up after a while," continued Veal, "and we found some real swell fellows from U.C. Berkeley Forestry. They got a helicopter out of San Francisco." While the small group stood around for several hours waiting for the helicopter, they kept the Tevis Cup riders moving along the trail. Dr. Cook, Veal, and several others carefully made their way down to the stranded horse. By the time the helicopter arrived, a TV crew that had heard of the event made its way to where everyone had gathered. "You know," said Veal, "cliffs and helicopters are not compatible." The helicopter crew wanted to call off the rescue, but Robie was adamant. "There was never a gray zone with Wendell," added Veal. "The helicopter kept trying to get close enough to get a sling around the horse. Rocks were rolling down the hill. Doc tranquilized the horse and finally we were able to get a sling on and they floated that horse up to Deadwood." From there the horse was trailered out, and it recovered without further incident. Veal continued his canyon patrol down to Foresthill. "We stopped in for a drink and watched our rescue on TV! The *Sports Illustrated* reporter got a much bigger story than he anticipated."

9

JAMES BEN ALI HAGGIN AND THE HAGGIN CUP

When 1963 rolled around, word spread as the Tevis Cup ride gained national recognition, and for the first time the ride exceeded fifty participants. Fifty-three riders started, and an impressive total of forty-four finished. Pat Fitzgerald logged the win that year aboard a nine-year-old Arabian gelding named Ken. However impressive Fitzgerald's win, it would be his wife, Donna, who would set seemingly unbeatable Tevis Cup records seven years later.

Despite the improvements to the veterinary panel, Dr. Barsaleau and others remained unhappy about the treatment of the horses. Even with the vet checks, there were many miles and many hours between vet inspections, and some riders simply overrode their horses. The Tevis Cup ride was beginning to attract the wrong kind of attention, and Barsaleau used that fact to promote his idea for another award, one that would commend horsemanship, and in a December 1963 article in *Western Horseman*, Barsaleau wrote, "To get the farthest, the fastest, in the best condition, and have enough horse to do it again."

Although various people had discussed the issue in the past, nothing was done until Barsaleau decided the time had arrived. With Will Tevis, Robie, Barner, and Betty Veal, he discussed an award that recognized superior horsemanship and a horse that finished the ride in excellent condition. While several people have claimed credit for the original idea, there is no doubt that Barsaleau's vision, persistence, extensive knowledge, and articulate abilities were responsible for the creation of the award.

Since the Tevis Cup was named after Lloyd Tevis, it was only fitting that the second award be named after his closest friend, his business

associate and brother-in-law, James Ben Ali Haggin. Born in Harrods-
burg, Kentucky, on December 9, 1822, Haggin derived his unusual middle name from his mother's family. Haggin's grandfather, Ibrahim Ben
Ali, was born in 1756 near Constantinople in Turkey. He was raised a
devout Muslim in a family of wealth headed by his father, Ali Ben
Mustapha, and was born to a Christian woman whom his father had
bought, after she was stolen from her family by Venetians. Ibrahim Ben
Ali himself married at the age of thirteen, and the young couple then
made an obligatory journey to Mecca. Upon his return, he married a second wife, Fatima (whose name appears regularly in the Haggin family
tree), and shortly thereafter he took a third wife, in keeping with Muslim law. At his father's urging, he joined the sultan's army.

His life took a dramatic change when two of his bunkmates were
found murdered and Ibrahim Ben Ali was seen as the prime suspect.
Professing his innocence, he was given five days to prove his claims; on
the fifth day he would receive a dish of black olives, indicating that he
would be put to death the next day. Imprisoned together in the sultan's
jail, an old Christian Spaniard converted him. Throughout the night he
prayed to his new savior and the next day instead of being executed he
was freed, as the two actual murderers had been found. However, freedom was an illusion. He was pressed into the sultan's army then fight-
ing a war between Turkey and Russia. He fought in many battles, and
was wounded several times. Ultimately he was captured by enemy forces
and imprisoned near St. Petersburg for two years. During that time he
befriended a lady to whom he ministered. Freed from prison, and
warned that if he returned to Turkey he would be treated as a spy, Ben
Ali headed to England. Eventually he sailed for America and set up
practice as a doctor in Philadelphia. He married, and his daughter Ade-
line Ben Ali married Terah Temple Haggin. They moved to Kentucky
where Haggin opened a law practice. James Ben Ali Haggin was the second of their eight children.

Unlike Tevis, Haggin was an accomplished horseman. For Tevis,
horses were a means of transportation and work; for Haggin, they were
a passion. He established a prominent Thoroughbred breeding farm in
Sacramento, and Rancho Del Paso produced many top racehorses, the
most famous being the 1886 Kentucky Derby winner, Ben Ali, named
for his mother's colorful family history.

Hearing of the Western States Ride, Louis Haggin donated the newest award in honor of his grandfather: a silver cup made by Tiffany and Company. The top ten horses would be evaluated, and Lloyd Tevis, grandson of the first Lloyd Tevis, summed up the award's purpose quite succinctly: "To be awarded to the horse in the most superior physical condition." Modern endurance rides usually award a best-conditioned award, a relatively objective honor based on certain physical criteria, such as general soundness after the event, ratio of completion time to that of the winner, and general recovery statistics. The Haggin Cup is much more, and has evolved over the years. Many people, especially noted horsemen, have come to regard the Haggin Cup as the most prestigious honor one can earn, and the award remains unique in both the sport of endurance and other equestrian pursuits as well.

"Mr. Tevis wanted to consider the top twenty finishing horses for the award," explained Barsaleau. "I wanted the top five. I felt there was too much time differential between the first horse and the twentieth horse to have a fair comparison. We compromised on ten." To this day the top ten horses are invited by the WSTF directors to be judged for the Haggin Cup.

✳ 10 ✦

Dr. Richard Barsaleau Earns a Buckle, and Marion Robie Closes Out a Decade

Dr. Richard Barsaleau had grown so intrigued with long-distance riding that he decided to join the competitors in the 1964 Tevis Cup ride. He would be the first veterinarian to compete, in part to learn what the horses faced throughout the entire ride. The veterinarians are only able to observe the horses at certain points. He wanted to see up close what it took for a horse to meet the challenge.

Barsaleau rode an Arabian mare he had bred himself, a mare that went on to produce two more Tevis Cup horses. "The mare was inexperienced," said Barsaleau, recollecting his first ride. "The October before, in 1963, I rode her in a hackamore class at the Grand National in the Cow Palace. I set out on the ride with John Rodgers, and we got lost a bit right after leaving Robinson Flat. It is easy to do out there. There was logging going on in the Cavanaugh Ridge area, and we took a wrong turn. After about fifteen minutes we realized we were lost and backtracked to find the trail. We thought it was the end of the world," laughed Barsaleau. This moment gave him insight into how easily a rider can get caught up in the competition and overlook the welfare of his horse. The experience cemented in Barsaleau's mind the concept of the ride veterinarians as advocates for the horses. He knew that while most riders had no desire to cause harm to their mounts, it was easy to get caught up in the moment.

Near the river crossing, Rodgers, Barsaleau's riding companion, was pulled. Barsaleau happened upon Nan Benzie, who had earned her first Tevis Cup buckle in 1961. "I give Nan full credit to my finish. My mare was inexperienced and Nan kept us going. That first finish was euphoric. I remember that first one."

Nick Mansfield finished his tenth Tevis Cup ride, the first rider to log one thousand miles over the rugged trail, and he did it consecutively. Perhaps even more impressive was that he accomplished this feat on the same horse, Buffalo Bill. The 1964 ride was the tenth annual ride, and Mansfield started a tradition that continues today. Since the inception of the ride in 1955, over sixty riders have achieved the distinction of completing the Tevis Cup ten times. However, few have done it consecutively as did Mansfield.

That year, Neil Hutton won the Tevis with a riding time of fourteen hours and ten minutes on his Arabian mare, Salalah. Perhaps the awarding of the Haggin Cup was even more important that year, if for no other reason than a political one. With all kinds of rumors, of horses being run into the ground and dropping dead, the SPCA began crawling all over the ride. In these early years, some horses did die and some riders were injured, but fortunately accidents like these were very few and far between. As veterinary standards became more rigorous, fatalities and other tragedies became almost nonexistent.

The SPCA actually held a hearing claiming abuse of the horses by both riders and the ride organizers. When one horse died, the SPCA attempted to prosecute the rider. The SPCA staked out several locations on the lower part of the ride attempting to put a stop to it and prove that horses were regularly being abused. "I hated to see the horses overridden," stated Betty Veal, "so I was glad when Wendell decided to do the Haggin Cup. Ina and I supported Doc's idea for the Haggin Cup." However, when Veal heard that the SPCA was trying to stop the ride, she was incensed. "We found out where they were going to be on the trail," she continued. "Fortunately I had a friend who had a ranch bordering that part of the trail. We just rerouted everyone through my friend's ranch, and around the SPCA people. They sat on the trail all night and never saw a single horse!" After compelling testimony by many of the Tevis Cup veterinarians, the rider was exonerated. The existence of the Haggin Cup as evidence of intent to ensure the horses' safety helped in the resolution of the case.

Participation in the ride took another jump in 1965. Eighty-five signed up to tackle the challenging route, and fifty-three of them realized their goal. By now the veterinary team was beginning to develop a solid science regarding distance riding that carries forward today. In addition to checking each horse for lameness, the vets check the pulse, respiration, and temperature for each horse. At mandatory rest stops, pulse and respiration are measured once again before the horse is released to continue down the trail. The vets use stethoscopes to listen to gut sounds, and look for signs of dehydration.

Year after year the Tevis vets built a very useful and valuable database of information. Vets see the horses approximately ten times throughout the ride. Some of the vet checks are in very remote locations and the vets have to hike in the afternoon before and camp overnight. Several of the vet checks are a "trot-through" where the vet watches the horse as it moves by. As long as the horse is sound and looks alert and relaxed it can continue. Other checks require only a quick pulse and respiration (P & R) check before allowing the horse to proceed. Robinson Flat and Michigan Bluff, the two one-hour vet checks, are much more comprehensive.

In 1965 Ed Johnson earned his first Tevis Cup victory on the Arabian stallion Bezatal, his first finish. Another stallion, Wendell Robie's Siri, won the Haggin Cup. This was an exciting victory for Robie as he had never won the ride when the actual Tevis Cup was awarded. Nick Mansfield logged his eleventh consecutive finish, the highest record in the history of the ride up to that point. Donna Fitzgerald earned a fourth buckle, and no one had any idea in 1965 that she would come to dominate the ride in a way no one has ever matched—and probably never will.

Another new face came to the ride. Juliette Suhr would make her mark and achieve a number of "Tevis firsts." From her home in Santa Clara, near the heart of the famed Silicon Valley, Suhr longed to return to her childhood love of riding horses. As a young war bride, her father announced, "You are a married woman. You will never ride a horse again." Suhr believed him, and for twenty years horses were completely absent from her life. "With three children to raise . . . I threw myself willingly into community activities. I became active in women's organizations, helped the PTA, warmed Little League benches for eleven years, chaired a Santa Clara County Mothers March of Dimes effort, canvassed the block for cancer research funds, chauffeured the Girl Scouts, wrote a newsletter for the local Goodwill chapter, and helped with fund-raising events for different organizations."

Suhr's life was full, or so she thought, until she ran into a friend who invited her to go riding. That was in 1962, and soon Suhr owned a half-Thoroughbred mare named Lady Kay. Early in 1964 Suhr heard about a ride in the Sierra Nevada. She called Wendell Robie and entered herself in the ride, having no idea what it would take to prepare for such an undertaking. Where her preparation and knowledge were lacking, Suhr had determination and enthusiasm on her side. However, these traits alone cannot get a horse and rider from Tahoe City to Auburn in one day. "I bought a new pair of jeans so I would look nice for the people and, as the waves lapped at the shores of Lake Tahoe, I climbed upon Lady Kay, and departed in the 5:00 A.M. darkness of a Saturday morning in mid-July." By the time Suhr arrived at Robinson's Flat, she and Lady Kay straggled in, last out of the fifty-three starters. Lady Kay was slightly lame and her pulse and respiration were way too high. Suhr was in no condition to ride any further herself. Her brand new, smart-looking jeans had rubbed her legs raw. Humiliated, defeated, and worn out, Suhr was forced to drop out, while her family optimistically waited for her arrival in Auburn.

Suhr did not remain beaten for long. "I had tried and failed, but the exhilaration of just being a participant in that ride lingered. For someone who had never ridden in rugged mountains, the high country called me and I knew I would return. The early rides among the rows of pear trees in my Valley of Heart's Delight were being replaced in my heart with the call of the high Sierras." Although Suhr longed to return to try the Tevis Cup, she realized that Lady Kay was not a one-hundred-mile horse. Apparently Dru Barner took notice of Suhr, perhaps amazed by her naïveté, and called her early in 1965. Barner wanted a younger and faster horse and told Suhr that she could borrow Chagatai, who was by now sixteen years old, but still quite fit and sound. Suhr knew Barner had won the Tevis on Chagatai and had finished a total of five times. She was both overwhelmed and thrilled with Barner's offer.

In 1965 Suhr arrived at the start of the Tevis Cup ride with a chance of actually finishing. Chagatai had been down the trail many times before and his old home in Auburn lay at the end of the route. Suhr wisely wore her oldest and softest pair of jeans, and both she and Chagatai finished the ride that year, no worse for wear. At the end, Suhr stated that she felt "ten feet tall," (a title she later used for a book chronicling the many adventures in her life). She helped organize the sport and was the first person to finish the Tevis Cup twenty times, earning the first two-thousand-mile belt buckle. Only five riders have earned this distinction, including Suhr's adult daughter, Barbara White, who holds the record for the most finishes to date, at twenty-seven.

Over the next three years, Ed Johnson and Bud Dardi traded off Tevis Cup victories. Johnson won in 1965 and 1967, with Dardi taking the two even years of 1966 and 1968. In between Dardi's two Tevis Cup wins, he captured the Haggin Cup in 1967, proving himself a capable, talented horsemen. Finishing the Tevis Cup ride is a challenge; to win these coveted trophies three separate times is quite a feat.

In 1966, Pat Fox once again found herself at the starting line, but this time she was on a horse, not watching from the sidelines. "I had watched this ride develop and I knew so many of the characters." Three years earlier Fox was asked to serve on the WSTF Board of Governors. She was one of the first women on the board and she served until 1989. "I attended all of the meetings. During the time I served, I watched the WSTF go from a club-oriented group to an internationally recognized one. When I first started we didn't know very much. I learned by trial and error."

Although she didn't really know what it would take to get from Tahoe City to Auburn in under twenty-four hours, Fox was comfortable riding in the backcountry. The Sierra Nevada mountains were her playground. "When I began riding in the mountains, I never got lost. I seemed to have a sixth sense. I learned to read all the trail signs like Watson's carved square '8s' and the marks around the Basque sheepherders' camps." Fox started out her first ride full of hope, but by Michigan Bluff she threw in the towel. She had given birth to her third daughter, Polly, earlier that year and she was just too fatigued to continue. In 1967 she returned, determined to earn one of the sought-after buckles. "When you saw someone else wearing one, it was like a secret. You knew what that buckle meant to one another." Fox wanted to join that elite fraternity of riders. Carefully and steadily making her way down the trail, Fox and her Arabian gelding Rhapso finished the ride and Fox earned the buckle she so desired. For the remainder of her life she wore it as a badge of honor. Even when plagued by Alzheimer's and robbed of her memory, her Tevis Cup belt buckle was one of the few things she still recognized before she died in early 2003.

Fox and her husband, Malcolm, remained Tevis Cup fixtures. Where Pat was more willing to take on a public roll by both competing and serving on the WSTF Board of Governors, her husband was quiet and preferred an unobtrusive presence. Although Malcolm enjoyed riding, he did not seek competition. However, each year he rode to the top of Squaw Valley and placed an American flag on Watson's Monument on the Fourth of July and for the Tevis Cup ride.

The 1967 awards ceremony—Pat Fox, fourth from right, front row. [Charles Barieau photo]

As the decade drew to a close, over one hundred riders now competed in this annual trek through the Sierra Nevada on a historic immigrant and mining trail. The long-distance riders and the veterinarians were learning more and more about the effects of long distances on horses and how to prepare them. A new term was buzzing around—endurance riding—and distance rides of twenty-five, fifty, seventy, and even one hundred miles were beginning to pop up. While there were more rides in the West, a few were emerging in the East as well, topped by the Vermont 100. However, none attracted the attention and participation of the Tevis Cup.

Riders crossing Emigrant Pass with Watson's Monument behind them. Note snow still on the ground in late July. [Courtesy of Western States Trail Foundation]

Paige Harper taking a break along the Western States Trail, circa 1960s. [Charles Barieau photo]

Local townspeople greeting Marion Robie as she arrives at Michigan Bluff to win the 1969 Tevis Cup. [Charles Barieau photo]

In 1969, of the 114 horses that started, 52 finished. The percentage of completions was dropping, due primarily to the larger number of riders entering. Over the years the Tevis Cup has consistently realized a completion rate fluctuating between 45 and 60 percent. For some, luck, good or bad, intervenes. On that particular day their horse steps on that rock with their name on it, or perhaps the horse gets overly excited and tires itself out early on. In some cases the rider gets caught up in the event and forgets to carefully pace his horse. And in some cases, riders arrive at the Tevis Cup ill-prepared to go the miles.

That same year, Walter Tibbitts won the Haggin Cup on his Appaloosa stallion, Ruff Spots Banner, the only Appaloosa ever to win either the Tevis or the Haggin Cup. Marion Robie, Wendell's granddaughter, closed out the 1960s by winning the Tevis Cup with her Arabian mare, Hailla. Robie beamed as his granddaughter accepted the prize, a vision he'd made concrete.

❧ 11 ❧

THE TEVIS CUP GOES TO SQUAW VALLEY

The 1970s proved a decade of great change for the Tevis Cup, and for the emergence of the sport of endurance riding. Several champion horses and riders now gained prominence, horses and riders who have established a legacy unparalleled to this day. In this decade, another new sport emerged as a direct result of the Tevis. Ultramarathon running is an even more widespread sport than endurance riding, with the original run on the Western States Trail the foundation and genesis of the sport. The trail so many immigrants found too difficult to cross provided a worthy challenge for endurance horses, and for runners.

Word of the ride had spread, and riders came from throughout the United States and other countries. Flying a horse around the world remains very expensive, complicated, and risky, in addition to the logistical problems presented by having to quarantine a horse, for anywhere from several weeks to a few months, so many of the foreign riders leased horses that were stabled near the Tevis trail. This desire for Tevis Cup horses helped fuel a small economy which led to endurance riding as a profession.

In addition to training and conditioning horses for themselves, a small number of horsemen living in the vicinity began training and conditioning experienced, reliable horses that riders coming from afar could lease, and those with the means could buy.

After twenty-five years, 870 riders had attempted the arduous ride and 507 actually finished. Given the large number of riders attempting the Tevis Cup each year, the Tahoe City post office no longer provided a practical starting point. In addition, the trail between Tahoe City and Squaw

Valley had become quite congested, as it was never intended for large groups of horses and riders. The WSTF governors looked for a more appropriate starting point, and they settled on Squaw Valley.

Alongside the expansive meadow a rustic stable offered boarding for some horses in the summer months and hosted a string of dude ranch horses that took tourists on guided rides around the meadow, and up into the small ridge separating Squaw Valley from Alpine Meadows. With plenty of parking and a horse-friendly atmosphere, Squaw Valley was a perfect place to start the ride. Squaw Valley was still basking in the glow of hosting the 1960 Winter Olympics and the worldwide recognition this conferred. An event that attracted participants from throughout the United States and even a few from other countries fit into Squaw Valley's image as a world-class destination. In midsummer, horses and riders assembled in the empty parking lot that filled with skiers in the winter months. Some people brought pipe corral panels and fastened them to the sides of their horse trailer. This allowed them to construct a portable corral for their horse. Others rigged rope corrals, and still others tied their horses to the trailer for the night or hobbled them to graze in the meadow. (Hobbles are leather straps placed around the horse's front feet and attached with a short chain. The horse can take small steps to browse the grass, but it is difficult for the horse to wander long distances. Horses don't need to lie down to sleep and most prefer not to, so being hobbled or tied does not affect their ability to adequately rest.)

The Tevis ride's veterinary standards and procedures were becoming more formalized and scientific. With all the vets now assembled at the starting point of the ride, they were able to evaluate each horse as a group. During the ride the vets were spread out at the various checkpoints, to reassemble at the conclusion of the ride. By performing an initial review together, they could discuss any particular characteristics a horse had, or any unique qualities in its gait, and note these tendencies on its veterinary inspection card. When the horse arrived at various vet checkpoints during its trek, the card would remind the vet of the horse's particular way of going and instead of automatically labeling the horse as possibly lame, the vet could compare his own observations with his memory of the horse at the preride check, as well as any comments noted by his colleagues along the way. Some of the vet check locations were so remote that it was necessary to hike in the night before and camp, in order to be in position to provide aid and to review the horses.

Serving on the veterinary panel was quite prestigious and, although he no longer served as the head vet, Dr. Barsaleau remained influential and active. He was proud of the fact that during his tenure he implemented honorariums for the veterinarians, a tradition that continues today. The veterinarians are the only paid group involved with the Tevis Cup. The rest of the functions of this massive undertaking are performed by volunteers, many returning to the ride year after year, just as the riders do. For them, the Tevis Cup is in their blood, also. There is something about this event that draws people in, whether to compete, volunteer, crew for a rider, or just follow along like a groupie. They are all Tevis afficionados, and as the years went by, more and more people became involved with this amazing undertaking.

For twenty years Squaw Valley provided a perfect starting point for the Tevis Cup ride. Riders and their crews could easily camp and horses could quietly graze during the night. At the 5:00 A.M. start, and then every two minutes, a group of ten horses would start up the mountain toward Watson's Monument. With a few slight alterations in the trail, riders still traveled one hundred miles before reaching Auburn and the ride lost no level of difficulty. In fact, it was arguably more difficult, as the horses had to immediately begin a two-thousand-foot ascent before settling into their pace and preparing themselves for more treacherous terrain ahead.

Despite the early hour, some of the local Squaw Valley residents got up before the sun to watch the crazy riders. Among those spectators were Malcolm and Pat Fox, who knew that the journey was possible after Pat accomplished it in 1967. Fox was dedicated to her horses and the mountains she grew up in. For decades she was the only person in the entire Tahoe–Truckee area who kept a horse in the high mountains year-round, simply moving her horse from her backyard to her garage, relegating the family's two Jeeps to the outside for at least six months. The local kids and their parents were used to seeing the tall, red-haired woman riding along the plowed streets on her Arabian horse, and they often called out to her horse by name. However, the tourists driving in to ski were always slack-jawed as they spotted Fox riding along the Main Road in the dead of winter. With their fancy skis and high-tech snow gear atop their cars, to the tourists Fox must have looked like an apparition from one hundred and fifty years ago. For Fox, separating horses and the mountains was inconceivable.

Although she never again competed in the Tevis Cup, Fox assumed a very important role. She and other select riders took on the role of drag riders. Because the majority of the trail goes through remote areas, the only effective way to assist any rider who may get in trouble is via horseback. In this modern-day world of instant communication, even cell phones do not work on much of the trail where the canyons block the signal. Just as they did one hundred fifty years ago, individuals have to help one another, often without the use of technology. Drag riders became an integral part of the Tevis Cup, helping ensure the safety of all participants. Beginning in the 1970s and into the 1980s, Pat Fox regularly volunteered to ride the section of trail between the start at Squaw Valley to Robinson Flat, while Jack Veal continued to patrol the canyons.

On August 15, 1970, Fox stood aside waiting for 164 riders to head out on their journey, their quest to complete the Tevis Cup. A little over half would make it to Auburn. The Tevis Cup truly is a test of the individual, and the ability to guide one's self and one's horse over a difficult trail gives the riders discoveries and experiences that stay with them a lifetime. Many riders describe facing situations and emotions never experienced before and likely never to be experienced again. Once they head out on the trail, they are alone. Like the early immigrants, miners, and others who came West in search of a new life, the chance for wealth, or an adventure, Tevis Cup riders embark on their journey accompanied only by their noble horse and a goal. The Tevis Cup is a journey of the self, testing the mind, the body, and the spirit.

Over the past twenty-five years, while the ride had changed, so had the way competitors prepared for it, many beginning to experiment with different and quite specific conditioning techniques. Where many of the early mounts were fit simply because they were working horses on ranches or used for timber cruising in the high country, by the 1970s horses were less an integral part of daily productive life. Most horses were maintained for recreational purposes and riders had to make a point to get themselves and their horses fit to travel these distances. Arabians proved to be the breed of choice. Thousands of years of selective breeding by Bedouin tribes across the Arabian peninsula had resulted in a light-boned, durable horse.

Linda Tellington-Jones (front rider) leading a group of riders out of Squaw Valley.
[Courtesy of Western States Trail Foundation]

Arabian horses had to travel over arid desert lands with the nomadic tribes who depended upon them, developing the capability to handle the stress of covering long distances and—genetically and metabolically—their bodies adapted to these conditions. These horses can maintain a sustained, elevated pulse and respiration rate indicative of strenuous exercise, then drop back to resting levels very quickly. The nomadic tribes prized their fine horses, and often a good horse was elevated in stature above the tribespeople. The Bedouin relied on their Arabian horses, and the horses relied on humans for their survival. For generations this symbiotic relationship continued, yielding a horse capable of physical extremes, and a heart willing to do whatever was asked. These characteristics were perfect for endurance riding, and Arabians have dominated the sport like no other breed.

Riders also have a crew that assists them throughout the ride, making sure the horse and rider are equipped with all the proper supplies necessary for their epic journey. Because ride organizers designate certain places along the trail, such as Robinson Flat and Foresthill, as areas where crews can access their horse and rider, equipment can be fixed, and supplies refreshed when needed. The start of the ride is usually chilly, as the sun has not yet risen, and the high altitude holds the cold air for hours, so riders often begin the ride wearing a sweatshirt or long-sleeved shirt, with a lighter shirt underneath. By the time they reach Robinson Flat, they have usually removed at least one layer of clothing. Riders can then change into a lightweight shirt for the heat of the canyons, and many choose to replace sweaty socks that can cause blisters while they both ride and run alongside their horses. Often crews change out a horse's saddle pad at the different access points, for much the same reason riders change socks. A few riders will even change parts of the equipment used on a horse. Some horses are quite headstrong at the beginning of the ride and need a more powerful bit; by the time they reach Robinson Flat they have usually settled into their rhythm, and the rider will opt for a milder bit.

Crews are integral for checking equipment and making sure the rider is carrying the correct supplies. A broken billet strap may be a minor inconvenience when tacking up to ride in the arena, but in the wilderness this can be devastating, and means a very long walk for the rider. A simple thing, such as forgetting a sponge, can jeopardize the horse's entire well-being. Riders usually carry a large sponge tied by a cord or long leather strap to a ring on the saddle. When they reach a small creek or other water source, they can simply drop the sponge into the water, saturate it, pull it up using the cord, and then sponge the horse's neck and hindquarters, thereby cooling the horse externally while the horse cools himself internally by drinking. A rock wedged between the hoof and a horseshoe can stop a horse in its tracks. Dislodging it with a hoof-pick is usually the quickest solution, but if the rider has forgotten this piece of equipment he must wait for another rider to provide aid.

Some of the vet checks that allow crews are more like Indy 500 pit stops than a trail ride checkpoint. Each crew member has an assigned task and the crew's job is to check and replenish without wasting valuable time, especially if the rider has his or her sights set on a top-ten finish. As the horse trots into a check that does not have a mandatory wait time, the crew strips the horse of its saddle and any protective legs wraps or boots. A designated crew person and the rider give the horse a quick once-over, before sending horse and rider to the vets for the official evaluation. In the meantime, someone checks all of the equipment, replaces the wet saddle pad with a dry one, and cleans off the boots that will go back on the horse's legs. The boots provide both protection from nicks and scratches, as well as some support, like many professional athletes who wear various elbow, knee, and wrist guards. Another crew member replenishes the rider's drinking bottles and snacks, and usually includes some high-energy treats for the horse as well. A good crew will also appraise the overall attitude of their horse and rider. Is the horse alert and demonstrating its typical personality? Is the rider tired but clearheaded, or has the heat affected the rider and should he rest for another fifteen minutes? A good crew can make the difference between a horse getting pulled, or making it through the entire ride without harm.

❧ 12 ❧

DONNA FITZGERALD AND WITEZARIF:
UNPARALLELED CHAMPIONS

The year 1970 would introduce a horse-and-rider team who embodied the very word "champions." Their accomplishments have never been rivaled, and may never be. That year would also introduce a finisher whose life was intertwined with the Tevis from the day he was born.

Pat and Donna Fitzgerald were well acquainted with the Tevis Cup, Wendell Robie, and many of the early participants. Pat earned his first completion in 1958 and Donna followed two years later in 1960. While finishing the Tevis Cup is notable in itself, in the 1970s Donna achieved an excellence surpassed by none. The Fitzgeralds represented the stalwart pioneering spirit of many early residents in the Tahoe area. The couple ran Stateline Stables in Stateline, Nevada, where people flocked in order to traipse through the scenic mountains on horseback and get a taste of the western way of life. Their experiences were more Hollywood than westward movement, but no one can dispute the incredible views offered the riders who paused on the vistas and ridges overlooking spectacular Lake Tahoe. The Fitzgeralds had a small bay Arabian gelding they used as a guide horse. "Witezarif was an unprepossessing individual in a corral full of Arabian geldings. Just standing there you would never pick him out as anything special," said Dr. Barsaleau with a twinkle in his eye as he eagerly recounted Witezarif tales. "He had a lot of heart. Following him down the trail it was like watching pistons, the way his hocks propelled him along. Many times I ate his dust for a goodly number of miles. Following Donna on the trail was just that, following, not catching up!"

Although plain to look at, Witezarif carried noble blood in his veins. Ted Jeary of the Hyannis Land & Cattle Company in Nebraska had bred the gelding, as well as a number of other quality endurance horses over the years. However, the Jearys weren't trying specifically to breed endurance horses. In fact, it was the Tevis Cup that planted the notion of long-distance riding in the minds of many riders. The Jearys ran a working ranch and wanted to breed hardy, sound horses, and Arabians had proven their sturdiness. The horses had to adapt to the harsh desert conditions, and be able to live on sparse rations and infrequent water stops, ideal capabilities for harsh ranch life.

Witezarif's heritage harkened back to champions. His sire, Witezar, was an American Horse Shows Association champion and a son of Witez II, an equine survivor of the Second World War. A number of other top endurance horses also trace their lineage back to this famous stallion.

As early supporters of Robie's vision, the Fitzgeralds had participated in the Tevis Cup each summer. They looked forward to the event every year and wanted good horses in order to compete. Donna Fitzgerald first owned a half-brother to Witezarif, named Razlind, and the gray gelding helped her earn buckles in 1965, 1966, and 1967. Initially Pat Fitzgerald was looking for a new Tevis Cup horse when he bought Witezarif, but it was Donna's link to the horse that created the unbeatable team. A tremendous horsewoman, she was firm but empathetic, and she seemed to speak "horse."

Outwardly quiet, Donna Fitzgerald was every bit as tough as the rugged men around her. She was neither intimidated by their ways, nor could they outride her. "Pat was a daredevil," recalled Jack Veal of the pair, "but Donna was just as good and just as tough. And to see her on a horse . . ." The Western States Trail seemed made for the pair. In fact, some old-timers took to jokingly referring to the trail as the "Witezarif Trail."

In 1970, Fitzgerald began a string of Tevis Cup wins that has never been equaled. Although challenged each year, Fitzgerald and Witezarif won the Tevis Cup four times, a streak only interrupted by a young upstart named Hal Hall. In 1975 Fitzgerald resumed her winning ways and captured two more Tevis Cup victories. While they also completed and won a number of other endurance rides throughout California and Nevada, Fitzgerald considered her Tevis wins to be the most special and meaningful.

Donna Fitzgerald and Witezarif. [Courtesy of Western States Trail Foundation]

As Donna Fitzgerald began her reign as Tevis Cup victor, Hal Hall came of age, growing to be a lanky sixteen-year-old. (Coincidentally, Hall was born in the same hospital where Betty Veal worked, and on the same day she sent out the first invitation to the inaugural Western States Ride.) Hall's parents weren't horse people, but they happened to live just down the street from Wendell Robie, and Hall spent many hours in the company of Robie and his peers. Hall got a hands-on education about horses, and learned much through trial and error. Robie was not always the most patient person, and Hall and others had to scramble to keep up with him, learning along the way. Robie rarely explained much, figuring that solving the problem was the best teacher. If someone didn't know how to ride along the challenging trails of the canyons, Robie knew that enough time in the saddle would either teach them, or make them give up. Either way, he didn't mind.

Hall talked his parents into buying him a horse. Hall developed a good work ethic and helped out in his family's pharmacy to help pay for its keep. He showed this first horse in local shows, where he befriended a young girl his age, Ann, who would later become his wife and share his passion. Hall also rode trails with Wendell Robie whenever he could. Robie enjoyed taking groups of riders out on the lower portion of the Western States Trail, and on these outings often held court, proclaiming his opinions and views on everything from horse care to politics. He had a rapt and loyal audience, and from these excursions Hall developed a love for both horses and trail riding, especially in the Sierra Nevada.

As the Tevis Cup grew and matured, so did Hall. With the approach of the 1970 ride, Hall knew he wanted to participate, but as a junior rider he had to find a sponsor first. Tevis rules state that junior riders must be at least twelve, and until they reach the age of eighteen they must have a sponsor accompany them throughout the ride, a requirement that persists to this day. If the sponsor is pulled during the ride, another adult often volunteers to step in and sponsor the junior rider for the remainder of the event. The Fitzgeralds loaned Hall one of the horses from their stables, with Pat acting as Hall's sponsor.

In anticipation of the ride that year, Hall conditioned himself so he could dismount and run alongside his horse where necessary. Not only did he successfully finish that year and earn his first of many Tevis belt buckles, he also journeyed to the newly formed Virginia City 100 ride in nearby Nevada. "I finished the Virginia City on my old ranch horse," recounted Hall, "and Ted Jeary from Hyannis came up to my dad and me." Jeary had begun following this new long-distance riding activity that seemed to be emerging. As an independent, self-reliant fellow, undoubtedly Jeary was attracted to the likes of Robie, Mansfield, Fitzgerald, and the many other colorful characters affiliated with the Tevis Cup. Jeary approached Hall and told him to come to Nebraska, as he had the perfect horse for the youth. Hall jumped at the chance, his father gave his blessing, and he was off to Nebraska to look for a new horse. "El Karbaj was a distinctive horse and the first time I saw him he was leading the herd across the plain. When they came into the corral, he was the most standoffish of all the horses. He was independent, and I liked that," said Hall. Something about the horse that acted indifferently toward people and assumed the dominant role in the herd appealed to the teenage boy. He embodied the very traits most teenagers begin seeking out: independence, confidence, and strength.

"I began saving the $1,500 I needed to buy the horse. That was a lot of money in those days," said Hall with a laugh. He slowly earned money from working in the pharmacy, but the prize money he earned when he won the Levi Strauss Ride & Tie, a forty-mile event, sealed the deal. Like endurance rides, ride-and-tie events had also begun to crop up, offshoots of the Tevis Cup ride. Held over much shorter distances, two people and a horse make up a team. One person rides the horse for a distance and then ties the horse. That rider then becomes a runner, and when the second runner in the team comes upon the horse, he hops on and then overtakes the first runner. Switching back and forth in this manner, the runners leapfrog through the course. Hall was a strong runner and a good rider, and the prize money gave him enough, when added to his savings, to buy El Karbaj and make a down payment on a pickup truck. "I bought pipe sides for the truck and hauled my horse just like the Fitzgeralds did. When I put the tailgate down my horse just learned to jump right up into the bed of the truck." The boy, now fast becoming a man, drove to Nebraska to pick up his horse. "It was funny, Ted hardly gave any of his horses Arabic names, but he named El Karbaj for the Arabic word meaning 'the cutter,'" continued Hall. "El Karbaj was related to Witezarif. They had the same dam, and my horse's sire was from the Witez II line."

In 1971, as Donna Fitzgerald was winning her second Tevis Cup, Hall started the ride on his new horse, a bona fide endurance horse. Although they were pulled at Michigan Bluff, Hall was enthralled. "He wasn't a runaway and he climbed great," said Hall of his horse. In 1972 Hall could finally ride the Tevis Cup as his own man. "I was turned loose and I finished second, right behind Donna. She was a dynamite horsewoman. She was fearless in the canyons. She would just gallop down. I wouldn't and couldn't keep up, but I could catch her in the climbs," Hall said with a grin. Although Hall crossed the finish line first, Fitzgerald was right behind him and had the fastest time. "In those days, with the staggered starts," explained Hall, "it was like chasing a ghost." Riders did not have a reference point for how they were doing compared to the riders around them. For most this did not matter, but for the twenty or so who had visions of a top-ten finish, knowing where you stood in relation to the others was important. Change was not possible on the matter of staggered starts at that time, for Robie was unrelenting. Although beaten by only a couple of minutes, Hall was honored with the Haggin Cup that year, quite a feat for an eighteen-year-old young man and a six-year-old horse. "My horse made it easy. We learned together." Over the years the pair finished the Tevis Cup twelve times out of thirteen attempts. Their only pull was their very first year. El Karbaj has had the second most Tevis finishes of any horse in history. A little Quarter Horse mare known as Thunders Lightning Bar was never speedy, but recorded an unprecedented thirteen finishes.

In 1974 when it seemed that Donna Fitzgerald was unbeatable, Hall broke her streak. "We were close all day," said Hall of that fateful day. "I competed against Donna a lot. I think it was that last climb at Robie Point that gave me the advantage." Fitzgerald went on to win the Tevis Cup two more times before relinquishing her hold; however, Hall was just getting started.

❧ 13 ❧

To Finish is to Win: The Formation of the American Endurance Ride Conference

When Hall finally competed in the ride in 1970, another woman rider was freshly introduced to the Tevis Cup that same year. Both would continue their careers to the present, and greatly influence the sport of endurance riding. Kathie Perry discovered endurance riding when she resumed her childhood love affair with horses. As a girl, Perry grew up around horses on her family's farm in Kansas. When her family moved to Fremont, a small town south of San Francisco, they were not able to keep a horse in the more suburban area. Perry focused on other activities, finished school, and married Ernie Perry in 1963. Several years later she had an opportunity to once again incorporate horses in her life when her older brother, Sam Arnold, bought several Quarter Horses. Arnold wound up marrying Robie's granddaughter, Marion. "Sam had heard about this horse ride in Virginia City where you rode one hundred miles in one day," said Perry of her introduction to endurance riding. "Sam talked Ernie into joining him on this crazy idea despite the fact that neither of them had any endurance riding experience." Naïveté served Ernie well as he managed to finish the ride. Arnold wasn't as lucky when he was pulled partway through the ride. Regardless of their results, both Perrys and Arnold were entranced with this new experience. "Endurance riding offered freedom," explained Perry of her attraction to the sport and its challenges. For most people life is structured. There are rules to follow, deadlines to meet, paths that must be adhered to. "There were only three rides at that time and no real rules," continued Perry. "Basically you had to stay on the trail and go through the vet checks. Everyone knew one another, as endurance riding was a very small group at that time. Everyone was so friendly and helpful."

Following their Virginia City 100 experience, Perry decided to check out the Tevis Cup. "I watched Donna Fitzgerald earn her first Tevis Cup victory aboard her amazing Witezarif. Hal Hall was riding El Karbaj that year and I just knew I had to do this." Perry went home knowing that their Quarter Horses were not going to make suitable hundred-mile mounts, so she began looking for an Arabian. "Hal Hall picked a horse from the Jeary's Hyannis Land & Cattle Company. He kept El Karbaj and I bought Prince Koslaif for Ernie." As it turned out, although the horse was intended for one person, he wound up with another. It was the pairing of Kathy Perry and Prince Koslaif, or "Kola," that resulted in the pair competing in over thirty rides, with regular top-ten finishes. "Kola was purebred Arabian, but he was a 'mustangy' horse." Indeed, Kola embodied all of these traits. He was never a horse that sought human companionship and acted as if he barely tolerated his human rider, although he was never rank or unruly. Kola was tough and attacked the mountain trails as though conquering them was his one goal in life.

While Perry and Kola were getting to know one another, and with Perry aiming her sights on the Tevis Cup, she took up a more pressing cause. Endurance riding was becoming more popular, with rides cropping up all around the country, but there was little coordination or standardization. "There was a lot of desire for a fifty-mile ride, so a group of us got together to form the American River 50," explained Perry of the start of what has become one of the most popular and well-attended fifty-mile rides in the country. Perry assumed the role of ride director, assisted by a core of experienced, able volunteers. Rho Bailey, Cliff Lewis, Dave Claggett, Hal Hall, Phil Gardner, and Robie's granddaughter, Marion, all lent their time and experience to the endeavor. All had been involved with early Tevis Cup rides and were some of the most experienced endurance riders anywhere. "As we got into developing the ride," continued Perry, "we realized there was a need to keep records and develop standards."

Like many start-ups, the American Endurance Ride Conference was born at a kitchen table. In creating the AERC, its organizers wanted to enable the association to fulfill several functions. There were only ten rides at the time, but it was clear that more were to follow. Endurance riding had struck a chord and provided an outlet and focus for riders not interested so much in show-ring competition, but wanting more than just a leisurely trail ride. Deciding on the structure and goals of the proposed organization resulted in long hours of debate and brainstorming. The personalities were all strong and sometimes things got quite heated, although all were working toward a common goal. To keep things proceeding, the Halls' house became an informal meeting place. "My parents had little interest or stake in the outcome of all of this. They simply tolerated my passion for horses," said Hall when recalling those early days of forming the AERC and setting the direction for the Tevis Cup. The Hall household became a frequent meeting place for the adults trying to organize a sport, and the Perrys' kitchen table more often held endurance riding information than dinner. Hall, a quiet teenager, became the group's scribe. "I was one of the few kids in high school who had a typewriter and knew how to type."

Hal Hall and El Karbaj. [Courtesy of Western States Trail Foundation]

Perry and the other early founders recognized the need for a set of rules. Using the guidelines set forth by the WSTF for the Tevis Cup, the newly formed AERC adopted the Tevis Cup's charter. The rules were simple and basic. Horses had to meet established criteria for soundness, pulse, respiration, and other veterinary specifications in order to continue down the trail. Riders had to follow a marked trail and complete the route in the set timeline, generally twelve hours for a fifty-mile ride and twenty-four hours for a one-hundred-mile ride.

Furthermore, the AERC allowed no medications of any sort, neither performance-enhancing nor therapeutic. While there was discussion regarding therapeutic anti-inflammatory medications to ease soreness or minor fatigue, these early founders realized that crossing the line from minor relief to masking more serious problems was a blurry one—and one they did not wish to mess with. Besides, many endurance rides took horses and riders into remote areas where no immediate aid was available. Therefore, they decided to err on the side of caution, and hold to the line at no medications whatsoever. In the past, some horses had become quite ill, and a few had even died during the Tevis Cup ride. No one wanted to see unnecessary deaths, and this core group knew that if they did not regulate themselves, regulation would come from the outside, giving them little say or control.

With basic rules established, the founders built on Robie's early vision and recognized the need for an entity to serve as a clearinghouse and historian. The WSTF kept comprehensive records of horses and riders competing in the Tevis Cup, but no records existed of general endurance performance. In order to have a true sport, one that grows and develops, one needs data, and the AERC was ideal to fulfill this mission. "We began with tracking the performance of horses, and then it evolved to tracking the performance of riders as well," explained Perry. By their very nature horses have a shorter competitive life than humans. While a horse may be able to compete for five to ten years, a person can compete for decades with a variety of horses. Tracking the performance record of horses led to analysis of breeding and the recognition that certain bloodlines were dominant in the top endurance horses. Solid data allowed people to plan, which contributed to the future and stability of the sport of endurance. As the AERC tracked performances and kept records, establishing an Endurance Hall of Fame was a natural result. Wendell Robie was an early inductee, as the founder of modern endurance riding.

The AERC also established various awards to recognize achievement by both horses and riders at different levels. Awards are the cornerstone to almost any sporting organization, and with a consistent set of rules, record keeping, and awards, endurance ride organizers willingly registered their rides with the AERC. Today, almost every competitive endurance ride in the United States is sanctioned by the AERC. Finally, the AERC adopted one of Robie's visions that was inherent, but often unstated, at the Tevis Cup. This philosophy—To Finish Is to Win—is why each finisher of the Tevis Cup receives a Tevis Cup belt buckle, emphasizing the achievement of the individual. Except for a small percentage of top riders and horses, endurance riding is all about individual accomplishment. "Can I ride my horse on this hundred-mile route in twenty-four hours?" ask most people, and then they see if they can.

Perry, Hall, Bailey, and the others were all protégés of Robie's in one way or another, and with the creation of the AERC they were carrying forward Robie's early vision. Although there was some friction between the WSTF Board of Governors and the AERC Board of Directors, both groups stayed focused on the goal of solidifying the sport of endurance riding. The groups were comprised of strong-willed individuals, and fortunately a few on each side were committed to bridging the differences, for it was clear that each entity had a tremendous amount to offer a burgeoning sport. The Tevis Cup gave birth to the sport of endurance riding and remains the pinnacle of endurance achievement. The AERC cemented the sport and helped propel it forward with a unified face.

While the sport of endurance was just getting organized and spreading to a national level, Robie, ever the visionary, was already looking down the road. He knew of an organization called the Fédération Equestre Internationale (FEI), which serves as the organization governing international equestrian sport, composed of the three Olympic disciplines of show jumping, dressage, and three-day eventing. In 1970, the FEI added competitive driving as a fourth discipline, although it was never planned to be an Olympic sport. Robie wanted international recognition and he was an effective and creative public-relations person. When he set his mind to something he was relentless, much like the eight-year-old boy aboard his pony collecting delinquent bills, and the young man determined to win the heart of the beautiful Inez.

No Hands Bridge in the daylight, with Foresthill Bridge in the background.
[Courtesy of Western States Trail Foundation]

FEI recognition of endurance riding was still twelve years off, but Robie already actively solicited competitors from foreign countries. In the early days of the ride, Robie heard of a Russian man who expressed an interest in earning a Tevis Cup buckle. This was during the height of the Cold War, and getting permission for Soviet citizens to enter the United States was not an easy task—unless you were Wendell Robie. Robie marched right past fears about Communism and the Cold War and wrote directly to President Eisenhower. He explained that—given the huge Siberian forest and the Sierra Nevada's expansive stands of old-growth timber—he and the Russian gentleman wanted to exchange information on forestry practices. Robie convinced the administration of the benefits of this exchange, and the Russian was granted permission to enter the country. Of course a horseback ride through the remote areas of the Sierra Nevada would provide a rare opportunity to bear witness to the variety and quality of California timber. Getting the foreign visitor to the United States was challenge enough, so Robie arranged for a horse so the Russian could compete, and a Tevis Cup buckle returned with him to his country.

Robie often demonstrated his strong political ties and his willingness to use them. One year in preparation for the ride Robie began cutting down some trees on U.S. Forest Service land to improve passage along a section of the trail. A forest ranger informed him that he was cutting trees on Forest Service land and must stop. Robie refused and again the ranger asked him to stop. Robie told the ranger to just call his friend, Dick. The ranger told Robie he didn't care who he called, but he had to stop cutting down trees. Robie halted, called President Richard Nixon, and with permission resumed the clearing he deemed necessary.

⇒ 14 ⇐

THE WESTERN STATES ENDURANCE RUN

As the sport of endurance was getting organized, a young college student learned of the Tevis Cup and decided it was a worthy challenge. Gordy Ainsleigh's experience created an offshoot of the ride that would become a worldwide event in its own right, still unimagined back in 1970. Ainsleigh was simply a post–Army hippie college student at the University of California at Santa Barbara. Ainsleigh was one of those guys who would get an idea and then simply follow it, regardless of the consequences. At that point in his life, the word "planning" was a foreign concept.

"I decided I wanted to ride horses, so I went down to the Rec Department and rented a horse—except it was no fun to ride alone. I kept on riding though, and started thinking that I spent so much renting horses, I might as well just feed one." Unfortunately for Ainsleigh, the waiting list to lease a horse was quite long, but there was a horse he could buy. "I saw this horse and tried him out in the stable area and he really lacked enthusiasm. The lady who owned him told me that he ran away with everyone and that was the reason I couldn't ride him outside the corral." In his glib, persistent manner Ainsleigh convinced the owner to let him try anyway.

"I opened the gate and that horse took off like a racehorse! We lapped the pasture and then finally I got dumped on the ground. I got up, caught that horse, got back on, got dumped again, and decided to buy him." The owner was shocked, but as a member of the college wrestling team Ainsleigh was not one to shrink from a challenge despite the fact that he knew almost nothing about horses.

"I used to take that horse up the beach and we would go for seven to ten miles. We would just keep running until he got tired and began slowing down. Sometimes I would get off him and run alongside him. When the tide would start coming in we would turn around and head home." The turns of nature—the tide influenced by the moon, and the daylight provided by the sun—were Ainsleigh's barometers, and limiters to his riding experiences. "I felt like that kid on Walter Farley's black stallion. I used to think that was a dumb notion until it was me out there riding bareback on the beach on my horse."

People around the stable where Ainsleigh kept his horse, Rebel, told him it would make a good endurance horse. He had no idea what that meant until he noticed a flyer about the upcoming Western States Trail Ride. "I'd never heard of it, but it sounded fun and exciting. I grew up in Nevada City, which is quite close to the finish, but I never heard of the ride." With the ride only four months away, Ainsleigh sent off his entry form. "I got a short note back telling me the ride was filled for that year and to consider entering earlier." Showing uncharacteristic planning and forethought, Ainsleigh sent in an entry form in the fall of 1970 for the 1971 ride, and got in. "I started training using my own method. I had this six-mile course and there was one small hill and one biggish hill of about 250 to 300 feet. I would let my horse run for as long as he wanted and then we would trot. Well, I had no saddle and trotting bareback was pretty uncomfortable, so I would get off and run. I had a plan and each time we would go a little farther. I figured when I could run the whole thing we were in shape!"

With the date of the ride looming and the term ending for the year, Ainsleigh realized he needed to transport his horse from Santa Barbara to Auburn. As a starving college student who spent every spare dime on his horse, Ainsleigh decided to build a horse trailer to tow behind his '56 Chevy. "This grad student buddy of mine knew about welding and said he would help me—the only problem was that we needed a welder." U.C. Santa Barbara had a fine welder in its Art Department, but the head of the department was not keen to let Ainsleigh borrow it for his home-made contraption. "There was this big slot in the roof of the building for the gases from the kiln. We just 'borrowed' the welder," said Ainsleigh. They set to work on the trailer, but toward the end of their escapade, Ainsleigh and his buddy were running out of materials. They had begged and borrowed material from every source imaginable, but finally they had to resort to stealing to complete their project. "I felt so bad," said Ainsleigh, "but I had to buy food, so I shoplifted nuts and bolts. I just left money at the store the next year to make up for it."

They were finishing their final welds when the custodian drove up and saw the welder that normally resided inside the Art Department. A few pieces were missing from the trailer as the custodian took custody of the equipment. "At least we didn't have to get that welder back through the roof; it was hard enough getting it out!" laughed Ainsleigh. Luckily, he deemed the trailer substantial enough to get his horse to the Tevis Cup. "I led Rebel up to that trailer and he wanted nothing to do with it." Ainsleigh spent over two hours trying to get his horse in the trailer. The Tevis Cup was only days away. "It was getting dark. I was tired and I just sat down and sobbed. Then I heard this 'clump, clump' as the horse climbed into the trailer. I couldn't believe it. That was just how that horse treated me.

"I got up to Auburn about a week before the ride and I knew nothing about overexerting your horse right before riding a hundred miles," explained Ainsleigh of his final ride preparations. "I decided to get a look at the trail and go for an afternoon ride from Auburn to Michigan Bluff." Michigan Bluff is forty miles from the finish line in Auburn. "I started at 2:00 P.M. and headed out. Around Todd Valley I missed a turnoff and got lost." With darkness approaching, Ainsleigh came across some houses in the remote area. "I went house-to-house and told whoever would listen that I was trying to get to Michigan Bluff." Even the intrepid people living in remote Todd Valley were amazed at the hippie sitting bareback on a horse looking for Michigan Bluff located miles away. Of course Ainsleigh had no supplies with him—like food and water—but one of the residents took him in and he spent the night with Rebel turned out in a pasture. In the morning Ainsleigh's host pointed him in the direction of Michigan Bluff and watched the young man and his horse fade back into the wilderness from which they had come. "I got to Michigan Bluff around noon and decided to keep heading up the trail. I went up the two canyons. They were huge. I got off going uphill." After going through the two steepest canyons of the trail, Ainsleigh gave Rebel a drink at Bear Creek and then headed back down to Michigan Bluff. He rested there and once again was aided by the local residents. Ainsleigh finally got back to Auburn on

Thursday, with the Tevis Cup only two days away. Although there was not extensive research and knowledge about training and preparing for long-distance rides in 1970, most Tevis Cup riders knew not to make huge demands of a horse the week before the ride. Ainsleigh was oblivious.

Gordy Ainsleigh. [Courtesy of Western States Trail Foundation]

Back in Auburn Rebel once again refused to get in the trailer. "I galloped him around the fairgrounds for awhile and then he climbed right in. For years that was our routine."

That Gordy Ainsleigh was even attempting the Tevis Cup was incredible. The fact that he actually finished the ride was just short of miraculous. Amidst the assembled horses and riders decked out in all their gear was Ainsleigh astride his horse with a bridle and a simple bareback pad with stirrups, which offers little support to the rider and makes riding in balance with the horse for any amount of time quite difficult and tiring. Attempting to cover the rigorous terrain of the Western States

Trail without a saddle is simply suicidal. There was a reason the Mongolians developed saddles with stirrups by the fourth century A.D.—but Ainsleigh obviously had not paid attention to that history lesson.

At the start of the ride from the Squaw Valley meadow, the mountain loomed before them. Ainsleigh decided to tail up the mountain to Watson's Monument before mounting to begin traversing the steep granite ridges toward Robinson Flat. Unlike other riders, who train their horses to climb the steep slopes with the rider behind them holding onto their tail, Ainsleigh had no idea of this method. To correctly tail, the rider unclips one of the two pieces of rein attached to the horse's bit. This way the rider can still control the horse's uphill pace from behind, akin to driving a horse as if in a buggy. Horses climb uphill much more efficiently than their human counterparts, so tailing is a critical component to an endurance rider's strategy and technique. Humans can go downhill with greater speed and efficiency than a horse, so riders often reverse the formula and lead their horses down steep slopes at a fast walk or easy jog-trot.

Ainsleigh's start up Squaw Valley was like a self-described bad cartoon. Rebel headed up the mountain at a gallop with Ainsleigh gripping his tail and attempting to stay on his feet behind the sprinting horse. After all, Ainsleigh had trained and conditioned Rebel to go as fast as he could for as long as he could, until finally slowing to a trot and then ultimately a walk. "Pacing" was not in their vocabulary. Rebel had learned his lessons well and churned up the rock-strewn mountain with Ainsleigh bouncing after him. Why he wasn't killed or at least seriously injured is a wonder. "I kept falling but I didn't let go," said Ainsleigh of their wild ascent up Squaw Valley. Finally, toward the top of their climb, Ainsleigh fell and couldn't regain his footing. He had to let go of Rebel's tail as the gelding continued on, seemingly oblivious to his companion's fate. Dick Threlfall, a horseshoer who was also competing on the ride that year, caught Ainsleigh's horse and brought him back to the skinned, bruised, and bleeding young man. With no concept of turning around, Ainsleigh mounted and continued his quest for Auburn.

Riding bareback also took its toll. "I had trained for six-mile stretches," said Ainsleigh, recalling his first Tevis attempt. "I don't know how we made it. I tried to quit so many times that day. My crotch was raw from that bareback pad." At one point Ainsleigh tried to quit, but there was no way out except forward. "I was dejected. I wanted to quit, but there was no facility, so I had to keep going. I just trudged on." Further down the trail Ainsleigh came upon a small creek. "I just fell into the water and sat there. Another rider came along and yelled at me, 'Get out of the trail at least.' I moved over a couple of rocks." A short while later Larry Luster, who completed his first Tevis in 1969, came along. He saw Ainsleigh pathetically sitting in the water on a rock. Luster got Ainsleigh going again despite his protests that he just wanted to quit.

To give him some energy, Ainsleigh tried drinking a concoction of milk and honey that he only threw up as soon as it hit his stomach. "I had heard milk and honey were good for long-lasting energy. All I did was throw up. Finally a friend took pity on me and crewed for me. He gave me Coke and that helped."

Seventeen miles from the finish Ainsleigh once again tried to quit, but the caffeine jolt from the Coke propelled him into Auburn with thirty minutes to spare. Ainsleigh earned his Tevis Cup buckle, but he paid a mighty price. Ten days passed before he could walk without a limp. Fortunately Rebel fared much better than his two-legged partner. When he was sufficiently recovered, Ainsleigh decided to head over to Robie's bank to get the results of the ride. "When I asked for the results they told me Wendell wanted to see me. I felt like a count! Wendell said he was impressed by me. I had no idea why. When Wendell told me that Paige Harper didn't make the time cutoff, I said, 'I thought if I could finish, anyone could.' Dru Barner chimed in with, 'We thought that, too!' There I was with long hair, and a beard—a cross between a mountain man and a hippie—standing in the presence of Wendell Robie."

In 1972 Ainsleigh returned to the Tevis Cup with Rebel, and this time he used an English saddle. His finish was much less traumatic that year, and he didn't suffer for ten days afterward. However, riding a horse along the trail was never easy for Ainsleigh. Because his horse had soundness problems in 1973, Ainsleigh had to skip the Tevis Cup, although he did come to hang out and follow the ride. "I was so dejected. This was my most important event of the year. I saw Dru and poured my heart out to her. She listened to my entire sob story and then told me maybe it wasn't the end of world. I couldn't believe it! This was it, but here she is telling me that even if my horse is lame, I am a good long-distance runner." Ainsleigh perked up. He had never thought about running the entire length of the trail. He had run the last fifty miles of the Castle Rock ride in nine hours, and Robie and Barner told him he should be able to do the whole length in eighteen hours.

Ainsleigh went home from the 1973 event and immersed himself in other aspects of his life, like school, though he did send in his entry for the 1974 event. Throughout the early months of that year Ainsleigh's horse was not sound enough to train, let alone compete in the Tevis Cup. "I was a terrible procrastinator. There were seven weeks to the ride and I had no horse. Panic set in. At six weeks out I decided to run the distance. I was in shape for twenty to thirty miles, but one hundred? No one had ever done it before. It was the twentieth anniversary of the ride, so I figured it was a great time to give it a try."

Ainsleigh realized he was attempting something unprecedented and he actually sought some advice where little existed. "A few people had run a hundred miles on pavement and a running track, but no one had ever done it on such terrain." Several years earlier a few elite soldiers from Fort Riley in Kansas came to train on the trail. Dr. Jim Edwards, one of the Tevis vets, remembers seeing the soldiers head out on the trail. "They had heavy gear, fatigues, boots. There was this theory that a man could outrun a horse." Partway down the trail, the soldiers gave up. They were suffering from nosebleeds, and they were delirious and wandering off the trail. Later the Army pronounced that completing the route in twenty-four hours couldn't be done. But no one told Ainsleigh of the soldiers' misfortune.

Ainsleigh tracked down one of his high school teachers from Colfax High School. Pete Hanson had gone to the 1968 Olympic trials, had coached a number of runners, and done some mountain running. Ainsleigh presented Hanson with his idea. "I showed Pete some sections of the Western States Trail. Even Pete thought I was a bit crazy, but the whole thing piqued his interest. We figured out that if I could average 4.1 miles per hour over twenty-four hours, I could get to the finish line. It seemed doable."

When Ainsleigh announced that he intended to run the route, Robie left the final decision up to Barner. Barner had been part of Ainsleigh's inspiration, so she wasn't going to call a halt at this point; Ainsleigh was on his way. Several of Robie's cronies placed $1,000 bets that Ainsleigh wouldn't make it to the finish. "I know they paid up on those bets," said Ainsleigh later, "but I never saw any of the money!"

In preparation for his undertaking, Ainsleigh decided to take advantage of a new substance touted to be much better than the old wive's tale of milk and honey he had tried before. In the late 1960s Gatorade had entered the market as a sports drink when researchers at the University of Florida worked to develop a drink that would help athletes competing under stress. They developed a drink that they tested on the football team. The formula contained replenishing fluids, and a balance of carbohydrates and electrolytes, the trace minerals sweated out during exercise. The football players said the drink made them feel better and the team's performance improved. The researchers refined their concoction, and in honor of the university's football team, the Gators, they marketed their new sports drink as Gatorade.

On the Thursday before the race, Ainsleigh loaded up a backpack with ten quarts of the stuff. "I rode my motorcycle to intersection points of the trail and planted quarts of Gatorade." Despite the fact that motor vehicles were prohibited along the trail, he rode from Last Chance to Michigan Bluff, the anchor points between the two extreme canyons, and placed his supplies along the route. That was about the extent of knowledge and preparation for such a supreme feat of human endeavor—a man with a terrific amount of willpower, and ten quarts of Gatorade.

On Saturday morning, August 3, Ainsleigh strolled up to the starting line at 4:50 A.M., ten minutes ahead of the first group of horses. "I will always remember that morning," recounts Ainsleigh. "I walked up to Betty Veal and the start consisted of 'Well, I guess I'll be going now' and 'Good luck, Gordy.' Off I went into the darkness." Before cresting Emigrant Pass heralded by Watson's Monument, the day's first light was just beginning to erase the night sky and hide the stars. "I stopped and looked back at Lake Tahoe. It was intensely beautiful. An amazing experience. For a moment I regretted turning away from all that beauty, but then I turned west . . . to face purgatory. I will always cherish that morning."

Despite his lack of a horse, Ainsleigh's ascent up Squaw Valley that year was much less traumatic than his first ascent in 1971. Ainsleigh headed onward at a steady, ground-covering pace. The terrain was grueling, but he kept going along the trail, slowly putting the miles behind him. As the day wore on and the midday sun burned overhead, Ainsleigh reached the canyons. "It was horrendously hot that day. One hundred and eight degrees. There was no technology at that time, so I just suffered, and suffered some more." Besides sophisticated training and conditioning programs, present-day ultramarathon runners wear lightweight clothing that helps cool them and protect them from the sun. They have running shoes designed specifically for trails, and they carry electrolyte-filled drinks and high-protein gels. Ainsleigh had none of these.

As he climbed out of the canyon toward Devil's Thumb, Ainsleigh came across a horse that had collapsed in the river. "The horse was shocky, overheated, and hypothermic. That horse was dying after coming out of the canyon, and for the very first time I realized I was at risk. I felt a chill that hot, hot day." After seeing the tragedy of the horse and facing his own mortality for the first time in his life, Ainsleigh decided to quit. He stopped along the trail, and a while later Paige Harper and Diane Claggett came along. Ainsleigh told them he was going to quit and they stopped.

"They really pumped me up," recounted Ainsleigh. "Diane massaged my legs and she flirted with me. It really rejuvenated me, the whole package, and I left feeling good. I had been really bummed out because my girlfriend at the time decided to spend the weekend with the girls when she knew this was the most important thing I had ever done. I don't know what I would have done if Paige and Diane hadn't come along when they did. I was really feeling abandoned." Ainsleigh's enthusiasm carried him to Michigan Bluff. He spotted his girlfriend who had decided to come encourage him, and seeing her he was once again buoyed. However, Gatorade alone was not doing the trick. Ainsleigh was depleting his body's energy reserves faster than he could replenish them. "A friend handed me a dry mix of ERG. Without that I may not have made it. Gatorade was just not enough." One of the first protein and electrolyte concentrates on the market, ERG provided Ainsleigh with much-needed fuel for the last third of his endeavor.

Leaving Michigan Bluff Ainsleigh acquired a running companion. Clyde Nunn volunteered to run with Ainsleigh for the remainder of the route. He was young, strong, and talented, but had no training for this kind of feat. Bob Lind, who became the Medical Director for what was to become the Western States Run, met Ainsleigh and Nunn seventeen miles from the finish. Nunn was exhausted, and Lynn proclaimed that Nunn's legs were shot, so once again Ainsleigh was on his own. "At that point I didn't feel one hundred percent, mentally."

Ainsleigh happened upon the perfect solution: a pretty girl. Kathy Clark was riding a very young horse on the route, and she had slowed down significantly, as her mount was struggling with the distance and the conditions. The exhausted runner and the pretty girl on the overwhelmed horse joined forces and carried one another toward the finish. "Here was this pretty girl and I figured it was time to impress her." Ainsleigh yacked for most of the way to the finish. Clark was flabbergasted that Ainsleigh had reached the eighty-mile mark and was now talking to her almost non-stop. "We talked all the way to Cool. I shut up in the last canyon and then chatted all the way to No Hands Bridge."

Once across the bridge, Ainsleigh picked up his pace and raced in, finishing the Tevis Cup route in twenty-three hours and forty-nine minutes. That same year 191 horses started and 88 finished. The completion statistics that year were: horses, 46 percent; man, 100 percent. "After my run in 1974, I became a member of Wendell and Dru's inner circle. I never did see any part of those $1,000 bets, though!"

In 1975 Ainsleigh had a challenger. The other runner tried to emulate Ainsleigh's methodology but he never once talked to Ainsleigh himself. While Ainsleigh ran the lower section of the trail at least ten times in the dark, the other runner never did any nighttime runs. "The other guy was on the course and on pace," said Ainsleigh of his challenger, "but at the Highway 49 crossing he wanted to be solo, so I let him go on ahead. He got disoriented and gave up at No Hands Bridge." With less than four miles to go, the other runner was lost, confused, and had no idea where the finish was; the Western States Trail took its toll.

In 1976 the news of Ainsleigh's feat attracted a hardy group of runners, including a colorful character known as "Cowman" to the locals around Tahoe City and Squaw Valley, though his birth certificate read Ken Shirk.

Growing up in Salinas, California, a small, farming community made famous by John Steinbeck's *The Grapes of Wrath,* Shirk attended the local high school. "We were known as 'the cowboys' and a couple girls started calling me 'cowboy,'" said Shirk of the genesis of his moniker. Inspired by having seen Ainsleigh in action, Shirk decided to try the Western States Run. "We were all so new to this," said Shirk of those early runners. "We used electrolyte mixtures, but that was about it. The whole thing was experimental and we were the guinea pigs."

Shirk went on to finish the run thirteen times and then he added two Tevis Cup buckles to his collection in 1982 and 1983. "I had ridden horses as a kid and I wanted to cover the trail on horseback. I knew that just like in running, big guys like me [Shirk is 6'2" and 230 pounds] have a disadvantage, but I knew I could do it because I could run much of the trail."

Shirk is one of the few people who have completed both the run and the ride. Although he now lives in Hawaii, he tries to return to both the run and the ride every year. "I love the trail, I love the event, I love the people. All of this is like a huge family reunion and I just want to be part of it," he explained with an expansive smile. Shirk noted that he competed in the second Ironman contest ever held, another extreme endurance event.

Word was beginning to get around about Ainsleigh's amazing accomplishment, and Robie, never one to miss an opportunity, approached him about organizing an event just for runners. "Wendell came to me and said, 'Let's make this a yearly event,' and I said, 'You mean with advertising and the whole bit?' and so we ran a classified in *Runner's World*."

That first classified ad simply said:

ULTIMATE CHALLENGE

100 miles cross-country in the high mountains and deep canyons of the Sierra Nevada

Fifteen people sent in applications for the 1977 Western States Endurance Run. Four started, and only one finished: Andy Gonzales, a protégé of Pete Hanson, set a course record of twenty-two hours and fifty-eight minutes. "Andy asked me how to get to Auburn in twenty-four hours and I told him, 'Walk uphill and run the flats and downhills.' Andy finished in just under twenty-three hours," recalled Ainsleigh of the first man to repeat his feat.

Riders began complaining that the runners were stealing the limelight. "I met with Dru and Wendell after the 1977 event. Dru felt the run was very important and that the run was going to change history." They set a June date for 1978, one full-moon cycle ahead of the Tevis Cup. Once again Ainsleigh entered the event. "Long-distance running was so primitive in those days. The whole thing was suicidal. It was just lucky that I had a young, strong body. I was raised in an apocalyptic religion, a branch of Seventh-Day Adventists, and I never thought I would make it to adulthood. As I was going along Red Star Ridge that year I was even more positive that the end had arrived." A recent fire had scarred the land and the trees were gone. There was no shade, just hot black soil that radiated the heat back up at the runners. With no shade and no breeze, Ainsleigh felt despair creeping in. "I saw my own graph heading to zero and I was plotting where I could get to. I just decided to put one foot in front of the other and decided to keep doing that until I couldn't anymore." Ainsleigh reached the finish once again and beat Gonzales's time set the year before.

"Now I am fifty-five years old," reflected Ainsleigh in 2003, when asked about the growth of the Western States 100. "Now there are over 350 runners and the run is a worldwide event." With improved technology and vastly increased knowledge, winning runners finish in sixteen hours and average runners cross the finish line in Auburn in nineteen hours. Runners have thirty hours to complete the course, though those who finish in under the twenty-four hour mark earn their own version of the Tevis Cup belt buckle. Ainsleigh is one of the few people in the world who have both buckles. He has eighteen finishes to his credit and Tim Twietmeyer holds the record, with twenty-one finishes and a total of five victories. A 2003 issue of *Runner's World* wrote of Twietmeyer, "The 42-year-old software manager has won the country's most coveted ultramarathon five times and finished among the top five twelve straight years."

In 1999, a young upstart, Scott Jurek, showed up in Squaw Valley for the run. Heading up Squaw Valley he took the lead and never looked back. Jurek was the first non-Californian to win the Western States Run, and he has dominated the event. In 2003 he equaled Twietmeyer's record of five Western States 100 victories.

Many ultramarathons, one-hundred-mile runs, have sprung up over the years, but the Western States Endurance Run remains a pinnacle of achievement for ultramarathon runners. Over three thousand runners have completed their personal journey over the old immigrant trail. Fittingly, the winning runner receives the Robie Cup, inscribed with "Worth marks the man. There all the honor lies. Not content with well or better; He has raced 100 miles. The winner."

Ken "Cowman" Shirk in the high country. [Courtesy of Western States Trail Foundation]

❊ 15 ❊

KATHIE PERRY

Hal Hall established his endurance dominance in his early years by winning both the Tevis Cup and the Haggin Cup before he was twenty-five years old, and in 1972 the newly formed AERC recognized El Karbaj as the sport's first national champion. Kathie Perry had to wait a bit longer, but by 1975, she was ready for her Tevis Cup challenge. Prince Koslaif had gained some experience at smaller rides, and Perry looked forward to her own Tevis journey, dreamed about and planned for since seeing her first Tevis Cup in 1970. In 1975 she managed to finish, and earned her first Tevis Cup belt buckle.

On July 22, 1978, 205 horses gathered at the start in the Squaw Valley meadow. This was the second year that the event started over two hundred horses and riders, a huge growth from the handful competing in the early days. The Tevis Cup had truly become a major event. Kathie Perry had two Tevis Cup completions under her belt and a good horse in Prince Koslaif. "In those days," said Perry thinking back to that memorable day, "everyone figured there were about twenty contenders for the Tevis Cup and the rest were riding to finish. That year everyone thought the contest would be between Potato Richardson and Elwin Wines." No one figured Perry to be a serious competitor.

Wines was pulled at Michigan Bluff and Richardson had the lead. The staggered starts made it difficult to tell who was leading the ride, but Perry found herself ahead of most of the riders. "Coming out of Cool, Phil Gardner on Potato's crew told me that Potato was twelve minutes ahead. I wasn't sure where we stood in relation to one another from the start, but twelve minutes was very close. I knew there were six miles left and I had quite a bit of horse, so I decided to pick up the pace." Despite having traveled ninety-four miles, Kola was still fresh and strong, and settled easily into a gallop. Having been ridden over much of the lower portions of the trail previously, when Kola crossed No Hands Bridge he knew "home" lay only a few miles away. Although Richardson crossed the finish line ahead of Perry, she had closed the gap, and crossed the finish line just minutes later. Until the official timers could perform their calculations, no one knew who won. "It turned out I beat Potato by just two minutes!" After one hundred miles, the finish had come down to a two-minute difference between the top horses. For Perry her Tevis Cup win was a highlight of her life. "Winning felt different. It was the difference between a silver medal at the Olympics and a gold medal."

Because of their intense involvement and interest in the Tevis Cup, the Perrys moved to the Auburn area, buying land on a point overlooking the American River. Perry went to work at Robie's bank, then known as Central California Federal Savings & Loan. "Wendell hand-picked just about everyone who worked at the bank, and if you weren't willing to do some Tevis Cup work . . ." Perry smiled as the words trailed off. Robie carefully built a team of people around him who grew to share his vision and implement it.

Kathie Perry and Prince Koslaif. [Charles Barieau photo]

"Wendell was beyond his time," explained Perry. "For all his vision, Wendell was very down to earth," she remembered. Like others in Robie's inner circle, Perry would trail ride with him. "Wendell was a great story-teller. At that time my nine-year-old son, Jimmy, liked to ride with me and he was intent on riding as far as he could." Like many boys, Jimmy was quickly bored by adult conversation and would ride on ahead. But when Robie launched into one of his many stories, Jimmy was content to ride alongside Robie, even slowing his horse's gait so he didn't miss a word. Robie could weave tales that made the listener feel as if he was part of the adventure.

Like many others, over the years the entire Perry family was involved in endurance riding. Jimmy earned his first buckle at twelve, and amassed a total of four during his youthful career. Their other son, Gregory, never rode, but did help crew for his parents and brother. "For years," said Perry, "whenever the Tevis rolled around, the entire Perry family showed up to ride, crew, cheer, and spend precious family time." Perry remembers a few years when the clan extended beyond their immediate family to friends and other Tevis afficionados. During the late 1970s and early 1980s, up to thirty people would base out of the Perrys' home during Tevis week. "People would camp in our front yard, crash in our living room, and any-where they could find space. There would be bodies everywhere. Those were really fun times," recalled Perry with a smile.

Over the years Perry went on to earn a total of fourteen Tevis Cup completions and induction into the AERC Hall of Fame. One of her fa-vorite finishes was the year she earned her one-thousand-mile buckle for ten career Tevis finishes. "I was riding a six-year-old horse on its first Tevis Cup, and my riding partner was a woman on her first Tevis Cup. That was an ultimate ride for me. The Tevis makes you set your own goals and ride your own ride. Each horse brings its own way of going down the trail, and the scenery always looks a little different. However, ultimately you bring your own handicaps to the Tevis Cup and you get to see what you can do with them." For Perry, being able to combine both endurance rid-ing and her family into shared experiences is the epitome of rewarding for her. "Endurance riding is my passion and my family is my love."

As the 1970s closed, records were made and broken, and the ride gained prominence every year. Donna Fitzgerald's six wins with the same horse may never be matched; Hal Hall won the Tevis Cup twice and the Haggin Cup once; and Julie Suhr earned a one-thousand-mile buckle for ten finishes. Kathie Perry helped launch the American Endurance Ride Conference and thus provide organization and history for this new sport; and finally, with the close of the decade, runners now tested their mettle on the same route that almost thirty years earlier, some men questioned the possibility of doing, even on a horse.

➴ 16 ➴

TEVIS CUP RESEARCH REACHES OUT

The twenty-sixth running of the Tevis Cup in July 1980 saw a record number of horses. Two hundred twenty-six horses left Squaw Valley that early morning. Since 1955, when the ride began, 2,652 horses and riders had started and 1,519 had completed the one-hundred-mile journey. Riders representing all of the states in the Union had competed, and riders from other countries had begun regularly speckling the annual start lists. Organized endurance rides were cropping up throughout the country, and AERC membership was growing rapidly. Endurance riding had struck a chord among a segment of horse enthusiasts. Many liked the combination of riding their horse through wilderness areas, coupled with an air of competition. Endurance riding seemed to bridge the gap between purely recreational riders who had little ambition to compete in horse shows, and show-ring riders representing many different types of competitive riding, like western, jumping, dressage, and the like. Endurance appealed to those who enjoyed riding trails and the rides often introduced them to areas they might not have explored otherwise. Horsemen and -women alike found that the sport offered an entirely new aspect of competing with their horse, one that didn't involve subjective judging and provided recognition for superior performance.

By far the most heavily attended ride in the country, the Western States 100 Mile Ride now set the standard for other rides, and the sport in general. Veterinary standards continued to improve, and the Tevis Cup provided field data for the burgeoning study of the effects of long distances on horses as well as human athletes. Early in 1980, the highly regarded University of California at Davis veterinary school contacted the ride's organizers about conducting an ongoing study of horses competing in the ride. Many of the official ride vets were from U.C. Davis and they and their peers recognized the opportunity presented them. Nowhere else were as many as two hundred or more riders and their horses gathered in one place in an attempt to ride one hundred miles within twenty-four hours.

By collecting data, veterinary medicine could help riders better prepare their horses before long-distance rides and take more effective care of them during the ride. The horse community had come to recognize the importance of electrolytes during strenuous physical exertion, but there were no comprehensive studies on nutrition, treatment of horses during the rides, and conditioning, though such research existed for horses in racing and other speed tests. And there were no significant studies on preparation for long distances. This research was needed not only for endurance horses, but for several other equine sports that required long distance tests, although not all at the distances required by endurance riding. Three-day eventing includes a phase requiring horses to gallop several miles over a course of natural obstacles, as well as slower work at distances of several miles. Like endurance horses, eventing horses are required to endure extended physical exertion. In addition, as with most studies, unexpected results are generally revealed that often benefit the larger population. This was the case with the University of California at Davis Tevis Cup study, which continues to this day.

Dr. Gary Carlson of U.C. Davis heads the ongoing studies, in addition to countless veterinary students, other vets, and volunteers. The Western States Trail Foundation helps support the research, financially and otherwise. Initial research involved simple things, such as recording why horses were pulled from the ride and at what locations, types of treatment any of these pulled horses received, and some additional examinations to follow up on those done by the ride veterinarians.

One direct result of these studies, when used along with the data accumulated by the ride vets, was improved veterinary examinations during the ride itself. As those within the veterinary community learned more about the effects of long-distance rides on the physiology of horses, they passed this information along to riders and those interested in endurance riding.

Both the AERC and the WSTF were huge supporters of educational activities for both veterinary science and riders. Both organizations held educational forums and clinics, and published pertinent research information in their various newsletters and other correspondence.

Tevis Cup veterinarians began to refine what they looked for at each vet check. In addition to checking each horse for soundness, by having the rider lead the horse at a trot along a smooth, flat surface, the vets carefully reviewed and recorded the pulse and respiration of each horse. They also used stethoscopes to listen to the heart, gut sounds, and the lungs. They then observed the overall demeanor of each horse, considering several points regarding its overall appearance. Did the horse look tired or exhausted? Did the horse display a willing attitude, or were his ears pinned and was he reluctant to move out? Was he sweating profusely, or worse, not sweating at all? When the vet ran his hands along the horse's back, loins, and flanks, did he flinch from undue body soreness? Did he have cuts or abrasions from the rocks or from interfering, or hitting an ankle with the opposing hoof? The ongoing studies helped the Tevis vets better recognize what was "expected" and what was abnormal.

Riders carry cards with them throughout the ride that they must provide for consultation at each vet check. The veterinarians in attendance note both statistics, like the horse's pulse and respiration, as well as more general observations. If a vet at an early check notes that a horse may be showing beginning signs of dehydration, vets further down the trail will carefully look for dehydration and note their own observations.

In addition, the veterinary committee established minimum and maximum pulse and respiration criteria horses had to meet at each vet check. Based on the various Tevis-related studies and data gathered during each ride, horses must meet very specific pulse and respiration criteria, or P & R, which varies at each designated stop. For example, at Red Star Ridge, the maximum pulse is 64 and the maximum respiration is 48. However, at Robinson Flat the maximum pulse allowed is 60 with the same maximum respiration of 48 breaths per minute. Based on the studies, the veterinary panel could establish limits that were within safety margins, thereby knowing where to draw the line.

The vets also considered "recovery rates," how quickly pulse and respiration dropped to normal levels after prolonged exertion. A fit, well-conditioned horse should recover within minutes. Continued elevated pulse and respiration rates were indicative of undue stress, which normally resulted in a horse being pulled. During the Tevis Cup vets erred on the side of caution, for once a horse left a vet check it could be several hours before the rider reached another checkpoint. No one wanted to risk a horse encountering some kind of health problem on a remote section of trail, where little to no help would be available, let alone vehicle access to get the horse transported out. Therefore, if there is any doubt as to the horse's fitness and recovery, the vets will pull it. The Tevis Cup maintains some of the strictest veterinary endurance standards in the world and has been a leader in this aspect of the sport.

As the years went on, the U.C. Davis study became more and more sophisticated. In 2001, Dr. Carlson and his staff performed an in-depth analysis of horses pulled from the ride. Generally these horses fall into one of two main categories: those pulled for metabolic reasons, and those pulled for soundness reasons. Metabolic problems consist of things like dehydration, improper gut or stomach sounds, pulse irregularities, and respiratory problems. Carlson was particularly interested in gaining a better understanding of the underlying conditions resulting in metabolic pulls.

Because a majority of pulls occur at Robinson Flat—thirty-six miles into the ride and the first of two vet checks with a mandatory one-hour hold, or rest, and because there is some vehicle access to the location—Dr. Carlson chose that location to perform his study. He set up a centrifuge in order to provide on-site analysis of blood and urine, utilizing a portable generator brought in for this purpose. Those entrants whose horses were pulled for metabolic reasons were asked if they wanted to participate.

Most riders were more than willing to have blood and urine drawn from their horses, when possible. Dr. Carlson was able to provide useful data within as little as fifteen minutes, and he performed more comprehensive research when he returned to the labs at U.C. Davis. His research on this specific issue helped the vets more effectively and efficiently treat the stressed horses, by helping riders better understand how to prepare their horses, and to recognize early signs of problems and how to remedy them before they become more serious.

Information and results from the various metabolic studies begun in the early 1980s were used by organizers at the 1996 Olympic Games in Atlanta, Georgia. One of the concerns about the Atlanta site was the effect that high temperatures and humidity would have on both human and equine athletes. In the equestrian community there was special concern for three-day eventing horses that are required to gallop and jump over a complex and difficult course that spans several miles. By utilizing the Tevis Cup data along with other research, the Olympic organizers learned to use large fans, water misting systems, and "cooling tents" to provide shade, all to help the horses recover after long, strenuous workouts. Because of the extensive research and preparation for the weather conditions, not one horse at the 1996 Olympics suffered any serious metabolic problems. Tevis organizers, especially the vets, were quite pleased about this, though most people were unaware of the Tevis Cup's influence on this outcome.

Mary Tiscornia, 1979 Haggin Cup winner, cooling off under the Swinging Bridge between Last Chance and Deadwood. [Courtesy of Western States Trail Foundation]

✵ 17 ✵

1980–1989: Boyd Zontelli, Rushcreek Ranch, and Becky Hart

With ever-increasing numbers of participants, the Tevis Cup went forward into the 1980s. In 1981, Boyd Zontelli returned to the Tevis Cup with a horse named Rushcreek Hans. Together they set a finish-time record of ten hours and forty-six minutes, a record that stands today, and probably always will. The average winning time since recorded times began in 1960 is thirteen hours, which equates to 7.5 miles per hour. Since the 1990s, winning times have slowed to fourteen and fifteen hours, perhaps due to even more rigorous veterinary standards and pressure to not overtax the horses. However, this in no way diminishes Zontelli's outstanding accomplishments.

"I rode as a kid, but going around and around an arena was boring. I wanted to recapture the excitement of the old days," Zontelli reminisced. The Southern California resident was out trail riding on his ranch in the Malibu Lake area when he came upon another rider. "This guy was training for an endurance ride and I rode along with him." Until then Zontelli had never heard of endurance riding, but the idea intrigued him and fit in with his goals. "I love to explore and I like to discover the bond with my horse. I was hooked from my first ride. It was very rewarding." The Tevis Cup was Zontelli's third endurance ride, and although it took him a couple of tries, his first finish in 1979 with Rushcreek Eaton was also a victory. "That year was a great lesson for me," recounted Zontelli. "I wanted to try really hard to win, but I wasn't willing to jeopardize my horse." Toward the very end of the ride near Painted Rocks, in the final ten miles, Zontelli realized his horse was tiring. "He was running out of gas and I had a very difficult decision to make. Loreley Stewart was just a couple of minutes ahead of me, and I had to make the decision whether to chase her down." Zontelli slowed his horse's pace and chose to go for the completion in honor of his horse. "I was coming down the trail toward No Hands Bridge and the gathering spectators started cheering for me. I was really confused because I knew Lori was ahead of me. I just kind of ignored them and headed on." As he came upon No Hands Bridge, illuminated by the full moon, Zontelli realized why he heard all the cheering. Stewart's horse was done, and had quit right in the middle of No Hands Bridge. Although she managed to coax him in at a slow pace for the final four miles, Zontelli passed her by. Refreshed by the slower pace, Zontelli's horse picked up an easy trot and cruised in for the win. "I was awed by that. I honored my horse, and he gave me the win."

Of his Tevis experiences, Zontelli says it is not one of his three wins, but a very special ride in 1984, that was the most exciting and means the most to him. "My daughter, Cheyenne, turned twelve that year and had been wanting to do the Tevis. We decided that she and my wife would ride together and I would go for it," he explained, in reference to his competitive nature. For Zontelli, everything that could go wrong, went wrong—but not really.

As he crossed over Emigrant Pass and left Squaw Valley behind, Zontelli missed a crucial yellow trail marker. It took him several miles to realize he was off the trail. Angry at himself for missing the trail, he turned around and headed back up the ridge. Along the way he encountered a loose horse, which he quickly caught and led along, figuring he would encounter the horseless rider. Approaching the trail junction, he came upon Pat Fitzgerald, who had been tailing up the ridge when his horse took off. "There I was, in last place with Pat Fitzgerald. He got back on and we rode off together for awhile."

A short distance later, Zontelli came upon a girl who had fallen off moments before. "She cried 'Help!' so I jumped off my horse." He landed on one of those notorious high-country rocks and broke his ankle. "I didn't know it was broken at the time, but it swelled right up and hurt like . . . well, you know." The girl thanked Zontelli for his assistance, got on, and rode off, completely oblivious to his injury and distress. Zontelli struggled to remount his horse with his injured ankle. Like the mountain men he admired as a boy, Zontelli gritted his teeth and suffered through the pain. "I could barely put any weight on that ankle so I had to ride off my knee." However, he couldn't quit. He had to at least get to the next available vet check in order to get aid.

Boyd Zontelli on his way to one of several Tevis Cup victories. [Courtesy of Western States Trail Foundation]

"My wife and daughter passed me as they were leaving the first vet check after Squaw Valley and I was just arriving. Ellis Ruby, from Rushcreek Ranch, saw me, and like a true cowboy gave me some aspirin, and sent me on my way." At Deadwood, Zontelli met up with his wife and daughter. "At least I wasn't in last anymore!" he laughed. However, the news wasn't good, as his wife's horse was soon pulled. Zontelli knew how much his daughter had looked forward to her first Tevis Cup. "She trained and conditioned her horse all by herself. She would get up hours before school to ride and take care of her horse. Then she would ride after school and then do her homework." Knowing she needed an adult sponsor to accompany her to the finish, and this time motivated by love and admiration for his daughter, once again, Zontelli decided to continue.

With some of the pain eased, and with fresh inspiration, the two continued at an easy pace. Because their horses had gone so slowly through the high country and the upper parts of the trail, they hit the canyons when the horses were quite fresh. "I will never forget it—we galloped the last canyon. It was such a thrill. Then coming out of the canyons toward Foresthill, the horses really picked up their pace. We passed a lot of riders." They vetted easily through Foresthill, and in the late afternoon headed out to the final third of their father/daughter journey. "I wanted to win, but when I realized that wasn't going to happen, I figured we would make it a father-and-daughter ride." Along the way they kept hearing stories of how a real horse race between Becky Hart and Loreley Stewart was unfolding in front of them. As they entered the final vet check at Lower Quarry, once again Zontelli was faced with a difficult decision. "Everyone told me that Becky and Lori were just a few minutes ahead of me and their horses were getting tired after battling it out most of the day. I had plenty of horse left because we had gone so easy in the early parts. My daughter turned to me and said, 'That's all right dad, I'll just pull here and you go win.' I couldn't believe it. She knew she couldn't continue without an adult sponsor." Zontelli only pondered his decision for a moment. "There really was no decision to make. We headed toward the finish and Cheyenne's mare, Rushcreek Shakina, just put her nose on Hans's rump and off we went." He then proudly let his daughter lead him across the finish line. "She rode in third, and was the youngest rider to finish so high in the Tevis placings. I was really proud of her," said Zontelli with a smile in his voice.

Zontelli has spent his adult life endurance riding. He serves on the AERC Board of Directors, and still competes to this day; but the Tevis always holds a special place in his heart. "Each ride is like a lifetime. You learn something about yourself each ride and that stays with you in the long haul." In September 2002, Zontelli guided his twelve-year-old granddaughter to her first endurance ride finish in a twenty-five-mile ride in Norco, California. "It's just very special," concluded Zontelli of his endurance experiences, highlighted by his time on the Western States Trail.

Zontelli's horses come from a strong and interesting lineage. Rushcreek Ranch in Lisco, Nebraska, has been a huge, working cattle ranch since the early twentieth century. In the 1940s, Tom Wells and his son, Preston, wanted to upgrade their herd of horses. They were a rough and difficult lot, made up of mustang crosses and some coarser horses acquired as the U.S. Cavalry was disbanded. Cavalry-bred horses had been held in high regard for many years, due to their careful breeding and training, but as the horse cavalry waned and the motorized cavalry waxed, the quality of their breeding and training diminished.

Although the American Quarter Horse eventually became the breed of choice for western ranchers, in early 1940 the breed was relatively unknown, especially in the far reaches of Nebraska. Preston Wells wanted to improve the ranch's herd of horses, so he contacted a family friend, Albert Harris, a successful businessman in Chicago who had studied various breeding lines of American horses. While in Europe, he became quite informed about Arabians and upon his return to the U.S., he helped found the Arabian Horse Registry of America. He suggested the Wells infuse some Arabian blood into their herd. In the first generation they found the foals to have improved temperaments and better conformation. The ranch hands found the horses easier to break and train, and excellent for ranch work. In addition, their Arabian breeding gave them exceptional stamina and durability. They didn't tire on long cattle drives and they remained sound, not succumbing to the rigors of work as other horses did.

As long-distance riding developed, riders began to seek horses better suited for these long distances. Like those from the Hyannis Ranch, Rushcreek horses went on to win many top endurance honors. Three different Rushcreek-bred horses have won the Tevis Cup: Zontelli's own two horses—Rushcreek Eaton and Rushcreek Hans—and Sam Arnold's Rushcreek Champ, who also won the Haggin Cup. In 1979, Carolyn Wells (at age 60), a member of the Rushcreek family, earned a Tevis buckle with Rushcreek's Faye. Rushcreek horses are so popular with endurance riders that there is a waiting list for each year's foal crop, and when new wranglers come to the ranch they aren't allowed to bring their own horse, but must use one of Rushcreek's Arabians. Although most sneer at first about riding a little Arabian instead of a stout Quarter Horse, their opinions quickly change when they realize what great horses Rushcreek produces.

While Zontelli set record times for the Tevis Cup, Becky Hart put endurance riding on the map. Until Hart's incredible accomplishments with a little bay

Arabian gelding, RO Grand Sultan, few outside of the endurance community knew about endurance riding, let alone any of its stars. Hart changed
all that. She discovered endurance riding in 1975 and never looked back.

Hart was a successful show rider, and in 1974 she was competing her
horse, Nusan, fondly called "Boo," at Arabian horse shows. She lived near
Julie Suhr and was vaguely aware of Suhr's long-distance riding efforts. In
1975 as Suhr was preparing for the Tevis Cup, she found herself without
a horse. Although Hart had never done any endurance riding, she told
Suhr that she thought Boo was in good condition and could carry her to
a finish. After going on several training rides together, Suhr agreed with
Hart's assessment, but she would only take Boo to the Tevis on one condition: Hart had to come crew. Suhr, ever the horseman, realized she did
not know Boo the way Hart did. Therefore, she wanted Hart at each of
the vet checks to help assess the horse's condition and attitude. Prior to
the initial check-in at Squaw Valley, Suhr asked Hart, "If you think this
horse can go a hundred miles, why aren't *you* riding him?" Hart replied,
"Are you kidding? Me? Ride a hundred miles? I could never do that." Suhr
and Boo completed the Tevis in 1975, her eighth; and in 1976, Hart
completed her first Tevis Cup. She returned in 1984 with RO Grand Sultan, or "Rio" as he was called around the barn, and began their ascent toward national and international prominence.

Although many endurance riders scoff at show-ring riders, there are
many attributes those same riders bring to endurance riding. The uneven
terrain, steep climbs, and twisting trails require a rider who does not interfere with the horse's need to constantly adjust its stride over unpredictable footing. A rider who does not stay in balance with his horse can
cause the horse to trip, stumble, and work much harder than it normally
would. In order to travel long distances, the horse cannot afford to waste
precious energy maintaining its footing due to a novice rider. Beginning
in the 1980s some savvy endurance riders who were without a strong
show-ring background began seeking riding instruction, often from
hunter/jumper and dressage professionals, obtaining more of a forward-
seat style, and learning to ride in balance, both of which are conducive to
endurance riding. Dressage brought an element of rigorous and exacting
training into endurance riding that was much needed.

While endurance riders had learned much about conditioning
since Wendell Robie's first ride in 1955, many riders underestimated

the importance of training their horses to willingly accept the bit and to respond effortlessly to a rider's commands. The horse's obedience is an important component in creating and maintaining the needed balance and harmony. By helping the horse balance itself and by regulating its pace, the horse is less likely to tire and to injure himself.

Dr. Barsaleau, highly regarded in the endurance community, made no bones about the important influence the show-ring disciplines had on a successful endurance horse and rider. "Training and conditioning are separate disciplines and they are not interchangeable. Training is the process of mannering and education for the horse." Barsaleau was often accused of "holding a damned horse show in the woods." Where other riders might be inclined to let their horses walk or trot along while going down the trail, he would ask his horse to leg yield, and perform other lateral work which creates flexibility, responsiveness, and suppleness, and was especially useful along the narrow, winding trails, for traversing steep switchbacks, or when galloping along through an open area, and over questionable footing. An unschooled rider might begin yanking on the horse's bit, trying to get their horse to veer around any poor footing, which often resulted in the horse breaking his stride, tossing his head, and generally disrupting his easy, fluid gait. Barsaleau felt that a horse with even average talent could often outperform a horse with great talent, but little training.

"It is atrocious seeing the riding," said Barsaleau of the many endurance riders he observed over the years. "They lack preparation, planning, and strategy." Barsaleau cited Marcia Smith, Erin McChesney, and Becky Hart as the finest horsemen, and all had varying degrees of show-ring experience.

As a testament to her superb horsemanship, Becky Hart and Rio won almost every major endurance award the sport had to offer, with the Tevis Cup as their first. While Boyd Zontelli was guiding his twelve-year-old daughter to her first Tevis Cup finish, Hart was battling for the lead with Loreley Stewart. Hart and Rio prevailed, and logged the first of two Tevis Cup wins. Two years later, in 1986, Hart again completed the Tevis Cup, this time edged out for the win by Stewart. Hart always rode her horses effectively and efficiently, her riding style only adding to her horse's performance, not hindering it.

With international recognition of endurance competition came national, continental, and world championships, and Becky Hart was among the first to compete overseas for her country. Like other equestrian competitions, the endurance championships had both team and individual competitions. In the Endurance World Championship, each country was invited to send a team of its four best horses and riders to the host nation. The finish times of the three highest-finishing riders counted toward the team standings, and the team with the lowest cumulative riding time was named World Champion, and presented with gold medals. Then the three riders with the fastest finishes overall were awarded gold, silver, and bronze medals as individual champions. Endurance riding now had the honor of international recognition, but many still regard the Tevis Cup as the ultimate achievement.

Following her second Tevis win in 1986, Hart and Rio went on to the 1986 North American Championship, joining with riders from other parts of the country, Canada, and Mexico. They showed that their Tevis Cup wins were not a fluke by winning the gold medal. In 1988 Hart once again returned to the Tevis Cup, and once again she and Rio had their names inscribed on the Lloyd Tevis trophy. As a member of the United States Equestrian Team, Hart went to Europe for the inaugural Endurance World Championships, where she was a member of the gold medal team, and also became the individual gold medalist. For the next two World Championships, in 1990 and 1992, Hart and Rio continued their dominance of the World Championship individual gold medal. In 1993 they repeated their victory at the North American Championships, and then culminated their stellar international career with a best condition award at the 1996 World Championships.

Though hardly anyone outside of endurance riding had previously heard of Becky Hart, her name and photo were now plastered across horse magazines of all kinds. She became a household name among horse-crazy girls, and those competing in hunter/jumper, western, and dressage shows, as well as various breed organizations. Such was the level of her accomplishment that in 1990, she was inducted into the AERC Hall of Fame, and both the American Horse Shows Association and *The Chronicle of the Horse* honored her as Horseman of the Year. In his endurance career, Rio logged over ten thousand competition miles, finishing all thirty-six of the one-hundred-mile rides he started in, and winning twenty-two of them. For Hart, Rio truly was the horse of a lifetime.

Although not as prominent today in the competition aspect of endurance riding, Hart continues with the passion that began for her as a young girl in 1974. She runs Skip Lightfoot's stables in the San Francisco Bay Area, and still trains and competes endurance horses.

In part because of Hart's influence, Lightfoot also became involved with endurance riding and currently owns some international-caliber horses. He had his own memorable Tevis experiences a decade later. Hart is considered an excellent instructor, and in addition to the lessons she conducts at her resident stables, she tours around the country giving clinics and seminars. She is a regular speaker at the various Equine Affaire expositions held around the country, which attract thousands of spectators and participants. Hart is regarded by many both in and out of endurance riding as one of the top competitors in the sport, and there is no doubt of the level of recognition she provided. Once again, the Tevis Cup was the launching pad.

Julie Suhr

Although she had finished her first Tevis Cup in 1965, Juliette Suhr longed to have a chance at the Haggin Cup, which for her represented an acknowledgment of superb horsemanship. After returning to riding as an adult, Suhr pored through books, asked questions, and tried to learn from any mistakes; the result was a rider who became a horseman. Just about anyone with a modicum of desire can learn to ride competently, but only those with the passion to understand the horse as a whole can be considered a true horseman. Dr. Barsaleau is fond of saying that he is a "student of the horse," and when someone referred to him as a horseman, he would correct them and say he was "working on it," understanding that learning about horses is a lifelong process.

Like Barsaleau, Suhr regarded each of her horses as individuals and sought to understand their distinct needs as such. In 1980, Suhr came across that one special horse that elevated her among the elite of endurance riding. HCC Gazal was another product of the Hyannis Land & Cattle Company of Nebraska. Like Rushcreek Ranch, Hyannis bred and produced a number of horses that had very successful endurance careers. Their Arabian and Arabian-cross horses were bred specifically for ranch work, but that same breeding and initial training made them ideally suited for the sport of endurance riding as well.

In writing of Gazal in her autobiography, Suhr described him as "a proud horse, blessed with desire. A tremendous athlete—there was only one way to ride a horse such as this one in an endurance race and that was for the top. I don't think he ever took a deep breath—he was born a cut above the rest." Initially Suhr's husband, Bob, rode the horse on his first endurance rides, limited-distance twenty-five-mile rides. Suhr took over the reins for the third of these twenty-five-mile rides, and Gazal was awarded as the best conditioned mount. The next night she wrote his breeder and said, "I have found my Haggin Cup horse. Give me two years and he will win it." Much to her delight, in 1983 Gazal carried Suhr down the Western States Trail and was indeed awarded the Haggin Cup. They repeated the feat again in 1984, and for a third time in 1986. No other horse has duplicated this accomplishment.

In 1986 Suhr had a chance for a rare double victory, the Tevis Cup and the Haggin Cup. However, one of the challenges the diminutive Suhr faced with Gazal was his headstrong nature. He was a big-strided horse, and his powerful haunches—which helped propel him up the challenging canyons—also created a great deal of thrust to contend with over a ride of such length. Although they remained ahead of the majority of the 269 horses that started that year's Tevis Cup, by the last ten miles Suhr was exhausted. She and her friend, Loreley Stewart, were the first two riders into Lower Quarry, the final vet check before the finish. If a rider presented his horse to the vets before the horse was adequately recovered he would be given an automatic ten-minute hold penalty. Suhr knew the first horse to recover and return to the final six miles of the trail would likely be the Tevis Cup winner that year. True to form, Gazal recovered quickly, while Stewart's horse, Risque Rocket, took a few minutes longer to reach the established criteria. However, while Gazal was fresh and willing to trot out, Suhr was completely exhausted. She was afraid that if she let Gazal settle into his huge, ground-covering trot she would not be able to keep him from breaking into a canter and then, ultimately, a gallop. The next stretch of trail, down to No Hands Bridge, is barely wide enough for one horse, and twists and turns among the rocks making it unsafe to traverse this section of trail at more than a walk or slow trot, especially given the steep drop down the rocky face to the ribbon of river below. The more Suhr struggled to slow her horse, the more he fought back. He knew the route, and also that the finish was just a short distance ahead. However, Suhr was fearful that she couldn't maintain control if she let him speed up, and was even more worried that she would not be able to stay on. When Gazal heard two horses approaching from behind him, he fought Suhr for his head even more. Gazal was competitive and liked to be in the lead, but his rider was attempting to quench his competitive nature. With reluctance, Suhr let the two faster riders pass, and with it she let go of the Tevis Cup.

For years after Suhr knew she had the top horse that day, but she felt her horse did not have the top rider. However, her disappointment was tempered with their third Haggin Cup win the next morning. "He put on a thrilling performance. He pranced, he danced and entranced. And he won his third Haggin Cup, a record that still stands," wrote Suhr.

In 1984 the Tevis Cup lost its creator. Although at eighty-nine years old Wendell Robie had slowed considerably, he was still active. For him, "retirement" meant quitting life, and Robie lived life to its fullest throughout all his years. He had grown the family's small, one-branch bank into the Heart Federal Savings and Loan Association, a cluster of savings and loans throughout Placer County. Robie had kept an active interest in skiing with the Auburn Ski Club, and his crowning achievement in this sport was the opening of the Western SkiSport Museum at Boreal Ridge, atop Donner Pass. "The center is what Wendell envisioned," said Bill Clark, the executive director of the Auburn Ski Club.

The Western States 100 Miles—One Day Ride was Robie's proudest achievement, and he collected his thirteenth and final Tevis Cup belt buckle in 1974 at the age of seventy-nine. Robie died on October 31, 1984, and at his funeral on November 6, longtime friend Jack Veal led a saddled, riderless horse in front of the funeral procession. Robie's boots were turned backwards in the stirrups, a tribute usually given to presidents, leaders of countries, high-ranking military personnel, and other dignitaries. "I loved that man," said Jack Veal, summing up the sentiments of many. Despite the loss of Robie personally, all of the things he was involved in—from his businesses to the Auburn Ski Club to the Tevis Cup—flourished, a testament to Robie's vision and ability to create things larger than himself; and perhaps more importantly, with the structure to continue even without the bold visionary at the helm.

That same year also saw the creation of a federal policy that put the Tevis Cup in jeopardy. The ride had survived animal-rights protesters and other challengers, but the passage of the 1984 Wilderness Act restricted access to a significant portion of the Western States Trail. In recalling that time, Hal Hall explained the dilemma facing them, "The federal policy surrounding the 1984 Wilderness Act stated that competitive and/or commercial ventures were prohibited in Wilderness Areas." The area surrounding Granite Chief, on the backside of Squaw Valley, including the famous Cougar Rock, was designated federal wilderness area with the stroke of a pen. Showing their solidarity, directors from both the Western States Trail Foundation and Western States Run combined forces to deal with this crisis.

They met with of the U.S. Forest Service, their congressmen, and various local and state leaders. While many were sympathetic to the issue, none would take up the cause. A grass-roots effort resulted in more than ten thousand letters flooding the offices of Congress, but still the Forest Service stood resolute. Both the run and the ride were competitive and commercial, and they could not pass through the newly designated wilderness area. The irony of the situation was that the very champions of the area were the ones being shut out.

Finally, with the future of both events in jeopardy, Hal Hall and John McCullough (both representing the ride) and Tony Rossmann (president of the Endurance Run), headed to Washington, D.C. "John and I went along to do what we could, but Tony knew the ropes," reported Hall. Rossmann was an attorney by profession and he was comfortable dealing with politicians, lobbying, and legislative efforts. To combat the brick wall they had run into, ride and run organizers had introduced their own legislation allowing them access to the Granite Chief Wilderness Area. "We had to convince congressmen to sign on to the legislation," continued Hall of his adventure in the nation's halls of congress. "How legislation works is that a congressional committee has to consider your bill. In order to do that you have to get their aides and analysts behind your proposal." The men knocked on doors, went into offices without any scheduled meetings, talked to anyone they could get to listen; in short, they lobbied, and they were successful.

Their legislation was scheduled for a committee hearing, and Hall, McCullough, and Rossmann knew they had one chance. "I wish you could have been there," said Hall of that day. "I wish we could have a recording of Tony's speech. It was fabulous and he was fantastic. It was all-American, Mom, and apple pie. As soon as he was done they voted to carry the legislation to Congress."

In a last-ditch effort to resolve the problem, following Rossmann's inspiring speech, the men headed over to the main offices of the U.S. Forest

Service. They didn't have an appointment, and they didn't even know if the appropriate people would be available to see them, but they got lucky, and found themselves face-to-face with the director of the Forest Service. "He took us in and met with us," said Hall, still incredulous almost twenty years later. "He really listened to us and we explained how we had gone through every channel, beginning at the local level." The chief understood their seriousness about maintaining access, but he made no promises, and the men left with no expectations. Their legislation was going forward, so it was just a matter of waiting for the process to unfold. They returned to California and resumed their daily lives knowing they had given it their best shot.

Five days later the director of the Forest Service announced that, once a year, both the run and the ride would be given special dispensation to travel through the Granite Chief Wilderness Area, putting reasonable limits on the two events. Since that day, the run has an annual maximum of 369 runners and the ride has a maximum of 250 horses. The legislation was dropped and the two events continued.

PART THREE

❧ 19 ❧

ORGANIZING THE WESTERN STATES
100 MILE RIDE: A DEDICATION TO THE IDEAL

The Tevis Cup and the entire sport of endurance underwent significant changes in the 1990s. For the Tevis Cup, it was a decade of change, a decade of growth, and a decade of amazing horses. By 1990, endurance riding had spread throughout the world, with rides held on all continents. Endurance became established as an international sport, complete with a world championship event. There were ten international rides in 1990, and by the middle of the decade, that number doubled to twenty.

By the start of the decade 5,024 riders had attempted the challenge of the Tevis Cup and 2,905 met the challenge. The event kept growing, and with growth came more demands. Several decisions within the Tevis organization greatly influenced the future of the ride.

The first major change was another new starting point. When Robie organized the first ride in 1955, his invitation letter stated that they would start in front of the Tahoe City post office. As the number of participants increased year after year, organizers changed the start to Squaw Valley, with its expansive valley floor that easily accommodated the horse trailers, 250 horses and riders (and crew), and the support vehicles. Starting in Squaw Valley was very popular with both ride organizers and the competitors. Access was easy, there was plenty of room for everyone to spread out, and spectators could easily mill about the temporary camps set up the day before the start of the ride and see the horses and riders off on their journey in the early morning hours.

As the years progressed, such wide-open real estate became very valuable, and outside interests began looking to the relatively flat land of the meadow for additional development and expansion. In part due to Robie's early efforts, the entire area now attracted tourists year-round, from around the world, for recreation and vacations. In this way, the future of both the ride and the run might fall victim to Robie's own success at promoting the outdoors. In addition, some within the WSTF wanted a permanent location they could call their own.

In his later years, Robie had formed the Wendell and Inez Robie Foundation, in part to help support many of their community interests and as a mechanism to give perpetual life to his dreams and visions. The Robie Foundation was governed by trusted, close friends of Robie's. In the late 1980s, realizing their time at Squaw Valley was limited, foundation members began the search for land with input from the WSTF Board of Governors.

The Tahoe-Truckee area is quite mountainous, and by the eighties all the relatively flat land by or near road access was unavailable or prohibitively expensive. The foundation's search team identified land along a ridge that ran parallel to the Truckee River between Squaw Valley and Truckee. This was primarily forest land, and access was via primitive, one-lane dirt roads. Given its location, the land was not suitable for development, and there was no infrastructure to provide for electricity, running water, or sewer connections, but that was not a problem for the foundation's directors. Marc Van Zuuk was instrumental in identifying and acquiring the land the Robie Foundation eventually bought.

Van Zuuk had a degree in engineering and worked as a land surveyor. His avocation was locating old roads and railway easements. In his spare time he pored through old maps and archived land records. As a member of Parlor 59 of the Native Sons of the Golden West, Van Zuuk came to know Jack Veal, who brought him to a Western States Trail Foundation meeting, recognizing Van Zuuk's talent and interests in historic routes. Because the Western States Trail passed through Forest Service land, a federally designated wilderness area, land owned by the State of California, as well as private land, obtaining the permits and easements necessary to conduct the ride was becoming increasingly challenging. The world was now a much more populous and litigious place than it had been in 1955. Van Zuuk recalled the first couple of WSTF meetings he attended in 1986. "I made the mistake of leaving a meeting early and they put me on the board! I knew nothing about horses." Now Van Zuuk owns a horse and enjoys pleasure riding. As he became involved with the ride, he got the Tevis affliction. "I don't have the endurance riding bug," he explained, "but I have a passion for trails, and that trail in particular." Van Zuuk became the resident expert on easement and access issues.

Van Zuuk also works tirelessly on trail maintenance and improvement. The work the WSTF does on the trail, and the techniques they have developed over the years, have been adopted by trail preservation groups across the country, setting the standard for trail maintenance, especially in wilderness areas. Jerry Fruth, an area vice president of the AERC, is very involved in trail maintenance and preservation from his home in Evansville, Indiana. In 2001 when he earned a Tevis Cup belt buckle, Fruth addressed the crowd: "I have seen trails all over the country, and if anyone wants an example of how trail maintenance and preservation are done the best, come to the Tevis Cup. As I rode I observed the engineering. It is marvelous."

Van Zuuk is constantly on the lookout for discarded or spare items that will aid in maintaining and preserving the trail. "You ought to see my collection of culverts," he explained proudly. "I have a stockpile of culverts I have collected from job sites that were too short for the job, but long enough for the trail." Managing erosion and water run effectively so that it does not wash away the trail, while remaining as noninvasive to the wilderness as possible, is an art form, and one which the WSTF Trail Committee has mastered. "When we go up in the spring," said Van Zuuk of springtime trail work, "we never know what the high country looks like until the snow melts." The manmade trail wends its way through some of the most spectacular natural settings in the country, and through their tireless efforts, the volunteers have managed to achieve a successful blending of the trail with its native environment.

Because of his expertise, Van Zuuk aided in the search for land on behalf of the Robie Foundation. The foundation tried to work with both the Forest Service and the California Department of Forestry to acquire land, but dealing with governmental bureaucracy proved onerous.

One day Walt Tibbitts, who served on the WSTF board, announced that a private wood products company was in receivership, and among their real estate holdings was a quarter section, or 160 acres, that met the requirements of the Robie Foundation. The site could be reached by several miles of winding dirt road off Highway 267 near Truckee, and a small meadow served as a natural amphitheater; although rustic, the site was perfect, and Robie Park became a reality.

The 1990 Tevis Cup started from this location, and over the years the Robie Foundation added basic infrastructure, necessary for hosting such an event and all the participants it attracts. The site boasts potable water, generators provide limited power, and the recently erected Barsaleau Pavilion provides a large, covered gathering place. In addition to the Tevis Cup, the Native Sons of the Golden West and the Boy Scouts, among others, have used the site for camping and wilderness activities.

"It's a great place for the ride to base and for all of us to enjoy ourselves," stated Jack Veal proudly. "We want to keep it rustic with enough infrastructure to be comfortable."

Another change for the ride came recently when, due to logistical difficulties with using Michigan Bluff for the first one-hour hold, ride organizers decided to use an area at Foresthill, only nine miles further down the trail. Although quaint and festive, getting all the vets, officials, crews, support people, and spectators, as well as the horses and riders, in and out of Michigan Bluff was very complicated. The town lies at the end of a narrow dirt road that twists and turns several miles off of Foresthill Road, the main road leading up into the heart of the Sierra Nevada. Michigan Bluff is perched at the end of the trail, and only recently did the town even get dedicated phone lines. "Yep, we had party lines, until sometime in the 1980s," said one longtime resident of the little town.

As a money-raising effort to fund various community projects, and to help out the tired, dusty travelers along the ride's route, every year the local townspeople would sell food and drinks to passersby. Some residents on the main street of the town even rented their front yards to the riders, as a place to rest from the exertions of the trail. The majority of horses, riders, and their crews lined the single street, and everyone enjoyed the festive setting.

The move of location to Foresthill did provide much easier access for everyone involved with the event. The area is atop a large plateau overlooking the majestic American River Canyon, and there is now ample room here for crews and family members to pull in trucks, trailers, and RVs. Logistically, Foresthill represented a great improvement for everyone involved with the Tevis Cup ride, but many still miss the quaint atmosphere once provided at Michigan Bluff.

In the town of Foresthill, local residents come to line the streets with chairs, and picnic throughout the afternoon; viewing the horses as they trot by is an annual event. Local businesses set up water misting systems to cool the athletes as they pass through, and many a rider finds a cold drink thrust into his or her hand by a local resident.

The townspeople love this event, and the riders definitely appreciate the show of support. Endurance riding is one of the loneliest of sports, and those moments of cheering voices and encouragement last many miles for these hardy souls, and their even hardier mounts.

A very positive development for the Tevis Cup was the appointment of WSTF board member Larry Suddjian as ride director. Suddjian brought a level of professionalism and organization to the ride that was never seen before. Tevis Cup organizers were feeling internal and external pressures to become more professional as the sport evolved. Outside groups continued to focus on animal welfare and land use, and more riders came to the Tevis Cup with a competitive focus. Participants were not as tolerant of bottlenecks at vet checks or communication difficulties.

Committed to Robie's visionary leadership, the Board of Governors continued to preserve the vision and integrity of the ride, while improving the handling of the annual event. "The ride evolved," explained longtime supporter Jack Veal. "It needed to go from a daredevil pursuit to a groomed, sophisticated event." Suddjian was the perfect choice. "It's about management: knowing horses and organizing people. This is basic event management," he explained. Suddjian wanted the Tevis Cup to maintain its reputation as the most challenging endurance ride in the world, and for the next decade, he did just that.

Suddjian implemented systems and procedures spelled out in what was to become his famous "Tevis Cup Bible," a blue binder over four inches thick that contained every piece of information Suddjian might need. This kind of information was critical, for among other things, Suddjian was responsible for lowering a river. Moses may have parted the Red Sea in biblical times, but the Tevis ride director is responsible for making a fast-moving, wild river safe for horses and riders to cross late in the ride. The river powers huge turbines that provide power to Sacramento. Normally water out of Oxbow Reservoir flows at over 2,000 cubic feet per second, which results in the deep, fast-flowing river where the Tevis Cup horses cross. At this rate of flow, the water is deep enough in the middle that a horse would have to swim, and the current could carry horse and rider downstream. In addition, when the horses reach the river crossing at mile 89, it is dark and they are fatigued. Suddjian had to coordinate with a number of private and local, state and federal agencies to reduce the flow from the reservoir. In a spirit of cooperation and in recognition of the importance of the ride, the Placer County Water District, the Federal Bureau of Reclamation, the Pacific Gas and Electric Company, the Auburn Division of Reclamation, and the California Department of Water Resources collaborated to reduce the river's flow. They took into account outflow from the reservoir, river flow and depth, anticipated electrical demands, and the speed the leading riders were traveling. In the late afternoon, a group of volunteers with wetsuits strung a rope across the river and attached glow sticks to it to provide a guide for riders as they reached the crossing in the dark.

In addition to all of the painstakingly compiled and updated data, the blue binder ensured consistency, as it was eventually passed on to subsequent ride directors who built on the organization Suddjian established. Both Dale Lake and Merv Pyorre, who followed Suddjian, said they would not have assumed the responsibility without the blue binder. Suddjian was proud of the fact that he had a Tevis Cup belt buckle, earned in 1985, and he enjoyed riding the Auburn trails from his home with his wife Candy. Furthermore, his Tevis finish helped him understand what the riders needed during the ride.

Suddjian identified key elements of the ride, and then put people in charge of those areas. He recognized the need for strong coordinators, a task made even more difficult given the fact that all were unpaid volunteer posts, except for the vets, who were paid a modest honorarium. Although Suddjian identified many excellent individuals, perhaps his most outstanding choice was Dr. Mitch Benson as chief veterinarian. Benson served as a vet secretary and then a ride vet since 1973. "My first time with this ride I rode with one of the official vets. That was in the days before I went to vet school," recalled Benson of his early Tevis memories.

Recognizing the importance of public perceptions, combined with the need to protect the welfare of the horses, chief veterinarian Dr. Mitch Benson built an outstanding team of veterinarians who have each brought an impressive background of experience and knowledge to the ride. A position on this team is coveted. Many participate, and stay with the ride for years, because of the stature of the ride and the chance to be part of something very special. Because of the vigilant vet checks and evaluations, the Tevis Cup remains virtually free of complaints from animal rights groups, and the Society for the Prevention of Cruelty to Animals has been impressed with the quality of care the horses receive.

"Each section of the ride has different demands," explained Dr. Benson. "The vet at a specific checkpoint needs to be familiar with the surrounding terrain when he applies the [health] criteria to the horse. The vet needs to know the distance to the next checkpoint and what the terrain is like so he can tell if the horse is demonstrating the physical condition to get to the next point. For example, the vet at Foresthill knows this is the last major stop until the finish line and that a tough canyon follows this stop. Also, it is hard to get horses and riders out after this point."

Throughout his tenure as head vet, Benson was very proud of the panel of Tevis Cup vets. They are an interesting group, and among the fifteen to

Tevis Cup veterinarians (left to right): J.C. Cook, Jim Edwards, Gary Cook. [Marnye Langer photo]

twenty vets who serve the ride each year, they have over two hundred years of combined veterinary experience. Dr. Jim Edwards of Chico, California, a jovial gentleman with a quick wit and knowledgeable eye, is the veteran of the group. He has worked for the Tevis Cup since 1969.

"The Tevis Cup is a great opportunity to work with colleagues and we work as a team. It's also such a prestigious event. It's the Indy 500 of the horse world, the granddaddy of endurance rides. I am honored to be a part of it. There is such a high degree of professionalism. Working the Tevis hones your daily skills," explained Edwards of his ongoing participation. Despite the fact that he has retired from daily vet care, Edwards puts the Tevis Cup date on his calendar every year. "I wouldn't miss it!" he says with a laugh.

Robin Kelly of Tahoe City, California, is a relative newcomer, having signed on as a Tevis Cup vet early in the 1990s. "More competitors are yearning to learn," she said of the rapport between vets and the riders. "The Tevis is an incredible event. This is a historic course and it is an opportunity for me personally to work with great athletes—horse and human," she stated of her involvement with the Tevis Cup. "I love it. Among the vets we are like a big family that comes together once a year for a reunion. We come from all over the country." Ray Randall of Bridger, Montana, echoes Kelly's sentiments. "This ride is a demanding, difficult ride. Just to complete it takes a lot of perseverance. I get to see good horses and I get to work with other vets who see a lot of different things. I can learn new things and different ways to do things. For me, the Tevis Cup is continuing education."

Dr. Gary Cook of Billings, Montana, and his family attend the Tevis Cup every year. Although he no longer works other endurance rides, he stays on with the Tevis Cup. His wife Joan serves as his vet secretary. She grew up in Reno, Nevada, and remembered spending long summer days hanging out at Pat and Donna Fitzgerald's stable. "One of my strongest memories is the smell of walking into their barn. They kept this huge barrel of molasses that they added to the feed for the horses. I will always remember that smell," she recalled fondly. Pat Fitzgerald eagerly shared his Tevis Cup passion with the young riders in the area and would often sponsor them on the ride. Under Fitzgerald's guidance, Joan Walker Cook earned a Tevis Cup belt buckle in 1966. "Pat really worked to take kids through the ride. Both he and Donna were good horsemen. I rode a little Morgan horse and I remember riding into McCann Stadium at the end of the ride. We rode out of the dark into these bright lights and all these people were sitting in the bleachers in the middle of the night. They cheered for every rider entering the stadium. It was such a thrill."

Although she enjoyed endurance riding, Joan Cook had no idea it would lead to meeting her husband. "My dad was crewing for Pat and Donna at the Virginia City 100, and I met Gary at that ride. He was the Nevada State Vet and based in Reno." Fresh out of vet school, the native Montanan found himself in the high desert of Reno, Nevada. Cook says she took pity on him. "He was lost. He had to get to all these ranches and they were spread out everywhere, so I rode with him on his calls." A relationship blossomed. "She took me riding with her," recounted Cook. "I had ridden a lot in Montana, but the plains are nothing like the desert!" His wife laughed. "The whole time we were out riding, he kept asking me, 'Are you sure you know where water is?' I think he was convinced we were going to get lost." They married in 1973 and moved back to Gary's hometown of Billings to start a vet practice.

In the mid-1980s the Cooks began working the Tevis Cup. Their son J.C. wanted to follow in his father's veterinary footsteps, and throughout his college years, he served as his father's vet secretary at the Tevis. In 2002 J.C. earned his Doctor of Veterinary Medicine degree, and was invited to join the Tevis Cup veterinary panel as the youngest member of the team.

Communication is a key component of the ride, and one made even more challenging by the remote aspects of the trail. "The logistical problem for the Tevis is that the first fifty-five miles or so take place where there is no infrastructure, neither electricity nor communications," explained Ed Reilly, who assisted with Tevis communications. "After going through two towns, it resumes in the wilderness for the last thirty-five miles." Effective communication was provided not by new technology, but old technology. Vets at remote checks needed to be able to call for trailers to pick up pulled horses, and record keepers needed to be able to update the head secretary regarding which riders made it through the checks and which were pulled. Reliable communication was critical, and local ham radio clubs and enthusiasts from around the Auburn area helped the Tevis Cup ride develop a viable communication system.

Volunteers are essential to any event of this magnitude, and more than six hundred volunteers participate annually to make the ride possible. Buck and Brandon Hyers, father and son, rode the Tevis Cup in 1981. They earned their buckles and were so impressed with all the help and assistance they received during their ride that they decided to volunteer the following year. Since 1982 the Hyers family has manned the Bath Road location, welcoming riders and providing the first services to them as they enter the mandatory one-hour hold at Foresthill. Coming out of the canyon in mid- to late afternoon, the riders and horses are hot, dusty, and tired. They are greeted by a water-misting system, troughs of cool water, buckets of carrots, and the Hyers, who gladly hose down the horses to help cool them off. "It's a virus," explained Buck Hyers. "We were inoculated with enthusiasm for this event. It's insane, but it is also a natural high. To finish is a rush, and we wanted to help after so many helped us during our year."

Working on the Western States Trail. Larry Suddjian, second from left (with shovel).
[Courtesy of Western States Trail Foundation]

Not all the volunteers are necessarily horse enthusiasts, but each one has a tale to tell of how the Tevis Cup has affected him or her personally. The volunteers all work together and under the leadership of Suddjian, the Tevis Cup organization became a finely honed machine. During their ten years of service, the combination of Suddjian and Benson brought skills, talents, vision, and a fantastic synergy to the Tevis Cup.

⇒ 20 ⇐

ERIN McCHESNEY

In 1990 Hal Hall completed his sixteenth Tevis Cup ride and logged his third win. However, this time it was not with El Karbaj, the Arabian gelding who had taken Hall so far, but a new mount, HCC Zarlusko. That same year a nondescript little bay Arabian by the equally nondescript name of Harry earned the Haggin Cup, with his owner Daniel Bunn. However, this would not be Harry's only moment in the limelight.

At the 1990 Tevis Cup ride, Julie Suhr accomplished her twentieth finish, becoming the first rider ever to accumulate two thousand miles on the Western States Trail. Suhr headed into that memorable ride with eleven consecutive finishes. "I figured I would be riding the most important ride of my life as I reached for the first ever two-thousand-mile Tevis Cup silver buckle." Suhr trained diligently on her three-time Haggin Cup winner, Gazal. She felt that this ride would be her final journey down the trail that had had such an impact on her and her family. However, Suhr's journey turned out to be much more difficult than she had ever anticipated. During a training ride in preparation for the Tevis Cup, Suhr and Gazal fell. Although Gazal galloped toward home unscathed, Suhr was not so lucky. A nurse at the hospital informed Suhr that she had broken her collarbone, but that it would heal in a couple of months. "A couple of months?" Suhr didn't have a couple of months; she only had five weeks.

Suhr was determined to make the ride, but she knew that there was no way she could survive all those miles on Gazal, who was a strong and bold horse. Suhr's friend Maryben Stover offered Suhr the use of her Quarter Horse mare, Rushcreek Q-Ball. She had crooked legs and a crooked white blaze running down her face, but Maryben told Suhr the mare was "smooth as glass and could be controlled easily with just a halter." Although Q-Ball had never done a hundred-mile ride before, she had a fast trot and a big heart.

"I began that last journey over the Sierra Nevada. It was a ride filled with nostalgia for I truly believed that, if successful, I would never attempt to conquer that trail again." Q-Ball did as her owner promised, and carried Suhr smoothly and safely along her journey. In 1994 Suhr's daughter, Barbara White, won the second two-thousand-mile buckle ever awarded. Over the next eleven years a total of five people have earned these ruby-encrusted trophies.

In 1991 a young woman came to the Tevis Cup and took the ride by storm. Earlier, in 1976, the McChesney family moved to the little town of Cool, nestled in the Sierra Nevada foothills near the Western States Trail. Erin McChesney's parents ran the Cool General Store and two of their employees, Karlon Keene and Diane Holt, taught the girl about horses. "My parents promised me I could have a horse when we moved to Cool. I worked in the store and earned enough money to buy my first horse, Chappo," explained McChesney of her introduction to horses. McChesney started riding at age nine and quickly became interested in endurance riding. In 1980, at age fourteen, she rode her first Tevis Cup and earned her first buckle. After finishing the ride she knew that someday she would return.

After finishing school, McChesney had the horse bug. In addition to her endurance interests, McChesney had developed a strong background in dressage and general horse training. Besides giving lessons and training other people's horses, McChesney showed her own Arabian stallion, Abu Shan, to the International Arabian Horse Association's Region 3 Second Level Dressage Championship. During that time, she decided to breed one of her mares, and the resulting filly was Cougar's Fete. "I worked for a commercial cattle ranch. When Fete was three we worked cattle and checked five thousand acres of grazing land."

For two years McChesney worked on the cattle ranch, and in that time Fete matured from an unbroke three-year-old into a well-conditioned, well-trained, five-year-old mare. McChesney also trained Fete in the basics of dressage. The mare was responsive, obedient, and could balance herself over difficult terrain. "I always knew I would do endurance with her, but waited until she was seven to do any rides with her. I knew she would be very successful. She has an incredible attitude of stature, independence, and acts like the alpha mare. She goes well alone, and seems to prefer it that way." A few horses push for the front and in so doing separate themselves from the group, going against their very nature as herd animals. These horses are very often the champions, whether on the racetrack or the trail.

McChesney set her sights on the Tevis, and beginning in 1990, she competed in several fifty-mile rides with Cougar's Fete and easily finished them. Despite her recent arrival to the sport, Fete even earned a reserve best condition award, which only added to McChesney's belief that her mare had much more in her. "I always felt she was a hundred-mile horse. Prior to the Tevis Cup she finished in the top ten of the fifty-five-mile Dru Barner Ride." McChesney used all of 1990 and the first half of 1991 to thoroughly prepare Cougar's Fete for the task facing her.

McChesney is adamant about preriding the route. "The Tevis is very difficult terrain and part of the ride is in the dark. Some riders come here cold, but generally the successful ones know the trail. I like to ride the last part of the trail to get my horse really familiar with the route. I would leave from Cool and ride to Auburn, which is the last seven or eight miles of the ride. Then I would put my horse in the trailer and take her home. I wanted her to know this part of the trail really well and to know it was the end. I knew we would be riding the last section in the dark and we would both be tired."

As the start date for the Tevis Cup approached, McChesney was logging 110 miles a week on Cougar's Fete, six weeks prior to the ride. Three weeks before the ride, she dropped to sixty or seventy miles a week. In the final two weeks, McChesney cruised thirty-five or forty miles on the weekends, and lightly hacked the mare around her farm on the weekdays. Distance competitors, whether human or equine, follow similar training and conditioning strategies. As a competition nears, athletes ease up on their workouts to allow their bodies to recover from the hard training and to store energy for the supreme effort that will soon be required.

Confident about her horse's training and skills, McChesney credits her strong background in dressage for her balanced, effective riding style, apparent from the moment you see her in the saddle. "I try to keep my horse balanced and ride to enhance her performance without interfering with the task at hand." Many riders, veterinarians, and ride officials feel that horses should have completed several one-hundred-mile rides before attempting the Tevis Cup, but Erin McChesney proved that solid horsemanship applied to an athletic, well-prepared horse can yield fantastic results. McChesney also knew her horse. "I really think she has such a good mind because of her early start," commented McChesney of the mare's calm, sensible demeanor. "Some of the horses on endurance rides make themselves so tired mentally by shying or being really nervous. That takes so much out of them."

McChesney started out cautiously in the early light of what was to become a memorable day. The mass start of more than two hundred horses in heavily wooded Robie Park can be quite chaotic as riders get caught up in the excitement of the moment, and already high-strung horses take the cue from their tense riders.

McChesney left Robie Park with about fifty horses in front of her. Passing through Squaw Valley, McChesney then began the first of the many ascents she and Cougar's Fete would face that day. The pair easily passed a number of horses and riders as they trotted up the rocky terrain leading to Emigrant Pass. This particular day would prove to be extremely hot, even by Tevis standards. At the bottoms of the canyons, the temperature approached 110 degrees.

Thirty-six miles into their journey, McChesney and Cougar's Fete trotted into Robinson Flat. Her crew informed her that she was the fifteenth rider in. For a brief moment McChesney allowed herself to feel excited, but she knew she had to keep her focus, for sixty-four arduous miles remained. She and Cougar's Fete had conquered the rocks and granite escarpments of the high country, but the grueling, heat-filled canyons remained, followed by the doldrums of encroaching night late into the ride. Since several horses were pulled, McChesney left in eleventh place from the Robinson Flat vet check. She and Fete made their way through the canyons along the North Fork of the American River in a steady fashion. They passed a few more horses and riders along the way. "It was terribly hot that day," recalled McChesney, "but we both do well in high heat. I also spent a lot of time preparing for the ride, trying to simulate the conditions and length of time spent on the trail."

As they entered Michigan Bluff, McChesney learned from her crew that she had four minutes in front. "I thought they meant I had four minutes between me and the horses that had left the check. It wasn't until I left Michigan Bluff that I realized there were four minutes between me and the rest of the riders." Once again McChesney felt that momentary thrill. "My crew decided we were going for first place, but I knew too many things can happen. I wasn't even thinking about first at that point."

It was in those final miles that McChesney's extensive training paid off. As the pair left the final vet check at Lower Quarry, Cougar's Fete really perked up. "She knew where we were and she was really confident on the very last part of the trail," stated McChesney. Since leaving Michigan Bluff, they had not seen another horse and rider in front of them.

Although the coolness of the coming night is welcome after hours of baking in the sun, the darkness can dampen even the hardiest of spirits. Fortunately, because of her preparation, Fete recognized that she was homeward bound and kept up her steady pace. The mare easily trotted the last six miles to the finish, where the crew awaited the pair's arrival. At 10:19 P.M. they emerged from the trees and trotted to the finish, amid cheers and clapping, after fifteen hours and nineteen minutes of riding time.

The following afternoon, McChesney proudly accepted the Tevis Cup during the awards ceremony. She then received the rare dual honor of earning the Haggin Cup, only the second time both cups have been awarded to the same horse and rider. Cougar's Fete was only the third mare to receive the Haggin Cup. "It took me a long time to digest winning both cups," said McChesney of her impressive dual victories. "Since childhood I had carried around the idea of winning one or the other of the cups someday, but it was simply a childhood dream that wasn't going to be realized. I am still awed by what Fete and I accomplished together. I am extremely fortunate to have had these experiences and they are still very personal for me. I gained a lot of recognition and notoriety as a result. I enjoy the speaking engagements and they give me an avenue to share my knowledge and experience with other people. But again, the experiences themselves are personal for me."

In the next several years, McChesney faced a number of difficult situations. "My life went through major upheavals," she explained when talking about that time period. In 1992 her mother underwent a mastectomy and this was further compounded by the fact that McChesney was pregnant and her marriage was not going well. In 1993 her first son was born and her second son followed in 1994. While struggling with two infant sons and running her horse-training business, her father had a heart attack. Her mother was then hospitalized with leukemia and died in 1995. McChesney felt like her life was falling apart. In order to begin putting it back together, she realized she had to get out of a marriage that was neither good for her or her young sons. "I went back to junior college to get my AA degree and filed for divorce." With so much pain in her life and so many demands on her, McChesney didn't have time to grieve or process all that was going on. Like a solid Tevis horse, she just kept putting one foot in front of the other, slowly putting the miles behind her. "I put blinders on," she said after her mother's death. "I was caring for my dad after his heart attack and my infant sons." Going into 1996, she needed some kind of boost. "I decided to ride Tevis that year. Basically I said, 'It's on the same day I won in 1991 and I need something good right now.' I had no intention of doing anything but trying to finish." Although few doubted her ability to guide her horse to a completion, no one figured that she could win again, on the same horse, five years later.

Coming into Robinson Flat, McChesney had a strong lead and left thirty minutes in front of the next horse and rider; however, other riders were not so fortunate. Dr. Benson commented that a higher percentage of horses than normal were pulled at Robinson Flat that year. "The change in the trail in the Cavanaugh Ridge area resulted in a more difficult route and the need for riders to go slower through that area," he explained. Often ride organizers have to make minor alterations to the route each year depending on the rate of snowmelt, impact on the trail following winter, and other factors. The weather was also hotter than normal, which created more stress on the horses and riders.

Riding the first canyons, McChesney maintained her lead and trotted into Michigan Bluff with no one on her tail. A *National Geographic* film crew was filming the ride that year for a documentary, and Cougar's Fete was scared of the microphone hovering only a few feet from her head while the vets prepared to examine her. "The film crew just swarmed us as we got into town, and my mare looked at that huge, fuzzy microphone that looked like some sort of dead animal," recounted McChesney of that particular moment. This stress caused her pulse and respiration to stay elevated, but once the film crew backed off, the mare's vital signs quickly came down to desirable levels. As soon as her hour-long wait was up, McChesney quickly remounted. She knew several serious competitors were only a short distance behind.

As they headed down the final third of the trail, Fete and McChesney picked up the pace. Knowing that the other front-runners were pushing no more than twenty minutes behind, McChesney did not linger at subsequent vet checks. A quick check of pulse and respiration, a big drink of water, a wave, and a call of "Good luck!" sent McChesney down the trail.

Gathered at Lower Quarry, crews waited, searching the darkness for a faint glimmer of a glow stick, or listening for the clank of a bit. They anxiously checked their watches, knowing the pace their rider hoped to maintain. "Was their rider late?" "Did the rider encounter a problem?" "Was the horse okay?" "Did something happen?" and then the eerie green of a glow stick light was spotted, shouts rang out, and then a few more minutes of waiting to see which rider was approaching. Was McChesney still in the lead? Had someone else overtaken her? At this point, the crews are almost as fatigued as the horse and rider they are supporting, and with that fatigue come wild visions.

To the relief and thrill of her crew, Cougar's Fete rounded the corner and burst into the bright lights of the vet check. McChesney smiled, and then quickly got down to business. Dismounting, she presented her horse to the veterinarians. All the waiting crews erupted in applause when the mare trotted out sound, and the pair headed down the trail again; their goal, the finish line, was only a few miles away.

At 10:38 P.M., to the cheers of the hundred or so people waiting at the finish line, McChesney and Cougar's Fete trotted from darkness once more. Her fist pumped into the night sky to punctuate her second Tevis Cup victory; McChesney completed the ride after a total ride time of fifteen hours and thirty-eight minutes.

At 10:00 A.M. Sunday morning, only seven of the Haggin Cup candidates appeared. McChesney presented Cougar's Fete first. "The first-placed horse looked really good, but not as good as in '91," said Dr. Benson after the vets finished with Cougar's Fete. Several other horses presented well during the Haggin Cup judging, but no decisive winner emerged. The vets convened a meeting with the Cup Committee to discuss their findings. "This year it was really close," said Dr. Benson, "and we had to resort to a hand vote. Usually we arrive at a verbal consensus, but this year it was really close. Although the [Cup] Committee selects the winner, they have never *not* followed the recommendation from the vet committee."

Wendell Robie called the Tevis Cup a "master's degree in horseman-ship," and in 1996, Erin McChesney certainly achieved this by winning both the Tevis Cup and the Haggin Cup in the same year, and for a sec-ond time. More remarkable, McChesney accomplished the feat on the same horse with a five-year break between her two wins. "It is an honor and a privilege to sit on a horse this good," McChesney told the audience when she accepted her awards. Her second set of honors set the tone for the rest of her life's pursuits. She remarried and is now Erin Klentos. Al-though no longer training horses professionally, she still enjoys riding, es-pecially on Fete. "The Tevis has been a wonderful influence on my life," she reflected. "I will never forget the wonderful gift that I was unbeliev-ably given twice."

☙ 21 ❧

THE JOSEPHINE STEDEM SCRIPPS CUP

When Roxanne Greene was fourteen years old, the Tevis Cup was already a legend to her. "I saw one of the Tevis belt buckles worn by a gentleman attending the Los Compadres Trail Ride in Palm Springs. He told about the seemingly impossible abilities of the Tevis Cup horses and riders," she recalled of her earliest Tevis Cup memories.

In 1976 Greene decided that she had to give the Tevis Cup a try. "I began with an international champion show mare who was eighteen years old." Greene carefully conditioned the mare and then, on the advice of her veterinarian, went up to Auburn a week before to ride sections of the trail between Michigan Bluff and the Auburn Fairgrounds. "On that first Tevis ride I knew some of what to expect, thanks to the advice and help of Richard Schmidt, DVM. Dru Barner and Wendell Robie gave me some pointers. Since that first year we have tried to get all the horses we have used over that section of trail at least once before the event." Greene finished the Tevis Cup and earned her first belt buckle. "The first ride for me was awesomely beautiful, and an affirmation that I could keep my mind and plans together for the time necessary to compete. The hours on the trail were magical." Greene's enthusiasm extended to her husband, Ernest, and their children, Jim, Rebecca, and Erin, who have all earned numerous buckles over the years.

Greene became very involved in the sport and still serves on the WSTF Board of Governors. Always a supporter of junior riders in endurance competition, and especially having watched her own children thrive in the sport, Greene wanted to establish a special award honoring the junior finishers of the Tevis Cup. "I have championed the participation of junior riders and I established the Josephine Stedem Scripps trophy, in honor of my grandmother. She always said the way for children to grow up and learn more responsibility is to give them grown-up tasks. I have always been amazed at the enormous responsibility and good sense displayed by the youthful endurance riders who have completed the ride. They care intensely for their mounts, and sometimes serve as the real leader when their sponsors are tired and everyone needs to display extra courage and horsemanship."

Roxanne Greene in 1976 on Dixie Dexter. Greene established the Josephine Stedem Scripps trophy for junior riders in honor of her grandmother. [Charles Barieau photo]

Although the cup was first presented in 1994, the names of every junior rider who completed the ride are inscribed at the base of the cup. Over ninety young riders have their names on the trophy and each receives a brass plate to put on his or her saddle.

In 2001, Greene made her twenty-fourth attempt at the Western States Trail. "I get very uptight before the ride," explained Greene, and she was more so as she was trying for her twentieth buckle, signifying two thousand career miles over the challenging trail. "Coming to the finish line was both a wonderful sense of relief and a feeling of personal victory over my sometimes lazy mind and my regularly inferior physical ability."

Junior finishers, 2001. [Marnye Langer photo]

❖ 22 ❖

Chris Knoch: A Man of Steel

During this era another star emerged with superior physical ability. Throughout the mid-1990s Chris Knoch seemed almost unbeatable. Knoch, a wildlife biologist, began his competitive focus at ride-and-tie events. A strong runner, Knoch and his various running partners earned many of the highest honors in these events, but the Tevis always beckoned. Like many others, Knoch saw it as the ultimate test of a long-distance horse and rider. The fact that he was such a strong runner only made the Tevis more appealing. In fact, in June of 1993, Knoch completed the Western States Endurance Run. He returned that July, determined to finish the ride.

Twice before Knoch had attempted the ride, and both times his horse was pulled. Knoch was a big man at six feet tall and weighing well over two hundred pounds. The fact that Knoch was such an accomplished distance runner helped his horse tremendously. Determined to earn a coveted Tevis Cup belt buckle, Knoch came to the Tevis Cup with a seven-year-old Arabian gelding named Saxx. "I bought Saxx two years ago. I was attracted by his attitude and willingness," explained Knoch. In his short endurance career, Saxx had already earned a total of six best condition awards, and Knoch and Saxx won the Memorial Day 100 in Redding earlier in the year. "Coming to the Tevis I knew I had a good horse," stated Knoch.

In 1993, there were several changes in policy governing the way the ride was run, and savvy horsemen were able to take advantage of one of them. Head veterinarian Mitch Benson, in conjunction with the entire veterinary panel and the ride's organizers, instituted a change to the one-hour-hold vet checks. Until 1993, the sixty-minute countdown began as soon as the horse and rider arrived at the vet check. "So many riders were pushing their horses hard, right up to arrival at the vet check," explained Benson of the change. "Many of the horses didn't fully recover until a good fifteen or twenty minutes into the one-hour period." The vets felt that as a result, the horses did not have an adequate rest period if so much time was spent in merely recovering a normal pulse and respiration rate.

After careful review, the veterinary panel established more strict pulse and respiration criteria for the horses upon arrival at the checkpoints they defined as "gate-holds," as well as several other vet checks throughout the ride. This meant that the full sixty minutes did not commence until the horse reached a pulse and respiration level established for each stop. As a result, smart riders learned to bring their horses into the check at, or near, the standardized recovery rates, so that the hold time started quickly. "'Recover-and-hold' gives the better riders and better horses a definite advantage," explained Benson. "Gate checks are used at most rides, and they reward good horsemanship and superior horses." Benson noted that significantly fewer horses were pulled for metabolic reasons than in past years. Riders who rode at a measured, steady pace were rewarded over those who raced their horses. As a marathon runner Knoch knew the importance of pacing, so he used the new gate-hold format to his advantage.

Knoch and Saxx started out the ride rather slowly, and steadily moved up through the pack within the first few hours of the ride. An agile, strong horse, Saxx tackled the steep, mountainous terrain like it was play for him. He just dug in and climbed. Although Knoch worried about the effects the high elevations would have on his horse, Saxx never seemed to notice. He powered up Squaw Valley and over Emigrant Pass. Standing on this crest where the Sierra Nevada begin their sloping fall to the west, Saxx paused, seeming to look for more peaks to climb. He didn't know the canyons waited ahead, and they would test his climbing ability perhaps more than the tallest granite peaks ever would.

Because of Knoch's familiarity with the trail and his knowledge of his horse, he knew when to ease back on Saxx as they approached Robinson Flat. Knoch was able to maximize his pace, and adequately cool his horse as they approached the first one-hour gate-hold in twenty-fifth place. Saxx was immediately approved by the veterinary committee. Saxx dozed and munched on the treats Knoch's wife Cheryl had prepared. Knoch rested and restored his energy as well. He was excited to see how relaxed and fit Saxx was, and hope soared within him that he would earn a Tevis Cup belt buckle. However, that cool morning among the pine trees of the high Sierra Nevada, Knoch had no idea how much he and Saxx would accomplish.

Some horses ahead of Knoch were pulled, and the pair left Robinson Flat in eighth place. Over the next thirty miles, the same group of about ten horses remained within two to three minutes of one another. Saxx tackled the arduous climbs in and out of the canyons with aplomb. Typically the canyons are brutally hot. Despite hopes for milder temperatures, the mercury approached triple digits. "In the second half of the ride I was worried about heat," said Knoch. To help his horse handle the stress, Knoch ran alongside Saxx for almost a third of the entire ride.

Steadily the pair pulled ahead of their competitors, and the trail was theirs—after leaving Foresthill, they never saw another horse and rider for the rest of the ride. After only fourteen hours and forty-four minutes on the trail, Saxx and Knoch emerged from the night to trot across the finish line in first place. "I really think being able to run for long stretches contributed to our large margin," said Knoch at the conclusion of the ride. Not only did he earn a well-deserved Tevis Cup buckle, he had also won the coveted Tevis Cup.

Knoch's unorthodox strategy caused some diehard Tevis competitors to grumble, some even suggesting that ride officials put limits on how much a rider could run alongside the horse. Even if the WSTF had wanted to pursue this avenue, enforcing it would be impossible, given the remote nature of almost all of the trail. Besides, this would not have been in keeping with Robie's initial vision. Mountain men, immigrants, and miners alike walked beside their horses or mules for miles on end. Throughout his time with the ride and up until his death, Robie had always said that each person should ride his own ride. If any rider wanted to run, and was able, he or she could run as much of the ride as he chose. Julie Suhr lamented that due to problems with her ankles and creeping age, she could no longer tail up the canyons. She had to rely on her horse to carry her every step of the way. There were a few grumbles, but no changes were made; furthermore, most people congratulated Knoch on his remarkable win.

In 1994 Knoch arrived at the Tevis Cup poised to win again. Finishing the ride is hard enough, but winning the Tevis Cup once, let alone twice, is extremely difficult. Knoch managed a repeat performance with his bay Arabian gelding. "The horse has been running good all year," said Knoch. "We've been saving him all year for this ride. I haven't done any ride-and-tie competitions, and only two fifty-milers, a seventy-five, and a hundred, which we won."

While many of the most competitive riders live on or near parts of the Western States Trail, Knoch lived in the San Francisco Bay area. During the week, Knoch rode in a state park near his home. "On weekends my wife and I would pack up on Friday nights and head to the Sierras. We would camp and then do lots of mountain trails for seven or eight hours a day. We did a lot of long, slow rides and gained familiarity with the trail." This riding also provided the mountain work necessary to prepare for the Western States Trail.

As the 202 horses queued at the starting area early that day, Knoch planned a slow, easy start. "We went out faster than I expected," he said. Instead of getting caught in the various bottlenecks that occur in the early parts of the ride, Knoch was ahead of most of the riders. "Not having to wait for horses in front of you not only saves time but it saves energy as well. Waiting can make some horses really anxious and fretful and then they are burning energy they will need later," explained Knoch.

Once over Emigrant Pass and with Watson's Monument at his back, Knoch settled Saxx into an easy pace as they descended the almost two thousand feet to Lyon Ridge, the divide separating the North and Middle Forks of the American River, known as the Foresthill Divide. With a quick trot-through vet check at Lyon Ridge behind them, the pair headed to Cougar Rock. Once past this obstacle, Knoch was able to let Saxx trot quite a distance, as the trail levels off for about ten miles. Approaching Robinson Flat, Knoch eased up on Saxx so he would meet the established criteria before their one-hour rest period. Knoch was well tuned to his horse's condition and, like many competitive endurance riders, he carried a heart monitor. Saxx was quickly accepted by the veterinary committee and was only six minutes behind the leader. Several horses ahead of Saxx were not immediately accepted by the veterinarians, so when Saxx's one hour hold was up Knoch left in sixth position.

They quickly passed three riders just before descending into Deep Canyon. "I wanted to catch up with Loretta Potts so I had someone to ride with in the canyons," explained Knoch. "Having someone to ride with can help perk up the horses," explained Knoch of his riding strategy. The canyons can get really hot and the horses are beginning to get tired, both of which can really sap a horse's attitude and willingness. Climbing out of the second canyon into Deadwood, Knoch finally caught up with Potts and her horse IVR Ranchy. They rode the third canyon at El Dorado Creek together and came into Michigan Bluff leading the pack.

During this second hold, both horses rested, with Potts leaving one minute ahead of Knoch. Despite the length of the ride, sometimes one minute can make a difference. "I didn't feel like I had as much horse at this point as I did in 1993," said Knoch. "His pulse and respiration came right down, but Loretta left one minute in front of me and I had to push to catch up with her."

Going into the Volcano Creek Canyon, Potts kept up a strong pace, forcing Knoch to match her, trotting and cantering all the way to Bath Road just outside of Foresthill. "I couldn't believe it," said an incredulous Knoch. "Her horse was so tough. He wasn't fading at all, and she rides the entire time." Knoch counted on spending a significant amount of time running alongside his horse as he had the previous year. This time if Knoch wanted to keep up, he had to remain mounted. "I didn't run as much this year. Last year I probably ran almost a third of the race myself. This year I probably only totaled about eleven or twelve miles, and I hardly got off toward the end of the race. In fact, at one point I got off to lead Saxx down a steep incline and he kept running over me so I got back on and stayed on until the end."

At Foresthill, Knoch got the advantage he needed. Although there was no mandatory hold, horses still needed to meet pulse and respiration criteria. Despite riding at a slightly faster pace than Knoch intended due to his desire to keep pace with Potts, Saxx recovered easily, quickly vetted through, and headed back onto the trail. IVR Ranchy, on the other hand, did not recover quite as fast, giving Knoch a precious ten-minute lead. Confident that he had plenty of horse left, Knoch continued to push Saxx and the gelding responded gamely. Pricking his ears, he headed down the last major descent to Ford's Bar. In the waning light, the pair pushed on.

"I had seen how tough Potts's horse was and I didn't want them cantering up behind me." Knoch wanted to establish a strong enough lead so that he could ease up on Saxx's pace. However, at Francisco's where a member of Knoch's crew was able to meet him for a few minutes, Knoch found out that another rider was making a bid for the lead. Although he would have preferred to ease up, he kept pushing Saxx's pace. All of Knoch's training rides along the trail began to pay off. "We had been over this part of the trail five times in the spring, and when Saxx saw the trail he was ready to go," stated Knoch.

They trotted and cantered all the way to Lower Quarry. "I actually walked in leading Saxx, and started feeding him handfuls of hay as we walked." The vets looked the horse over and gave him the go-ahead to proceed to the finish, just six miles away. "I let Saxx eat for a few minutes,and then taking more handfuls of hay, I started walking him toward the road. I tightened his girth and then continued down the trail."

Chris Knoch on Saxx—1993 victory. [Hughes Photography]

∾   ∾   ∾

Saxx continued his easy pace, tired but not exhausted. The full moon lit their way down to No Hands Bridge, up to Robie Point, and then to the finish line. The strong, steady pace had eliminated his competitors, and he finished the ride with a time of fourteen hours and forty-eight minutes.

"When we trotted into the stadium it was so great. There was no weariness. I was happy with Saxx's condition. I was ecstatic with the whole thing." Knoch's meteoric rise in the sport of endurance established his reputation as a tough competitor and capable athlete. Knoch felt that his ride-and-tie experience prepared both him and his horse. "Ride-and-ties are a great place to get experience on a young horse. The races are fast and mentally tough. They are really a mind game for the horses because they have to deal with being out in front by themselves and then being tied while a bunch of horses go past them. The whole pace is fast and they learn about vet checks, to eat when they get a chance, and to drink when water is offered. I think the ride-and-tie events make horses tough."

✹ 23 ✸

WIN BY A NOSE

Even though 196 entrants started the Tevis Cup August 12, 1995, the ride became a contest between two courageous, tough horses. At the end of the trail, over thirteen hours after they started, just half a length separated Matthew Mackay-Smith on WC Freiheit from Chris Knoch on Saxx, a difference that could have been critical had the riders or the trail been different.

Mackay-Smith arrived in California with "Fred," his eleven-year-old Anglo-Arabian gelding, about a week before the Tevis Cup. Mackay-Smith was well prepared for the arduous trek following top-ten finishes in two one-hundred-mile rides earlier in the year; however, he didn't come to win the Tevis. Mackay-Smith's philosophy is more abstract, and in keeping with Wendell Robie's vision. "I try to maximize my performance and that of my horse. If we happen to be the best that day, so much the better," he said. "I ride one mile at a time. I make sure the horse has a representative experience the first mile and then add the next mile to that. I add mile after mile, one mile at a time. Finishing alone is not an objective. I don't want the horse to have a bad experience."

Once in California, Mackay-Smith took three days to preride the trail, then concentrated on the lower portion, primarily the last fifteen miles. Like many experienced endurance riders, Mackay-Smith knew that Fred would be traversing these final portions of the trail in the dark. Imprinting the route on the horse would help him navigate the final miles on the day of the ride.

Chris Knoch and Saxx returned to the Tevis as the heavy favorites, following their back-to-back victories the previous two years. Although picking a Tevis Cup winner can prove difficult, there was no doubt that if betting was allowed, Knoch would have been an odds-on favorite. Saxx had continued to rack up completions on other rides, including a number of top-ten finishes and best condition awards. Earlier that year Knoch and his wife, Cheryl, had moved to Alturas, California, where Knoch continued his work as a wildlife biologist. He spent the spring and early summer riding Saxx, now nine years old, at the high elevations in the basin and range area of this far northeastern corner of California. "I felt Saxx was in the best condition ever," said Knoch.

Not realizing that their paths would converge, the two men, one a tall, stately, elder Virginia statesman, and the other a young, brash, husky biologist, each started the Tevis Cup expecting his own individual journey.

Mackay-Smith started out slowly with about fifty horses ahead of him. By the time he reached Squaw Valley, ten miles into the ride, Mackay-Smith had moved up about ten places. He and his mount climbed the steep grade up to Emigrant Pass, and then encountered a fairly deep snow-bank as they headed over to Granite Chief. Fred was moving in his typical free-going way, easily navigating the difficult rocky sections composing the first third of the trail. He led a pack of horses through and up out of Elephant's Trunk, along Red Star Ridge, and on into Robinson Flat. Fred recovered quickly and was clocked in for the one-hour hold in seventh place. Knoch and Saxx were only three minutes behind, Saxx having easily traversed the high country.

Mackay-Smith left Robinson Flat with only three or four horses in the lead, and cruised easily down into the first canyon. Knoch was close behind and caught up with the pair at Dusty Corners, forty-four miles into the ride. "I heard of Matthew and I knew who and what he is, but I had never met him. He is like an icon to me. He was completing his first Tevis the same year I was born. Riding with him for the remainder of the ride was fantastic. I was taking notes," said Knoch. Mackay-Smith knew of Knoch too. "I had heard that Chris was a 'mountain attacker.' I offered to let him have the lead in the canyons." And so began a journey that would provide memories for both men for the rest of their lives. Knoch accepted Mackay-Smith's offer and took the lead into the next canyon. However, he soon had to yield the trail to Mackay-Smith and his mount. When Knoch saw the way Fred handled the steep climbs, he was flabbergasted.

"I couldn't believe what I was seeing. I thought I had the greatest mountain horse of all time, and then I met Fred. He pushes with his rear end and takes about a three-foot stride behind. His front end just glides uphill, steering. It's intimidating to me," said an awed Knoch.

Standing at 16 hands, Fred demonstrated a big, ground-covering trot. Saxx, at not quite 15 hands, had to trot and canter to keep up along the gradual slope toward Last Chance. On the steeper parts of the trail, Mackay-Smith got off to lead his horse. "I think that when Chris saw me get off it both relieved him and made him feel comfortable," recalled Mackay-Smith. Knoch was impressed at the older man's fortitude and his ability to keep pace on the downhill sections. "Matthew is vigorous and goes downhill at the same rate I do," said Knoch with a touch of amazement. Mackay-Smith put so much pressure on Knoch that he only ran short segments of the trail, mostly when he joined Mackay-Smith to lead their horses down some of the steepest sections of trail.

Up until this point of his career, Saxx had never been seriously challenged, especially going uphill. Fred changed that. Both horses went up the first of the three canyons in thirty minutes. "Thirty minutes up the canyons is considered suicidal by some, but neither horse was stressed," said Mackay-Smith. Because of their pace, Knoch did not dare to get off and run for fear of falling behind Fred and his rider. At Deadwood, they caught up with the handful of front-runners and flew through the vet check. Most of the leading horses were eliminated as contenders in the second canyon between Deadwood and Michigan Bluff.

It was clear that the contest was now between two determined men, and two hardy horses. The men had assessed one another and each knew the other had enough horse to finish. Leaving Michigan Bluff in the early afternoon, Mackay-Smith and Knoch knew that there was no one in front of them and no challengers behind them; with an open trail in front of them and a lot of trail left to cover, their focus changed to one another. Although the two men were competitors, they also became friends over the next forty miles. "We visited and chatted like monkeys," said Mackay-Smith, thoroughly enjoying Knoch's company as they rode down the trail toward Auburn. Several times Knoch commented to his riding companion, "This is the most fun I've ever had on an endurance ride." Of all the topics they discussed, however, the one topic both men consciously avoided was the end of the trail.

As they tackled the remaining canyons, they maintained a running dialogue that kept pace with the horses' steady footfalls. The horses never faltered and neither did the conversation. "We had lots of giggles," commented Mackay-Smith. At one point they played a childhood game, each taking turns making up a newspaper headline about the other and the ride. For Mackay-Smith they concocted, "Old, Crotchety Hall of Famer Extracts One More Win," referring in part to Mackay-Smith's AERC Hall of Fame induction in 1984. For Knoch the headline went something like "Young, Blond, Adonis Three-Peats," referring to Knoch's previous two wins.

The two rode into Foresthill and out again, side by side. Both horses were quickly passed by the veterinarians. "As the ride progressed," noted chief veterinarian Mitch Benson, "it became apparent that the two horses were continually recovering better than those around them." Benson felt that both Fred and Saxx fit into the "superior" category. The two men rode through the town of Foresthill, encouraged by the cheers of the local townspeople. The men waved as they turned the corner off Main Street and headed back to the wilderness with only their camaraderie and their noble horses.

By now the sun was dipping toward the western horizon, and the trees cast long, dark shadows. At this point horses are often beginning to feel the fatigue of the distance traveled thus far, and their riders are weary. For Mackay-Smith and Knoch this was not the case. Both horses were traveling easily, and the two men were so engrossed in their newfound friendship that the hardships of the trail swept past them.

After the long, steep descent out of Foresthill down to Ford's Bar, the men headed to Francisco's. Coming out of the California Loop, Saxx pulled a shoe—a common occurrence on long rides. For a moment Knoch was distressed. "Fortunately he pulled the shoe off clean, so I stuffed the shoe padding in and put the EZ Boot on." Knoch started out slow, but Saxx was comfortable with his replacement shoe and they quickly caught up to Mackay-Smith and Fred.

Mackay-Smith could have turned the situation into a tactical advantage, but instead he pulled up Fred and slowly walked down the trail, waiting for Knoch and Saxx. "If I had gone on, Saxx would have gone insane," said Mackay-Smith of his choice. "Besides, these were two gallant horses giving a spiritual example of what horses can do. I couldn't take the ride out of the hands of the horses, so to speak, and make it cheap human strategy. At that point we were the stewards and pilots of our horses."

The two cruised into Francisco's. Although Knoch knew he had no margin for error given the close competition, he erred by not checking the water buckets supplied by the checkpoint volunteers to cool the horses. Although darkness had settled in, summer heat blanketed the canyons for several hours, and the horses still needed refreshing water sponged over their bodies. The buckets of water, supplied by volunteers on the ride, had been sitting in the afternoon sun, and without checking the water temperature, Knoch had drenched Saxx in warm water. He was puzzled by Saxx's sudden high respiration level since the horse normally recovered quickly and easily, until he felt the water. As soon as Knoch rinsed Saxx with cooler water, his respiration dropped, and the vets cleared him. Fred had already passed the vet check, but Mackay-Smith chose to wait for Knoch while Fred enjoyed a few extra mouthfuls of hay. "Matthew is a true gentleman and competitor," said Knoch of his new friend.

With the tough climbs and drops behind them, the riders approached the river crossing. The horses easily forded the American River at Poverty Bar, churning through the wide, cold river. Fred and Saxx trotted and cantered the remaining five miles to Lower Quarry. When Dr. Benson saw Fred and Saxx at Lower Quarry he was impressed with their condition. "It's not unusual to see lots of individual races unfolding within the greater race. But it is uncommon at the ninety-mile mark to see two horses so well matched. At this point one horse has usually proved itself superior. Neither horse faltered all the way to the finish," continued Benson.

As they left Lower Quarry, both riders knew the one thing they had not discussed all day was facing them—the finish line. Soon they would both have to address the one thing they had avoided, and neither knew what the outcome would be. Mackay-Smith believed that he had speed on his side, and was confident that Fred could outgallop Saxx at any point. Although Knoch recognized Fred's strength and size, he knew Saxx had the heart and drive to win, and in a tight race to the finish Knoch was confident that Saxx could outsprint the big, gray gelding.

Word had spread of the exciting race unfolding, and at the Highway 49 crossing the two men were surprised by the number of people lined along the highway to cheer for them and their two courageous horses. In years past, Knoch's crew had met him at the crossing to provide final words of encouragement before meeting him at the finish line. This year there was no time to slow down, as Mackay-Smith was pressing on and Knoch had to keep up.

After they crossed Highway 49 they made their way to No Hands Bridge. Coming around the blind turn to the trestle, Knoch could see about two dozen people milling about, hoping to catch a glimpse of the horses and riders. "Matthew started yelling, 'Here we come! Don't move,' and then he turns the corner and takes off at a gallop across No Hands Bridge," recounted Knoch. He pulled off his $100 sunglasses he had forgotten to give his crew at Lower Quarry, kept his eyes on Mackay-Smith to his left, tossed his sunglasses to the right, where he hoped Cheryl, who was seven months pregnant, would be able to catch them, and took off after Mackay-Smith and Fred. Saxx quickly made up the distance between him and Fred, reaffirming Knoch's belief that his horse could outsprint Fred. Off the bridge and down the trail they blazed until they turned the corner toward the switchbacks where Mackay-Smith slowed to a trot. "Then he turns to me and says, 'Well, we pleased the crowd.' At that point I made a conscious decision to let Matthew have the lead," said Knoch, shaking his head in amazement.

Matthew Mackay-Smith leads riders up to Elephant's Trunk during his 1995 victory. [Gus Wiseman—Photoworks For You]

Most of the remaining five miles the men rode side by side, where the trail allowed. Knoch remained confident that his horse could catch up in a quick sprint to the finish. Fred led the climb up Robie Point, where the horses cantered along back to the single-track trail. Knoch mused that they were an hour ahead of his winning times in both 1993 and 1994, but the horses were still strong. After Robie Point, the trail traverses an area thick with trees, where there is no room to pass, and a bad step along the narrow trail could send a horse sliding down the steep slope to the river below. They turned a corner and crossed a little creek, with Saxx right on Fred's tail. Soon the trees thinned, the trail veered upward, and the finish beckoned only several hundred yards away.

As the horses burst out of the trees they were momentarily stunned by the lanterns lighting the area. Knoch knew that the only way past Fred was to go around him. Left meant a precipitous drop into the canyon, so he went to the right, requiring Saxx to scramble along the steep bank in his attempt to get abreast of Fred. Saxx's first bound put him alongside Fred's haunch. Another powerful bound brought Saxx to Mackay-Smith's knee. In the next stride he lost his footing on the steep bank. He quickly regained his traction, but could barely reach Fred's neck, as the two horses surged across the finish line.

After one hundred miles and thirteen hours and fifty-six minutes, the contest came down to a final, gallant sprint at the finish. Dr. Mitch Benson made it a point to be at the finish to see the epic duel. "Had the trail been a little different or a little longer, the outcome may have been different. Saxx closed on Fred incredibly strong and fast. The nature of the trail and the length of the sprintable distance was to Chris's disadvantage," recalled Benson of the thrilling finish.

For Knoch, second place had never been so fulfilling. To have been beaten by such a superb horse and rider was not a disappointment, but an honor. Both men discovered that day that there were two champions on the trail, both with the capacity to win. While Mackay-Smith and Knoch could have chosen to tie, there remained an unspoken agreement between them to uphold the nature of the competition, part of Wendell Robie's vision when he founded the Tevis Cup. Competition fosters excellence, and there was no doubt of the excellence of both Fred *and* Saxx. With both horses checked and passed by the final veterinary committee, Knoch concluded their trail game of "headlines" by declaring the final headline, "Fred by a Head."

Matthew Mackay-Smith at Elephant's Trunk, 1995. [Photoworks
For You]

In accepting the Lloyd Tevis Cup at the awards ceremony, Mackay-Smith
spoke eloquently about the ride, its history, and its spirit. "There are a few
of you who know, and many who suspect and have an idea of how unique
and extraordinary this event is. You must exercise full attention and energies to preserve this experience. It is your sacred duty. This ride cannot be
duplicated, and you cannot create it again. The Tevis Cup is a very, very,
very precious institution. I am anxious that this ride will not be victim-
ized by those who see it as a mass-marketing project. Organizers must not
dilute the uniqueness of the ride in fear of decreasing participation. Don't

lose what is special about the Tevis. Keep the quality. This ride is comparable to the quest for the Holy Grail." Through Mackay-Smith's words, and the actions of more than two hundred horses and riders each year, Wendell Robie's vision lives on.

⇻ 24 ⇺

CHRIS KNOCH TRIES FOR A THIRD VICTORY

In 1996 Chris Knoch returned again. While he yearned for a third Tevis Cup victory, he also wanted the Haggin Cup. Although Saxx had won best condition awards at other endurance riders, he had never been a serious contender for the Haggin Cup, always finishing with fast, dominant times which sapped some of Saxx's reserves.

Although Knoch had two victories and a close second under his belt, he was not as confident coming into this year's ride as he had been in years past. Three weeks earlier in another one-hundred-mile test, the Race of Champions in Utah, Saxx had "tied up" early in the ride, building up too much lactic acid in his muscles and starting to cramp up. Although this condition is not serious if caught early and treated promptly, Knoch pulled the gelding from the competition, not wanting to risk any permanent physical damage. Knoch was completely baffled by the incident as Saxx was well conditioned and had never demonstrated any tendencies to tie up. However, Saxx responded well to treatment, and Knoch and his wife made the decision to go ahead with their Tevis plans. In order to realize his goal, to represent the United States on the World Championship team, he had to finish the Tevis Cup.

1996 was the same year that Erin McChesney returned to the Tevis Cup seeking a bright spot in her life. Where she rode Cougar's Fete boldly along the trail, Knoch was more cautious. "I didn't want to do anything to stress him," said Knoch of his mount. "All I needed to do was finish. Besides, I knew we would move up in the canyons." If Knoch could have had his wishes fulfilled that year, he would have said that winning the Haggin Cup would make his Tevis experience complete. Barring some freak occurrence, Knoch knew he could finish. Deep, down inside he wanted the Haggin Cup, and he knew he needed to finish in the top ten.

Finding himself in contention for the win in past years, Knoch had to keep pushing Saxx, so the gelding was never in the most ideal condition the following morning at the Haggin Cup judging. This year Knoch planned to go fast enough to finish in the top ten, and slow enough to ensure Saxx was in prime physical condition the next morning.

With McChesney carrying a strong lead, Knoch cruised into Michigan Bluff in thirty-second place and quickly vetted through. This was the first time Knoch was not leading the riders at this point in the ride. With an easy recovery, Knoch returned to the trail only twenty minutes behind McChesney. At Foresthill, with a quick trot-through vet check, Knoch had gained a few minutes on her. While McChesney left Foresthill as soon as her horse cleared, Knoch took a few extra minutes to have a farrier check Saxx's shoes. This year he was taking no chances, and making sure his horse was as sound as possible was paramount. Since he didn't anticipate racing to catch up with McChesney, Knoch figured he would spend some time running alongside Saxx.

Waiting at Lower Quarry, Cheryl, Knoch's wife, began pacing nervously. Fifteen minutes passed, and then twenty. Every time a call crackled over the ham radios, Cheryl or one of the other crew members would check with the volunteers manning Lower Quarry to see if Knoch was listed on an updated pull list. Each time his name was absent. Cheryl and the rest of Knoch's crew watched McChesney vet in, and after a few minutes head back down the trail. Thirty minutes passed and finally the pair trotted into Lower Quarry. Knoch knew that trying to catch McChesney would be suicidal, so he opted for a bit of rest. There were no other riders close to him, so he had the luxury of letting Saxx snack on some hay. Knoch chugged water as an anticipated source along the way had been dry and he felt signs of mild dehydration.

Knoch's crew dashed out of Lower Quarry, parked down by Highway 49, and hiked down to No Hands Bridge. In the rising moon they gathered at the edge of the historic narrow-gauge trestle bridge. They could hear Knoch and Saxx long before they saw them, as the horse and rider traversed the rocky switchbacks above. Urged on by a resounding cheer, Knoch and Saxx headed across to face the final miles alone, while their crew clambered into their truck and drove to the finish line.

Once again Knoch's crew anxiously waited. There was no communication available once riders left Lower Quarry until they reached the finish, and members of the crew kept checking with ride officials to see whether Knoch's name appeared on the pull list, while people stood around in clumps, speculating. What none of them knew was that Saxx had pulled a shoe and Knoch had to put on an EZ Boot. Knowing he had time on his side, he slowed Saxx even more, as there was no point risking the horse hurting himself. Knoch noticed that something didn't sound quite right as he crossed the bridge. "I looked down, and he was missing a front shoe. I don't know how long it had been gone, but it was really rocky just before the bridge."

Finally at 11:50 P.M., more than an hour behind McChesney, Knoch and Saxx cruised to a very impressive second place, and their fourth consecutive Tevis Cup finish. The next morning Knoch was hopeful that he had a competitive horse for the Haggin Cup judging. Although Saxx's exam went well, he did not trot sound on the circle probably due to losing the shoe. Knoch was disappointed, but pleased with his horse's strong performance. This impressive finish also ensured that he would now be representing the United States in the World Championships, and he credited his valuable Tevis Cup experiences with the accomplishment.

PART FOUR

⇾ 25 ⇽

CHANGES IN ENDURANCE

As Wendell Robie's Tevis Cup ride entered its fourth decade, the types of horses used for the ride, as well as the equipment, attire, and knowledge about long-distance riding, had evolved tremendously. "Long-distance riding in the early days," reflected Dr. Barsaleau, "was pretty experimental. We went in pretty 'cold turkey' and had to figure things out as we went along." Riders in the 1960s and 1970s did not have extensive knowledge about equine physiology as it pertained to long distances.

For the most part, the earliest generation of Tevis Cup horses were working horses. Nick Mansfield rode Buffalo Bill and his other horses to check cattle and to lead his riding ponies through downtown Reno; Donna Fitzgerald led dude ranch rides out of the South Lake Tahoe Stable on Witezarif; and Wendell Robie examined acres of timber astride his horses. Many of these horses were ridden every day and—through steady, regular riding—they developed a high degree of fitness. "There are some constants to getting a horse ready for the Tevis that have not changed," explains Dr. Barsaleau. "Regularity of work is a basic. The Tevis is a physiological fitness test. Ever-increasing distances combined with slight increases in speed will put a good base of conditioning on a horse. Witezarif worked primarily at a walk and slow trot, but he was incredibly fit because he worked regularly for long, steady periods of time."

These early horses, whether Arabian, Quarter Horse, Thoroughbred, or crossbred, were mainly working horses, and for them the Tevis Cup was just another day that happened to be longer than most. Although Arabians dominate long-distance rides, certain types of horses do well, regardless of their breed. These horses must be thrifty, and they must also be hardy, tough individuals, both physically and mentally. Many riders will tell you that a mentally tough horse can outlast a horse that is physically tough, but mentally weak. Like many of the riders, the horses are faced with challenges they've never before seen and probably never will again, unless they face the Western States Trail once more. Rarely did these horses encounter problems unless their riders decided to race instead of riding at a pace more suitable over the distance. "A few horses got into serious metabolic trouble," stated Barsaleau, "and mostly it was due to the rider overriding the horse. No horse ever died from a lameness, but severe metabolic distress can kill a horse."

Dr. Jim Edwards, who served his first stint as a Tevis vet in 1969, remembers many of the early horses and riders. "These were working ranch horses with big men riding them. They used heavy western saddles, rode in chaps, and often carried heavy gear on their saddles. Usually the men rode the entire distance and didn't get off and on a lot."

As endurance riding became popular throughout the 1970s, changes abounded. "I remember hearing about these newfangled 'electric lights' sometime in the '70s," recalled Pat Fox. "I hadn't been on a hundred-mile endurance ride for a couple of years. I never liked riding difficult trails in the dark, so I was really excited about the Tevis that year so I could see the 'electric lights' everyone was talking about." However, when Fox arrived at the check-in that year, she found out the "electric lights" she had heard about were really "electrolytes."

Although electrolytes help an athlete—human or equine—replace critical trace elements and minerals lost during heavy, prolonged exertion, overuse can cause problems also. "There are always some people who think that if a little is good, more is better," said Dr. Edwards. "I've seen riders give their horses huge doses of electrolytes, and that can cause more problems than not having enough electrolytes. The horse might not drink enough and then he has this concentration of electrolytes in his gut. To compensate, the electrolytes draw fluid out of the horse internally and then the horse is even more dehydrated. I've even seen some people put salt on their horse's tongues to get them to drink. It doesn't work," said Edwards, shaking his head. "You can't substitute all of these fancy things for good common sense, and riding your own ride." Barsaleau echoed some of Edward's sentiments. "If people just find the pace that's suitable for their horse, they can finish. People try to make the trail fit the horse. Some horses just can't do the Tevis. The terrain is difficult and riders have to pace their horses. Donna Fitzgerald was a great judge of pace."

However, those horsemen who combined sound practices with the developments in technology and improvements in knowledge regularly finished the Tevis Cup with sound, fit horses. By the 1990s, the tack for the horse was much lighter and designed to not rub the raw spots caused by sweat. Saddles are styled like English saddles, but most often are made out of lightweight synthetic materials, rather than leather. Most endurance riders have moved from the heavier western saddles of the past, used by cowboys and recreational riders, to the lighter-weight English saddles, or the McClellan saddle of the U.S. Cavalry. Both are anywhere from ten to twenty pounds lighter in weight. Riders also use stethoscopes and carry heart monitors to track their horse's pulse and respiration along the route. "In the '80s, some rides gave stethoscopes as completion awards," remarked Dr. Edwards.

Riders now use a variety of models to condition their horses. In the 1970s there was no formal model, with the exception of Tom Iverson's interval training. Iverson researched equine fitness as it pertained to racehorses and used the concept of interval training to see if it would increase speed. Interval training applied well to endurance riding. The horse works at a high-intensity pace, then drops back to a slower one. Once the horse's pulse and respiration drop and hold at a certain level, the rider then picks up the pace. By working this way the horse increases his stamina as well as his ability to cover longer distances at a greater pace.

Research on conditioning has yielded volumes of data that riders now employ as they prepare their horses. Endurance riders often know the physical tendencies of their horses better than riders in any other equestrian discipline. They know their horse's resting pulse rate, what the pulse rate should be at a trot, and the horse's upper limit—a higher pulse rate that the horse can maintain, without experiencing undue stress. They also know when the horse's pulse and respiration are too high or when the horse is taking too much time to return to acceptable levels. Top endurance riders, like any top rider in any equestrian sport, are the ones who tell the vet that the horse just isn't "right" on a given day.

Despite the many advances, Barsaleau, Edwards, and many top riders are emphatic that there is no substitute for basic horsemanship. "People sometimes get caught up the day of a ride and start racing," explained Edwards. "They have to remember to ride their own ride; the ride they trained for, at the pace they trained for. Only a small minority of riders on any endurance ride—but especially the Tevis—are the 'hot shoes,' the ones who can win. The rest are riding for the finish." Both Edwards and Barsaleau maintain that a savvy rider with a decently conditioned and prepared horse can complete the Tevis Cup riding at a steady walk and trot.

Hal Hall subscribes to what he calls a "midnight pace," when he feels he has a horse ready to try for a top-ten finish. This pace usually gets him to the finish line around midnight after about fifteen or sixteen hours of riding time. Otherwise, he will ride an inexperienced or less competitive horse at a slower, steadier pace, finishing in a ride time of eighteen to twenty hours. Like other veteran endurance riders, Hall takes pride in the fact that his horses are not used up after a Tevis Cup ride—they are tired, but not overly stressed. "I expect to see a horse that looks used," said Barsaleau, "but not used up. There is no reason for a horse to be used up."

Endurance riders themselves have benefited from changes in technology, especially in sportswear. The traditional riding gear of heavy pants, tall leather boots, and chaps is not conducive to riding a horse for long distances. "Anyone wearing 'tennies' in the Tevis Cup during the '70s was considered a freak and a health nut," laughed Dr. Edwards. However, lighter footwear made it easier for riders to walk and run alongside their horses. Now riders frequently wear an athletic shoe designed for cross-country or trail riding. The shoes have the lightweight aspect of a running shoe, but are sturdier and provide more foot and ankle support for both riding and walking along rocky terrain.

Riders have traded jeans for lightweight spandex and Lycra riding tights. Not only is the material comfortable and form-fitting, it also wicks away sweat and prevents blisters and rub spots. Some riders still wear cowboy hats and baseball caps, mainly to keep the sun out of their faces, but most riders now have opted for safety helmets. Equestrian safety helmets are constructed more like bicycle helmets, with their vents and bright colors, than the traditional velvet hunt caps once worn by show-jumping riders. Of all the equestrian disciplines, endurance riders are definitely the most colorful, and the least bound by tradition.

Some endurance riders prefer to use splint boots, bell boots, and leg wraps to protect and support their horses' legs while traversing difficult terrain, while some carry EZ Boots, in case their horses lose their shoes on the trail. Many endurance horses wear a rubber or plastic pad between the hoof and the horseshoe to provide relief from concussion and sharp rocks. Other riders prefer to let their horses travel naturally. Barsaleau is in the latter group. "I want a horse that travels correctly with a wide enough stance that he doesn't interfere with himself. If you condition a horse slow and you calculate your exposure to difficult terrain, the horse will not hurt himself." Some of the top competitive riders agree with Barsaleau's principle, but as they are striving for victories and positions on international teams, they want to eliminate as many potential problems as they can. Even the most correctly traveling horse that is well prepared can still whack his leg on a low-lying tree branch, or stumble and cut himself as he recovers his footing.

The sport has also benefited greatly from improvements in feeding and nutrition. Riders understand that there needs to be the proper balance between the amount of carbohydrates and proteins the horse eats, especially prior to a long ride like the Tevis. Furthermore, supplements, particularly those focused on joint health, have become quite popular for both horses and humans. Endurance riding has come a long way in a relatively short amount of time, and the knowledge gleaned about long-distance riding has benefited many other horse sports.

❧ 26 ❧

MARCIA SMITH:
THREE IMPRESSIVE VICTORIES

Like all horse-crazy little girls, Marcia Smith begged her parents for a horse. She was lucky because a neighbor had a horse she could ride, and Smith's parents told her she could have a horse as soon as she could take care of it herself. "When I finally got my horse, I had to stand on a chair or a bale of hay to put the bridle on," recalled Smith. Throughout the 1970s, the young Smith tried lots of different horse activities. "I did a little bit of everything, as long as it was on a horse!" She competed in gymkhana, and to hone her riding skills, Smith learned some dressage, and even rode with some of the local hunt clubs.

With college looming, Smith sold her horse and put the riding part of her life on hold. After graduating from vet school at the University of California at Davis, Smith met Tom Johnson, a polo player. "When Tom and I got together, I got another horse. I played a little polo and started doing some long-distance running." Johnson really took to running as well. He and Smith did some ride-and-tie events together, but ultramarathons were Johnson's forte. He has completed the Western States Run four times, winning the race three of those times—in 1990, 1991, and 1993—and has competed in ultramarathons all over the world, including one in Mongolia.

In 1990, Smith decided to try endurance riding, although she didn't think she had the legs to ride that far on a horse. "A friend loaned me this horse for a hundred-mile ride in Nevada. I called him 'The Train.' It was all I could do to hold on to him and stay on. My arms were so tired, and then at fifty miles he finally eased up. We finished, and I was hooked. I just loved endurance riding, the people, and the horses. I was so impressed riding the Arabian horses. They want to do the work and they like the job."

In 1990 Smith heard of a good endurance horse that had some soundness problems. "I really liked Harry when I saw him," said Smith of her first Tevis Cup horse, a bay Arabian gelding. Chuck Stalley, Harry's owner, told Smith that he had leased the horse to Dan Bunn for that year's Tevis Cup. "We agreed on a price," said Smith of her purchase of Harry, "and I gave him a check. I told him that if Harry was sound after the Tevis Cup, he could cash the check." Smith volunteered to crew for Bunn, which afforded her an opportunity to get to know her potential new horse better. Bunn had a great ride with Harry, and finished in the top ten. The next day he was deemed the most superior of the top-finishing horses, and earned the Haggin Cup. "After he won the Haggin Cup I didn't think I'd be able to buy Harry, but Chuck honored our deal. I was really stoked."

Realizing she now owned a competitive endurance horse, Smith set about working on Harry's soundness problems. Like many experienced horsemen, Smith, a small-animal vet herself, did not call a vet; she found a good farrier. A skilled farrier can keep the most problematic competition horses sound; at many top international events, whether they are for endurance, show jumping, or dressage, competitors will fly in their own farriers to help keep their equine partners sound. Many horsemen throughout the Sacramento area brought their horses to Blake Brown, a master in his profession. Photographs of champion reining horses, three-day eventers, hunters, jumpers, dressage horses, and horses from many other disciplines filled his display case, along with appreciative notes, cards, and letters from grateful owners. Brown consults with a horse's vet, as well as applying his own extensive knowledge to every new equine client he acquires. Smith knew that if anyone could help her keep Harry sound, Brown was the man.

Smith aimed Harry for the 1991 Tevis Cup. "I rode with Erin [McChesney] from Robinson Flat to Michigan Bluff and then I got pulled."

Undaunted, Smith headed home to learn more about her new horse and her new sport. "I asked everyone about conditioning programs when I started in endurance," reflected Smith. "The Tevis is not a fast endurance ride . . . Long, slow distances are important. Hill training is important." Like many endurance riders, Smith rode her horse three to four days a week, including at least one long, slow ride. Each week's distance ride is a little longer, with the goal of helping the horse peak at the ride. "Hills, hills, hills," states Smith as if a mantra. "The best training for any given race is to train on the terrain or similar terrain. Many riders and runners are surprised to discover that the Western States Trail is a downhill course. Runners develop sore quads and horses develop sore shoulders." A top athlete herself, Smith also knew that she needed to be in good condition for the Tevis Cup. "I try to be fit for the Tevis. Rider conditioning is a huge factor on a slow course like ours. Riders are in the saddle longer, so they get more sore and tired than on a faster hundred. I also feel, when racing, if the horse is moving at a pace that I could match on the ground at that moment in time, I should be on the ground." The amount of time a rider spends in the saddle is dependent on his or her level of fitness. Some riders stay mounted the entire ride, and if their horse is properly conditioned it can cover the miles without undue stress. Many riders tail up the canyons and other steep climbs, and then there are the extreme athletes—those like Gordy Ainsleigh, Chris Knoch, and Tom Johnson—who will run almost as much as they ride.

Based on Harry's proven ability to handle the difficult Tevis Cup trail, and her own desire to face the challenge once again, Smith applied her endurance knowledge and aimed her horse for the 1992 event. As she prepared for her Tevis Cup quest, Smith found it relatively easy keeping Harry fit with several ten-mile rides during the week, and one long ride on the weekend. Keeping weight on Harry was another matter. Despite the alfalfa hay, eight pounds of grain daily, and constant grazing in a lush, green pasture, Harry wasn't one to easily gain weight. Athletes, whether equine or human, cannot afford to carry any extra weight, but those covering long distances like the Tevis Cup and the Western States Endurance Run need a reserve. A horse without enough body weight can tax itself severely enough that it will need several months to adequately recover before resuming regular work.

Because of the cycle of the full moon that year, the ride was held in August, and temperatures in the Sacramento Valley had already registered over 100 degrees, day after day. Those riders able to safely negotiate the treacherous rocks of the first third of the trail would be blasted with heat in the canyons as they progressed down the trail.

Smith's knowledge of equine physiology and strong riding skills, combined with Harry's long-distance talent, made for a winning combination. Competitive by nature, Smith was hoping for a strong finish, but she knew she couldn't arrive planning to win; however, she did know she could plan for a ride that would fit her horse. A stickler for details, Smith made sure her crew knew their individual responsibilities, and that everything she needed was packed, labeled, and organized. Smith didn't want her crew wasting time fumbling around looking for needed items when they should be taking care of Harry, checking equipment, or filling water bottles. Smith's almost fanatical attention to detail is her hallmark and a key element of her tremendous success.

Coming into Robinson Flat that morning, Smith was among the first eight to ten riders. Harry was alert and fresh, and easily passed the vet check. "Usually I come into Robinson Flat in the top twenty or thirty, but a lot of horses pulled early." Like the previous year's winner, Erin McChesney, the pair left Robinson Flat in the lead.

For much of the afternoon, Smith had the steep canyons to herself. "Harry could skate downhill faster than I could run," said Smith of her decision to stay mounted for the long descents. "I tailed up the canyons, but I almost lost him tailing up to Michigan Bluff on the honor system," explained Smith. She would occasionally use what endurance riders refer to as the "honor system," which means tailing up a climb without unclipping a rein to help maintain some control of the horse. Harry started uphill toward Michigan a little faster than Smith could go. Fortunately Smith was strong enough to hang on to his tail and was able to shout a few strong "whoas" to Harry, and he slowed enough so that she could get abreast of him and grab a rein.

After Michigan Bluff Smith headed back to the trail still in the lead. By late afternoon, after leaving Foresthill, Shellie Hatfield had caught up to Smith. The two women pushed one another's horses, testing stamina, will, and courage. Harry and Xanthium, Hatfield's horse, kept answering one another's challenges. Despite the approaching darkness and the many miles logged, the two horses continued vying for the lead, and the riders encouraged them.

Smith, however, became worried that the competition was escalating beyond reason. "It was getting too aggressive out there and I was afraid that someone was going to get hurt," she said afterwards. As a result, the riders agreed to tie the race, and then backed off their pace. This was only the second tie in Tevis Cup history.

The next day at the Haggin Cup judging, Harry repeated his 1990 victory, becoming one of only four horses to earn the honor of winning both the Tevis Cup and the Haggin Cup in the same year. Sam Arnold and Rushcreek Champ did so in 1976, Erin McChesney and Cougar's Fete won both cups twice in 1991 and 1996, and a fourth horse was added to the roster in 2003—but his story is yet to be told.

With these two impressive victories, Smith had arrived on the endurance riding scene, and was only beginning to demonstrate her talent and skill. "The Tevis Cup is the beginning of the sport. It is the most important single ride in endurance and it is everything its name implies, but I set my sights on international rides. They seemed to be the top of the sport." Along with her international aspirations, Smith also set a Tevis Cup goal. "After Harry won, a goal started to form. I decided to try to win the Tevis three times on three different horses, and all that implies."

In 1993 Smith participated in her first international endurance competition, the North American Championships, precursor to the Pan Am Games. Though she had to bow out, she knew there would be other rides. With Harry getting older, Smith began the quest for another mount.

Knowing Smith was looking for another top endurance horse, David St. Charles contacted Smith to talk to her about his chestnut gelding, On A High, known around the barn as "Elvis." Although Elvis had done lots of rides, metabolic problems plagued the ten-year-old Arabian. "David asked me if I would take him for a year. That was at the end of 1994," explained Smith with a grin. "Tony Benedetti told me that I could win with Elvis. That horse could do anything, but he had metabolic issues." Smith was just the person to team with Elvis. Her solid horsemanship, veterinary knowledge, and her attention to every little detail was just what Elvis needed.

In 1995 Smith and Elvis rode for the United States at the North American Championships, and that year she not only finished, but won with the fastest time in the event's history. "It was a fabulous day from start to finish," recalled Smith, who still grins when thinking about that day. She also knew she had another Tevis Cup horse.

The 1997 Tevis Cup ride was especially important to Smith. Although she was automatically qualified to compete in the Pan Am Games as an individual, given her 1995 gold medal, Smith wanted an opportunity to also ride as a team member. In order to do that, she and Elvis needed a strong finish in the Tevis Cup, as the Pan Am Games were scheduled only two months later. As the sport of endurance developed international strength, the Tevis Cup not only retained its stature but became more and more important. Most riders found that if they and their horse could complete the Tevis Cup, they could face almost any route in the world. Horses and riders have to qualify for international rides, and often the Tevis Cup is used as a qualifying ride.

Several times FEI officials asked if the Tevis Cup organizers wanted an international designation on the ride, but they declined. Larry Suddjian explained that having FEI sanctioning on the ride would put the structure of the ride in the FEI's hands, a level of power and authority that the WSTF Board of Governors was not willing to relinquish. In addition, some of the standards and rules governing international riders are less stringent than the Tevis Cup's. For example, FEI riders only have one mandatory rest period. The WSTF Board of Governors chose to keep the Tevis Cup separate, and the ride's stature has only increased.

Knowing that Elvis's tendencies to have metabolic problems would be severely tested by the Western States Trail, Smith carefully formulated her plans and strategies for the gelding in 1997. She knew that keeping him calm in the beginning portion of the ride, traveling at a measured pace, and keeping him hydrated were all key components to a successful finish. Smith and her crew calibrated their watches at the beginning of the ride, with Smith making calculations down almost to the minute. She makes a plan that is most suitable for the horse she is riding and the existing trail conditions, and does not arbitrarily deviate from that plan. If a rider challenges her, she only increases her horse's pace to match the challenge if she knows her horse is up to it.

Smith planned a slow start for Elvis. "This is his first Tevis," said Smith of the thirteen-year-old, Polish-bred Arabian gelding. "This is not an optimal trail for him. He raced on the track and then his endurance rides have been on the flat roads." Elvis was accustomed to going fast for long distances, the change to difficult terrain and a much slower pace foreign to him. "My plan is to go slow over the rocks and hills and go fast where I can." Based on that, Smith rode carefully through the rocky area of the Granite Chief Wilderness. Despite her caution, she led the 223-horse field into Robinson Flat. Several horses and riders were hot on

Smith's heels, all pushing for the lead, but Smith remained true to her own ride plan. Elvis quickly recovered at Robinson Flat, and an hour later they headed back out on the trail with a slight lead over the batch of horses and riders that would be chasing them through the canyons.

Chuck Mather and Mark Richtman were both pressing for her lead, as were Kathy Majors Thompson and Shirley Delsart. At the Swinging Bridge, Thompson caught up with Smith. This was Thompson's first Tevis Cup, and she was glad for the company. "It's especially helpful riding with Marcia," said Thompson. Smith was happy to have a riding companion who did not want to challenge her for the lead, and was willing to ride at a reasonable pace through the canyons. Smith could stick to her plan and enjoy some company. The pair stayed together and rode into Michigan Bluff at 2:20 P.M. While their horses were resting, other horses and riders began trickling in.

As they watched the other front-runners come in, the sixth rider was actually not on a horse, but on a mule. Frank Smith and his chestnut mule, Little Buckaroo, had steadily made their way through the pack. The crowd went wild as the pair trotted in, and Smith, in his quiet, unassuming manner, tipped his hat, stuffed his T-shirt deeper into his back pocket, and trotted his mule to the vet check.

Based in nearby Grass Valley, California, he is a professional mule skinner. During the summer and fall months, Smith leads strings of pack mules into the high country for hunters and other adventurers. With all of the backcountry riding Smith regularly did in the course of his pack trips, Little Buckaroo was very fit and ready to tackle the miles.

Throughout the ride, Smith and his mule gained a fan club, and word spread of the mule skinner making his way down the historic trail; an icon of the past's miners and immigrants, who traversed the same route over a century earlier. At each checkpoint, Smith and Little Buckaroo were greeted with loud cheers and applause.

While Frank Smith relaxed during the one-hour hold, Marcia Smith and Kathy Thompson headed back out on the trail. They continued riding together as the sun began to set behind the tall pines. During the California Loop, about seventy miles into the ride, Elvis hit his slump point. Despite having company, Elvis tired, and was reluctant to maintain his pace. Whenever this occurs, Smith knows what to do. "I sing. Singing lifts my spirits and my horse's. I only know one song and I sing it over and over again." Her song? "Jabberwocky" from *Alice in Wonderland.* "Twas brillig, and the slithy toves, Did gyre and gimble in the wabe. All mimsy were the borogoves, And the momeraths outgrabe," sang Smith. Recognizing the familiar tune, Elvis was willing to continue down the final switchbacks before reaching relatively flat trail along the American River.

At Lower Rock Quarry, the final vet check before the finish, Smith gained her first distinct advantage. Thompson's Arabian stallion, LS Zane Grey, did not vet through as quickly as Elvis. Thompson did not want to overly stress her gray Arabian stallion. She preferred a good finish with a confident horse rather than to try for a win and exhaust her horse with the effort. For her a finish *was* a win, and she figured she could still finish in the top ten and be considered for the Haggin Cup. Since LS Zane Grey was used as a breeding stallion, a Haggin Cup win could mean even more than a Tevis Cup win. Knowing she had a strong horse, Smith galloped out of Lower Quarry toward No Hands Bridge, making the most of her several minutes' lead.

"You know, before the ride and during the beginning, I said this was not Elvis's type of course because it is rocky and hilly. Now I have to re-think that. The Pan American Championships are rocky and hilly," said Smith with a smile.

At 9:32 P.M. Marcia Smith emerged from the darkness and cantered across the official finish line of the Tevis Cup to hear spectators singing a rousing chorus of "Happy Birthday to You." Smith smiled her characteristic shy grin and said, "It was a great way to spend my birthday." She had a lot to smile about after winning her second career Tevis Cup.

Fifteen minutes after Smith secured her second victory, Thompson and LS Zane Grey entered the stadium to take the customary victory lap for the assembled audience. The Tevis finish was especially exciting for Thompson and her husband since they bred LS Zane Grey themselves. "He just proved that he has what it takes to do the hardest hundred-mile ride!"

Almost two hours passed before the next horses and riders made their way to the completion of their journey. As midnight approached, Frank Smith and Little Buckaroo made their way into the stadium, and the crowd erupted into cheers. Smith looked around as if searching for the cause of all the commotion, not realizing it was for him. As he crossed under the banner marking the symbolic finish line, Smith tipped his hat to the crowd, which then cheered even louder. "Well, now that's done," said Smith in his characteristic understated manner. Little Buckaroo was the first mule in more than twenty years to finish the Tevis Cup in the top ten. "He looks great," said Dr. Cook as he performed the post-ride vet check. "He looks like he was just out for an evening stroll." "We finished in '96 and we've moved up in '97," said Smith. "He was stronger this year. He had a lot more bottom, and he's toughened up. Last year he wasted a lot of energy—this year he knew what to expect and he just put his head down and kept going along. Yep," said Smith, more to himself than anyone else, "he showed me a lot more mule at the end."

The next day the Haggin Cup judging was far from an easy task. The top ten horses had all finished within a three-hour span of one another. As always, the entire veterinary committee convened to evaluate them. Mitch Benson reiterated that the Haggin Cup is more than a best condition award. "This award is a little different," explained Dr. Benson. "We evaluate the horses throughout the ride, at the finish, and then this morning. The Haggin Cup was intended to recognize superior horsemanship as demonstrated by the superior condition of the contestant's [winning] horse."

Marcia Smith, as the first across the finish line, was the first to present her horse. Elvis looked well recovered and trotted sound on the circle, but displayed a cranky demeanor, with his ears pinned back. He acted reluctant to trot out, although there was no doubt that he was quite sound. "It is one of the hardest things to deal with," said Smith of her horse's sullen attitude. "I've tried everything, like carrying treats, but he just won't perk up. It's just how he is." Unfortunately, Elvis's presentation counted against him during the judging, yet nothing could take away from his Tevis Cup victory.

Ona Lawrence's Dandy McCoy was the sixth horse to face the scrutiny of the veterinary panel. While Lawrence had completed eighteen one-hundred-mile rides prior to the Tevis Cup, and represented the U.S. on several teams, this was her first Tevis attempt. She was hoping for a top finish, and sixth place more than met her goal. "The Tevis Cup is incredibly tough," explained Lawrence. "Nothing compares to it. In fact, I didn't like the first part—it was scary." The early section of the ride can be quite daunting due to the challenges presented by the rocky terrain. "I was really careful about the rocks," she explained with a touch of awe. Since her horse is not comfortable wearing splint boots or any other type of protective gear on his legs, Lawrence kept to a very slow pace in the beginning of the ride. She knows her horse well and is a master at regulating her pace throughout a long-distance ride. In order to be as prepared as possible, Lawrence took up running to condition herself. "I had to make myself fit. I hate to run, but I made myself run for the Tevis Cup." Although she ran alongside her horse going down the canyons, she decided to ride him going uphill. "He was a real brat coming up the canyons, so I got on and rode him!"

When Frank Smith presented Little Buckaroo as the seventh of the ten Haggin Cup contenders, there was no doubt that the shiny chestnut mule was the crowd favorite. Smith had groomed his mount's coat to a copper sheen and they looked ready for a halter class. "I like it when the riders turn out their horses," said Dr. Barsaleau of Smith's presentation. "It is nice to see some aspects of the horse show world appearing on Sunday mornings," he explained in reference to the Haggin Cup judging. "It is nice to see top people setting a good example."

As Smith led his mule up to the vets, the audience erupted in cheers. Smith once again stuffed his T-shirt in his back pants pocket, and planted his hat more firmly on his head. Although he acted nonchalant, the mule's beautiful turnout revealed Smith's pride in his animal. Only one mule had ever won the Haggin Cup before, and that was in 1974 when Eva Taylor's Hugo topped the field. When Little Buckaroo trotted out on the circle, the crowd gave their vote of approval with cheers and applause. The audience left no doubt that Smith and his mule were clearly the popular choice. However, the veterinarians had a difficult task. "Mules are very hard to evaluate when comparing them to horses," explained Dr. Benson. "It's really hard for us to evaluate the mule's gait because he moves so different from the Arabians we're used to watching. We have to remember that it's normal for the mule to shuffle and amble, and determining his impulsion is very hard. What's normal for the mule is abnormal in the Arabian."

After reviewing the top ten horses, the veterinarians and other members of the Cup Committee sequestered themselves to discuss the candidates. At the awards ceremony later that afternoon, Marcia Smith and Elvis were presented with the Tevis Cup. Smith reiterated that pacing is key to success in the Tevis Cup. "So much of your pace is dictated by the course. This is a hard ride. There are other rides that are more competitive in terms of the number and level of competitive endurance riders, but this ride is unique and it is really hard. The terrain is very difficult. It is a big challenge and it is on a historic trail. The heat is tremendous, the steepness of the canyons, and the rocks by Emigrant Pass all make it really hard. This is the most difficult ride I've done."

Ona Lawrence's name was called as the winner of the Haggin Cup and she jumped up and down excitedly. "It was just my husband and me all day long and we were just beat at the end. Normally we get up during the night to walk the horse and put ice on, but we just wrapped his legs and went to bed!" Although the crowd was rooting for Frank Smith's mule, the Cup Committee unanimously chose Dandy McCoy, although they did give serious consideration to Little Buckaroo. "Ona's horse was by far the best moving and showed the least effects of the trail," explained Dr. Benson. "He had impulsion, fluidity to his gait, and a positive attitude. He was superior to the others and on par metabolically."

For the first time since 1992, the completion rate for the ride dipped below 50 percent. "The quality of finishers was better than in '96," said Dr. Benson, "but we had a lower than the normal percentage of finishers. The weather was good. It's always hot in the canyons. Good weather can be a curse and blessing though. In cooler weather the riders seem to push their horses harder. All of the major metabolic problems were in the first part of the ride when it was cooler. The trail conditions were rockier than normal. Riders I know who are not complainers were commenting how rocky Granite Chief Wilderness Area was. Well over half the injuries were due to the rocks."

Smith's 1997 Tevis victory represented the second leg of her Tevis goal. As she looked toward a third shot at the Tevis Cup, Smith wanted to improve her own riding. Drawing on her own childhood experiences with dressage, Smith decided to further her education. "Dressage training makes all the difference in endurance horses. A balanced and supple horse can trot over terrain that other horses must walk over. Even at a slow trot this will make a big difference over one hundred miles." Smith did not have to look far for assistance. She admired Erin McChesney for her endurance accomplishments, and recognized her skills with dressage training. "I consider Erin the master," said Smith. Unlike other dressage trainers, McChesney clearly understood how dressage applied to endurance riding and especially a trail as difficult at the Tevis. "I have taken lessons in basic dressage from Erin. This has made a huge difference in my horses and in my satisfaction with them."

The next year, in 1998, Smith began the Tevis Cup on her third horse, Saamson CC, a nine-year-old Arabian gelding. "I wasn't planning to buy a horse," said Smith of her acquisition of Saamson. "A friend was looking for a Tevis Cup horse. I went to Deb Cooper's, but the horse I looked at didn't suit our needs. Deb asked me to look at another horse." Saamson had a long winter coat encrusted in mud. Smith wasn't impressed, but Cooper told her the gelding was good, fast, strong, and clever through the rocks. "Then she also told me that he was rank. He reared, bucked, and would run off." Undaunted, Smith and her husband looked him over; Johnson led Saamson at a trot so Smith could evaluate his way of going, and then they bought him. "We didn't even ride him!" said Smith of their newly purchased horse.

"The first time I saddled him at home he went crazy," recalled Smith. Quickly it became clear that Saamson was not going to work out for Smith's friend. "Tom took over the early riding duties," she continued. "Saamson has a stallion mentality. You have to ask him—you can't tell him what to do." Gradually Saamson settled into his new life, and Smith and Johnson liked many qualities of their new horse. Perhaps Saamson would be able to handle the Western States Trail. "When he is tired, he doesn't like going uphill," said Smith. "The last section of the Tevis suits him because he is going downhill and home. He just chugs along."

The 1998 Tevis was one of Saamson's first one-hundred-mile rides. A steady traveling horse, Saamson carefully made his way along the trail. "Saamson is slow down hills and does better with me on the ground," explained Smith of some of her strategies with her equine partner. "I run down in the lead and then I get on him to ride up." They finished in second place, a very credible performance, but not the third win Smith was looking for. Unlike some other riders, such as Hal Hall and Barbara White, Smith does not make riding the Tevis an annual goal. In 1999 she passed up the Tevis in order to attend the Pan Am Games in Manitoba, Canada, where she finished ninth. She returned to the Tevis trail in 2001.

With 225 riders assembled at the mass start at Robie Park in August 2001, Smith wanted to set a starting pace fast enough to get in front of the majority of the riders. Although Smith was in the leading pack heading into Squaw Valley, she slowed Saamson as they began the rocky ascent up Squaw Valley. With many miles remaining, Smith didn't want to rush her horse and risk a misstep or bruised hoof. "I rode through the rocks with two other riders, Bev Grey and Mort Johnson," recalled Smith. Arriving at the Red Star Ridge vet check, the horses had to pass a quick vet check. "We instituted a gate-and-go at Red Star," explained WSTF President Chuck Mather. "This required horses to meet a sixty-four pulse rate before continuing. The idea was to force riders to slow down and let the horses drink before continuing on to Robinson. It seemed to work, as we had fewer metabolic problems."

While many riders now carry heart monitors, Smith relies on her stethoscope. "I am fast enough with a stethoscope that it takes me only seconds to get my horse's pulse. I'd as soon not deal with a heart monitor during a race." Smith and her husband, Tom Johnson, use heart monitors during training, but rarely in competition. "They are just one more thing to take on and off," explained Smith. "We are an athletic family. We use heart monitors during our own training, as they are a valuable tool. They can inform us when a very eager horse is working too hard, when a smarter horse is slacking off, and when a problem is brewing, like there is too high a rate for the work being done." Smith and her riding companions easily vetted through Red Star and headed out to Robinson Flat, the rest of the riders strung out behind them.

Sometimes the vet checks can get clogged with arriving horses and riders, but the gate-and-go and gate-hold formats help the flow of the ride, especially for those riders trying for a conservative finish. Riders don't waste time waiting unnecessarily in the checks and the vets are able to properly monitor the horses. Because of the new format at Red Star, horses did not come into Robinson Flat in large packs. "The change helped slow down and spread out the horses," commented Dr. Ray Randall, a member of the veterinary panel. "The horses weren't bottlenecking at Robinson and it was better for the horses. There never was much of a line for vetting."

Smith led into Robinson with Saamson having covered the rocky first third of the trail easily. "I disproved Mitch's theory of 'first in to Robinson is not first across the finish line,'" said Smith laughingly in reference to Dr. Benson. He felt that most riders reaching Robinson early had pushed their horses too hard and would not have enough horse left to cover the remaining miles. However, Smith's knowledge of the trail and its terrain, her veterinary expertise, and her superior horsemanship were the ingredients for her continuing success at the Tevis Cup, and endurance rides in general. "Marcia Smith should serve as an example to other riders. She is focused. She gets off and runs when she needs to. She keeps her perspective," stated Dr. Jim Edwards.

Heading out of Robinson Flat and into the canyons, Smith was lucky as that year the temperatures were significantly lower than normal. "Around noon I had to go down to the Swinging Bridge because there was a report of bees," explained WSTF President Chuck Mather. "I didn't find any bees, but when I looked at the temperature indicator on my watch it was only 88 degrees. Normally, the bottoms of the canyons reach 100 to 110 degrees in the middle of the day." While Smith appreciated the cooler temperatures, she wasn't worried about the heat. "My horse can handle the heat, so actually I was hoping it would be hot."

Going through the canyons Mort Johnson fell off of Smith's pace, giving her a commanding lead, but being in the lead was not necessarily an advantage with Saamson. "He doesn't like to be alone out front for long periods of time," said Smith. She trains her horses alone so they get used to being by themselves and not relying on a buddy. "I have to entice him. I get off and run and I give him horse cookies, *lots* of cookies. I knew I would have to get off and run, so I worked up to ten to fifteen miles a week."

During her one-hour hold at Foresthill, Smith talked about her running. "Now that I've gotten into running shape, I think I'll continue training for the National Ride-and-Tie Championships. You know, Tom won it last year," said Smith proudly. "We don't have kids so competing is our focus and a cornerstone of our relationship. We are both intense, focused, competitive individuals. I am a detail person and Tom is a 'big picture' person. It's a great combination. We both understand the sport of endurance, whether running or riding. The keys are pacing and patience."

Cleared from her one-hour hold, Smith gave her horse and her equipment one last look before remounting and heading out on the final third of her personal Tevis quest. Keeping to her mantra of "pace and patience," Smith and Saamson covered the distance to Francisco's faster than their training times. "The vets thought Saamson looked great," said Smith of her trot-through check. They easily made the river crossing, with the water low enough that Saamson did not have to swim. She met up with her crew for a final time at Lower Quarry, where after passing the vet check she let Saamson enjoy a few mouthfuls of feed before heading to the finish only six miles away. At that point, even Smith was feeling excited about her performance.

She tried not to think about the fact that she was on the cusp of achieving one of her lifetime goals of three Tevis Cup wins on three different horses. "I kept telling myself that it's not over until it's over. I told myself to focus, but I was getting more confident. We were in the flow," said Smith of her final six miles. The finish was near, her horse was strong, and the closest riders were over an hour behind her.

Later that night, at 10:18 P.M., Smith made Tevis history as the first person to win the ride three times on three different horses. "One of my lifetime endurance goals was to be the first to win the Tevis Cup on three different horses. I did it tonight," said a beaming Smith. "We had a good ride, all day."

Marcia Smith on Harry, 1991 Tevis Cup winners. [Hughes Photography]

Winning the Tevis Cup three times on three different horses vaulted Smith into an elite fraternity of Tevis Cup riders. Her accomplishment is on par with Donna Fitzgerald's six wins with Witezarif; Erin McChesney's dual Tevis Cup and Haggin Cup wins two different years on the same horse; Barbara White's record 26 finishes; and Julie Suhr's three Haggin Cup wins with HCC Gazal.

For one family, Tevis Cup memories span four generations. Kenneth and Maxine Sly were early supporters of the WSTF and the early Tevis Cup ride. Based near Placerville, the elder Slys raised their family in a rural setting. Embodying the same pioneering spirit and roots as Wendell Robie, the Fitzgeralds, and other early participants of the Tevis Cup, Maxine Sly earned the family's first Tevis Cup buckle in 1967, and her husband, Kenneth, followed suit in 1972. More than thirty years later, in 2001, while Marcia Smith was garnering her third Tevis Cup win, Kenneth and Maxine Sly's great-granddaughters Brittany McKenzie and Carolyn Finston, earned Tevis buckles in what has become a family tradition. Growing up, McKenzie had crewed for her other family members as they tackled the ride. "Doing the Tevis Cup is like a family tradition. You just do it," explained twelve-year-old McKenzie, the youngest finisher in 2001. "Most of the family has done the Tevis Cup, starting back with my great-grandparents."

McKenzie longed for a horse, and when her family moved from Southern California to El Dorado Hills, adjacent to Placerville, Sports Kheki showed up for Christmas. With her own horse, McKenzie could finally compete in the Tevis Cup instead of crewing. In addition, she was finally old enough to ride. Her aunt, Karen Ducher, pledged to sponsor McKenzie and her own daughter, fourteen-year-old Carolyn Finston. The three riders spent a lot of time training and preparing for the Tevis Cup. McKenzie rode in a limited-distance ride of thirty miles, and then a fifty-mile endurance ride. "I was nervous at the start," she said of her Tevis beginning. "The rocky parts were hard." She paused and then added, "The canyons were hard too."

Aided by other family members—all wearing T-shirts emblazoned with "Sly Family Crew" and pictures of previous family members who finished the ride, with the year in which they accomplished the feat—the three Sly family members made their way down the trail. They wouldn't cross the finish line first, but each would be a winner just for completing the ride. When they arrived at Francisco's it was after midnight, a time when most twelve-year-olds are sound asleep. McKenzie was tired and stressed. "I was afraid I would pass out. I wasn't sure I could make it, but everyone helped me. I ate a little and I drank a bit, and then I threw up. After that I felt much better!" Heading back on the trail for the final miles, McKenzie was nervous. "I was afraid of riding at night, but the moon was bright and that gave me some comfort. After awhile it wasn't too bad," related McKenzie.

Like many Tevis riders ahead of her, McKenzie dug deep to find out what was inside of her. The Tevis reaches deep within a person's core to see what that person is made of. Riding into the wee hours of the morning, Brittany McKenzie found rocks within her as solid as those she crossed earlier in the day. Standing on the awards podium the next day with her cousin and the other junior rider finishers of 2001, McKenzie spoke confidently into the microphone, a bit older, a bit wiser, and a bit more worldly than she had been twenty-four hours earlier. "I want to thank my entire family, and especially my grandmother, Carol Simpson. I can't wait to do the Tevis Cup again!" As a reward for their achievement, the two girls received brand new belts from their family so they too could sport their Tevis Cup belt buckles for all the world to see.

Carol Simpson beamed at her granddaughters up on the stage. She had watched her four children earn their Tevis Cup belt buckles, she had earned one herself in 1988, and now she was watching her granddaughters earn theirs. "This is just wonderful, unbelievable," she exclaimed. "I grew up around this trail and I just love this event." Regardless of where the large Sly family lives, the majority of them make a point to be at the Tevis Cup each year to cheer on some family member. For the Sly family, and many others, the Tevis Cup is an annual pilgrimage and a chance for family and friends to come together.

The reach of the Tevis Cup has touched more than families—it has affected entire countries. Endurance riding had so spread throughout the world that by 1995, there were twenty annual rides being held, and by 2002 endurance riding had expanded to include 186 international rides. Japan was one of many countries interested in this new sport. Crowded Tokyo and its surrounding cities don't offer the wild expanses of the American West, and the Tevis Cup embodied that vision of adventure, freedom, and a true test of the spirit. Interested in learning more and wanting to become participants in the international endurance scene, in 1996 the Japanese Equestrian Federation sent representatives to the oldest and hardest ride in the world. Japanese veterinarians teamed up with the Tevis Cup vets. Japanese riders joined crews, and a Japanese team filmed the ride for a documentary. They studied the ride, the organization, the riders, the horses, and the trail itself. They left overwhelmed and impressed, but determined to return for a Tevis Cup belt buckle.

In 1998, Shinobu Katayama, a thirty-three-year-old show jumping rider from Tokyo, represented Japan in the Tevis Cup. Not only did she earn her first Tevis Cup belt buckle, she also became the first Japanese rider to ever complete the ride. Katayama had been a part of the Japanese contingent that studied the ride two years before. Although her expertise was in the show jumping arena, she was taken in by the allure of the Tevis Cup. She vowed to return, and Cindy Barton, who lives near the trail, agreed to help her prepare. "She has great determination," said Barton of the ambitious Japanese rider. "When I saw her ride, I knew she had the riding skills to complete the ride." Since bringing a horse from Japan would be too costly, and given that the majority of horses in Japan are Thoroughbreds, Katayama asked Barton to help her find a suitable mount. Besides, as a first time rider, Katayama knew that an experienced horse would give her a better chance of finishing. Barton did her job well. She leased Debbie Victor-Wilson's seventeen-year-old Arabian gelding, Ayinsur, who had finished the Tevis Cup three times.

What Katayama did not know was that Victor-Wilson planned to retire Ayinsur, and she felt that helping the Japanese earn their first Tevis Cup belt buckle would be a fitting final ride. While Marcia Smith and Kathy Thompson were vying for a win, Katayama was after her own victory that same July day. She rode at a cautious pace, more concerned with completing the ride than finishing in a certain time. After riding through the wilderness for twenty-one hours and forty-nine minutes, Katayama crossed the Tevis Cup finish line. "It was great!" said Katayama with a grin. "Everyone was so friendly. This is very different from show jumping." Unlike show jumping, the endurance rider spends hours with his horse in remote areas negotiating challenging terrain. "The darkness was hard," continued Katayama. "We had some moon and I just followed the horse's lead. The horse knew the finish and we just cantered in!"

Upon hearing that she had piloted Ayinsur on his final ride, Katayama was stunned. "I had no idea this would be the horse's final ride," she commented. Victor-Wilson explained that she didn't want to tell Katayama of Ayinsur's impending retirement. Both Victor-Wilson and Barton felt that Katayama had enough pressure without the two of them adding more.

Since Katayama's ride, other Japanese riders have journeyed to the Tevis Cup, and their experiences in the challenges of the Sierra Nevada have helped them compete successfully in international competitions such as the Endurance World Championships and the Endurance World Cup. Riders from every continent have made the pilgrimage to the Tevis Cup.

However, most of the stars tend to reside closer to the trail. Between 1990 and 2003, nine Tevis Cup winners and six Haggin Cup recipients lived near and regularly trained on the trail. Some ride the trail for years before achieving top finishes. Undoubtedly, to finish in the top ten, regular conditioning and training on segments of the Western States Trail dramatically improves the odds.

❧ 27 ❧

POTATO RICHARDSON

In 1998 a longtime Tevis Cup participant, and arguably one of the most colorful of all Tevis personalities, finally got to see his name inscribed on the prestigious Tevis Cup trophy. Potato Richardson is a fixture, and he can seem larger than life, since his ability to embellish permeates his entire existence. Richardson says he grew up in Michigan, one of eleven children. "My dad's name was Stew, so my mother gave me and all my brothers middle names that were vegetables, and my sisters all had flowers as their middle names." Richardson says he came to California during the late 1960s, although his destination, upon leaving home in Michigan, was Alaska.

He decided to stop off in Long Beach, where his brothers, Rutabaga and Cabbage, lived. He quickly fell in love with the area and decided to finish his college studies in Southern California. Richardson then moved north to Sacramento, where he crossed paths with Paige Harper, an early Tevis fixture and close friend of Wendell Robie. Richardson was immediately taken with the notion of riding a horse along this historic trail. For an adventurer like him, the Tevis Cup just presented one more challenge. However, when he first set his sights on the ride, Richardson had no idea it would become so much a part of his life.

Richardson was comfortable around horses, having grown up around them. He began searching for a horse for the 1973 ride, but despite the good advice he received, Richardson could not have made a worse choice for a Tevis Cup mount. "I went out and bought this Appy," he said. Richardson had to learn about his misguided decision the hard way. "That Appy was a terrible horse. He could detect an uphill grade better than a civil engineer. When the grade would change, that old horse would just quit. One time I got off him and put my ear to the ground. I told him that I didn't hear any change in the ground. When the vets finally pulled me, they said, 'The horse won't make it and you look worse.' I told them, 'Thank you,' and promptly sold that horse to some family."

While many people would give up after such a miserable introduction to the endurance world, Richardson only became more determined. He admired Paige Harper's Tevis Cup belt buckle and he wanted one of his own. It took him a few more tries, but he finally found the right horse, in the form of an Arabian mare named Cailana. She carried Richardson to his first Tevis Cup completion in 1975, and he has not missed a ride since.

Richardson's passion for the Tevis ran so strong that he searched for property near the trail. He found a rustic ranch in Greenwood, nestled in the foothills in gold country, just ten minutes away from the trail. Richardson spends as much time as he can riding the trail and preparing his horses, and has made the ranch and the Tevis Cup his vocation.

Richardson's enthusiasm for the Tevis Cup is contagious, and he has acted as a sort of unofficial ambassador for the ride. During his travels in Europe, he told anyone who would listen about the amazing long-distance horse ride in the Sierra Nevada mountain range. European fascination with many things American, and especially the Old West, only enhanced Richardson's stories. He discovered that some of his foreign friends wanted to try the Tevis Cup, and so was born "Camp Tevis." Richardson was instrumental in opening the Tevis Cup to the world. "I run this camp. The riders come over for a couple of weeks before the Tevis and they stay at my place. I feed them, I take them out on the trail, and I give them some strategy. Hell, I've got friends from France, Hungary, Germany, Austria, Brazil—all over—that come ride with me."

In order to accommodate the riders, Richardson needed horses, and he needed good horses. If people were going to come from across the oceans and dedicate themselves to completing their Tevis journey, Richardson knew they needed suitable horses. He didn't want to bequeath his first Tevis experience on anyone else. Cailana was such an outstanding horse for Richardson that he began to research her lineage. He discovered that she was from the famed Witez II line. Richardson began carefully breeding Cailana to quality Arabian stallions, hoping to further improve her Witez ancestry. He also acquired other horses in order to maintain a competitive stable of endurance mounts for those in search of a Tevis Cup belt buckle, but without a suitable horse. Furthermore, while many horses have completed the ride without practicing on segments of the trail prior to the official competition, just as many horses spend some time on the trail getting acclimated to its unique characteristics. Most riders agree that familiarity with the trail only improves one's chances of completing the journey.

As Richardson began racking up one finish after another, victory remained elusive. In 1978 Richardson was the first rider to cross the finish line, but in those days the ride still began with staggered starts. Therefore, the official winner could not be determined until the actual ride times were compared. Although Richardson crossed the finish line first, Kathie Perry was the one awarded the Tevis Cup at the awards ceremony. In 1986 Richardson earned a coveted thousand-mile buckle recognizing his tenth completion. He continued to help riders fulfill their personal Tevis dreams, to breed endurance horses, and to enjoy his unique lifestyle. However, that shiny Lloyd Tevis Cup remained unconquered.

In 1998 all of that changed. Richardson's plans, dreams, and hard work all came together. Twenty-three years earlier, Richardson had earned his first Tevis Cup belt buckle on Cailana. In August 1998, Richardson embarked on yet another Tevis Cup journey; this time on Fille de Cailana, the daughter of his foundation mare. "Fille is bred for this," stated Richardson. In keeping with the mare's competitive nature, Richardson set an early pace. They were in tenth as they crossed Emigrant Pass, the spiny ridge marking the ultimate crest of the Sierra Nevada. With over thirty miles behind them, Richardson and Fille trotted into Robinson Flat in third. Richardson's son Range was riding with him, but the senior Richardson was concerned that the fast pace he was setting was too much for Range and his horse. "I told him he better slow down because I was going too fast for him and his horse." Range heeded his father's advice, set his own pace leaving Robinson, and ultimately finished twenty-sixth for his second Tevis Cup finish.

Fille recovered quickly at Robinson and Richardson was able to leave in first. This time he knew if he maintained the lead for the remainder of the ride and had a little luck on his side, he would be the winner. Staggered starts were a thing of the past, so Richardson didn't have to rely on complicated time estimates. In planning his strategy, Richardson likes to quote a famous football coach. "You know, Vince Lombardi said that you should use all the moves because you never know which one will win the game." Richardson employed every bit of strategy he could, combined with over twenty years' experience on the ride. He took advantage of Fille's drive to hold the lead. "Fille just hates to be second. When she sees a horse in front of her, she snaps like a rubber band. I call her my 'little Ferrari.' And you know," said Richardson with a wink and a sly smile, "we never saw the ass of another horse after Robinson Flat!"

As the sun continued its steady climb, raising the temperatures to almost 100 degrees in the depths of the canyons, Fille continued on, seemingly undaunted. In the early afternoon, Richardson rode into Michigan Bluff.

Richardson cruised through Michigan Bluff, where the locals still came out to cheer for the horses and riders, and after a cursory vet check, trotted up Main Street and then quickly dropped out of sight as he headed into Volcano Creek, the final major canyon of the journey. Although most riders reach this point at sunset, when temperatures are dropping, front-runners like Richardson are still facing the brutal heat. Fille was proving her hardy bloodlines, however, and came into Foresthill alert and strong. While a few horses and riders trickled in during Richardson's wait, he left in the lead—but with a serious challenger on his heels. Marcia Smith and Saamson, the previous year's winners, continued their push for yet another Tevis victory. "I didn't have to sing this year," said Smith in her typically understated manner. She pushed to catch up to Richardson, but not at the expense of her horse.

As the ride neared its end, Smith was gaining on Richardson. He entered Lower Quarry, the final vet check before the finish, with Smith only minutes behind. Both horses easily vetted through and headed into the darkness, and the final few miles. Richardson recounted the final miles of his victorious ride. "Leaving Lower Quarry that night and crossing Highway 49 for the last part to the finish, Fille heard Marcia Smith coming up behind us, and I just gave her a squeeze with my knees. She broke into an easy gallop and went across No Hands Bridge and made it real easy to the finish." Smith finished eleven minutes behind Richardson. Richardson earned his first Tevis Cup victory and he was thrilled, "This has been an incredible day." He could not say enough about his wonderful horses, especially the little, 14.1-hand Arabian mare who helped him fulfill his quest.

Richardson played to the crowd as he and Fille took a victory lap around the stadium and reveled in the limelight, his moment of glory. He strutted around, told wild stories of his hours on the trail, and talked to anyone who would listen. As colorful and boisterous a personality as he is, Richardson was humbled by this accomplishment.

As the horses and riders trickled in throughout the night, everyone kept count of the first ten horses and riders across the finish line, for these would be the Haggin Cup candidates. In addition to Richardson and Smith, Sandy Brown finished third, just four minutes behind Marcia Smith. Brown had completed a few twenty-five- and fifty-mile rides near his home base in Salt Lake City, but was riding his first hundred-mile ride and his first Tevis Cup; results made even more impressive given that he was riding a mule. Frank Smith and Little Buckaroo had been crowd favorites in 1997, and now another mule had finished in the top ten. "I'm still pinching myself," said Brown of his third-place finish with Ruby. "I bought her when she was six months old and she was narrow as a rail," recalled Brown, as he held his hands about six inches apart, referring to the mule's slight, bony frame. Now eight years old, Ruby had matured into an elegant, substantial mare. At 17 hands, Ruby towered over the 14- and 15-hand Arabians surrounding her. Generally, larger, more heavily muscled horses have to exert a lot more energy to cover the same distance as a slightly built Arabian with long, lean muscles; however, Ruby was well conditioned, Brown rode her well, and she handled the distance with aplomb. Based on his mule's steady distance progress, Brown aimed for a first-place finish.

"I decided to give the Tevis a try. My goal was to figure out the trail and do well next year," explained Brown with a grin. He was quick to credit Frank Smith with some good advice. "I met Frank at a mule race in Idaho. Then I saw him again at Robie Park this year, and we went for a short ride the afternoon before the ride. He gave me some good pointers, which gave me confidence. He really inspired me."

Brown incorporated Smith's advice into his own ride strategy. "I didn't want to go out too fast, but I wanted to get out toward the front and then stay behind the leaders. I didn't want to work my way up from behind. At Squaw Valley I was in the top ten, and then I moved to third or fourth after climbing out of the Valley. It was an easy hill for us!

"At Robinson I was out third behind Potato. My crew told me to take it easy and I decided third was okay. I ran a lot, probably thirty-five to forty miles of the ride. I didn't want to fag her out. After the canyons and the incredible heat, I walked a lot until Marcia Smith caught up with me late in the ride. I wasn't sure about No Hands Bridge, so I rode with Marcia." Brown knew Richardson was ahead of both of them, traveling at a good clip. "I decided not to get greedy, so I told Marcia I wasn't going to ride fast," Brown said. "I knew halfway through the ride that I could go for the Haggin Cup, so I didn't want to risk Ruby by racing her to the finish."

During the Haggin Cup judging, Ruby appeared alert and, just as Smith had with his mule the year before, Brown turned her out for the Cup Committee as if he were competing in a championship show. The Cup Committee presented the Haggin Cup to Sandy Brown and his mule, Ruby, only the second mule in the history of the ride to earn such an honor. "Not since 1974 has a mule won the Haggin Cup," said Brown proudly, referring to Eva Taylor's Hugo.

Like many riders who came to the Tevis Cup in the 1980s and 1990s, Brown got his start at ride-and-tie events. Raised in Texas, Brown grew up around horses. "I did rodeo and some arena stuff. I moved to Utah in 1977 and I got into trails and running." He found a nice Thoroughbred mare to use for ride-and-tie events. He bred her to a 13-hand jack, and the resulting offspring was Ruby. "I just let Ruby come along with us to races. She ran alongside us." What a sight Brown must have been in his running gear, with his sleek Thoroughbred mare, and a gangly, big-eared mule foal ambling along.

In the fall of 1998, when the WSTF Board of Governors met to review that year's ride, they also discussed the 165-pound minimum weight requirement for any rider in contention for either the Tevis Cup or the Haggin Cup. As the tack and equipment grew lighter, and more women became top competitors, people started asking to have the weight requirement removed. After much discussion the Board of Governors rescinded the rule. Research among other horse sports, by organizations like the United States Eventing Association, found that a weight handicap did not make a significant difference between lighter and heavier riders. However, many of the smaller riders complained that requiring their horses to carry lead weights was unfair to the horse, as the weight was static and could not shift to stay in balance with the horse.

Julie Suhr wrote eloquently of the issue in an article in *Ride! Magazine:*

> I have always felt that endurance riding is a sport we enter according to our individual assets and liabilities. It is the sport for young and old, male and female, skinny and heavy. It is a sport for dedicated people, be they housewives, construction workers, veterinarians, pilots, or teenagers. You name the profession and I can almost certainly find a rider from it on that great trail. It is totally unfair, but so is life. If you can't accept that, then go somewhere else where rules are legislated to shine brightly upon your particular assets.
>
> The San Francisco 49ers have never asked me to join their team. I am a woman, weigh 124 pounds, am 75 years old, have terrible ankles, and can't run. I am sure there are a dozen other reasons the 49ers haven't called. Neither has the National Football League offered to change its rules to make it "fair" for me. I literally have not a single asset they want.
>
> At the same time, if a 49er fullback wanted to ride the Tevis Cup, I bet I could beat him to Auburn because I have traits and characteristics that stand me in good stead—experience, light weight, and a modicum of horse and trail savvy. His football assets would most likely be a liability. I don't want to change the endurance rules to make it "fair" for him any more than he wants to change the football rules for me.
>
> If we could create one rule to make our sport more equitable to all, I would be for it. But endurance is a sport that will never be fair, and trying to fix one inequity opens a Pandora's box of other inequities, some far more important than weight.

In 2001 Cathy Rohm entered her first Tevis Cup, having completed her very first endurance ride in December 2000. "I saw the Tevis years ago when I went with some friends to Foresthill to watch," said Rohm of her earliest memories of the ride. Rohm showed Arabian horses, but never thought she would take to endurance riding herself. "I met Potato through work and we became friends," she explained of her involvement.

Rohm rode Fayette de Cameo, a Shagya Arabian Richardson himself had bred. The mare was only six years old and inexperienced, but she and

Richardson gained a lot of mileage riding the lower portions of the trail and other routes from his ranch in Greenwood. Rohm and Richardson both finished in the top ten, and the next day at the Haggin Cup presentation, head veterinarian Jamie Kerr presented the award to a very surprised Rohm. "This is the best day of my life! We had a master plan and trained together," exclaimed Rohm. For once Richardson was quiet, content to smile broadly from the sidelines as he watched Rohm (now his fiancée) and his horse receive their accolades.

Richardson had another day in the limelight in 2002. On July 20 Richardson decided to ride Fayette de Cameo himself. Although he won the ride for a second time, his victory was marred by claims of unsportsmanlike behavior, which cost him a chance at a second Haggin Cup win.

Richardson took a dissenting view. "To me, it is ridiculous [being disqualified from Haggin Cup judging]. The other riders should have let me through. I was late because when I got up my headstall and reins had disappeared. I was upset over losing my gear." Richardson rode the entire trail with two lead ropes attached to a halter. He *is* known for his unorthodox methods.

Richardson was quite outspoken about his Haggin Cup disqualification. "The second win is not as good as the first [1998]. In 2001 my horses finished second, third, and fourth, and we won the Haggin Cup. I feel good about [winning] the Tevis Cup again this year with the same mare. We have over an hour on the next closest horses." He was enthusiastic about his horse as he told stories about her birth. "I was having a party at my ranch one evening when the dam just walked up to the fence near the house and foaled right there. I carried the foal in my arms down to the barn." He raised and trained the mare, which has now earned the Haggin Cup and the Tevis Cup in two consecutive years.

In 2002 Hal Hall added a second Haggin Cup win to his many Tevis Cup honors. Bogus Thunder and Hall completed their first Tevis Cup in 2000, and had four finishes out of five hundred-mile rides. In December 2001, Hall was among a handful of U.S. riders to receive an invitation to compete in the United Arab Emirates President's Cup held in Dubai. Accompanied by his wife, Ann, and their two children, they and the horse flew to the Middle East. "It was a great experience," said Hall, and they finished fifteenth out of fifty-eight starters.

Where Richardson set a fast, winning pace for his Tevis Cup ride, Hall stated, "I ride what I call a 'midnight pace.' I don't have set times for certain checkpoints, but I do have an idea of how much time it takes me between points. I ride by the feel of my horse, by the weather, and my knowledge of the trail. This year I covered the second half faster than the first half, which is unusual." Midway through the ride, Hall told his wife that he would see her in Auburn at midnight. "He was five minutes late," she said with a grin.

Coming into Robinson Flat, Hall was twenty-first, and they easily vetted in and out. He is very careful to have his horse arrive at the vet checks as close to the established pulse and respiration criteria as possible. At Deadwood, Hall had moved up, and by Michigan Bluff he was in twelfth place. "As usual the canyons were muggy and humid, but he [Bogus Thunder] was really going. I didn't have to get off much. My horse doesn't tail well, but at Last Chance coming up to Devil's Thumb, there are thirty-three switchbacks and no flat ground. I got off to lead in that canyon and my horse's nose was in my back pushing me up!"

Hall knew Richardson was ahead of him by at least an hour, but he made no attempt to catch him. "There were places I knew I could have cut an hour, but I would have risked it all. I like to have something left in my horse's tank, and if I had taken off that hour I would have risked my horse even finishing." Hall stuck to his plan and rode his horse accordingly. "I wanted to lead [my horse] into Foresthill so we could vet quickly." Sitting ninth, they quickly passed the vet check and rested for the second one-hour hold before heading down into the remaining canyons in the waning afternoon heat.

Throughout the latter half of the ride, Carol Ruprecht of Newport Beach, California, on Findefar, followed Hal along the trail. "A couple of times after Foresthill I gave her the lead, but her horse refused to go out in front, so I just kept pulling her along." There are unspoken trail codes, and one is acknowledgment or deference to the horse and rider helping pull your horse along as fatigue sets in. This would come into play as the ride neared the end.

At Lower Quarry, Hall caught up to and passed the few riders ahead of him. "I just rode the ride I wanted. My horse recovered quickly, so I left and I figured I could just cruise in." Hall left in second, and Ruprecht left some time later in fifth. After crossing No Hands Bridge, Hall heard a horse coming up on him fast. "This was not the sound of a horse trotting behind us," stated Hall. As Ruprecht caught up to him, Hall realized he could no longer stave off a race to the finish; they were now riding for second place. She never said anything, but kept pushing along and ignored a tenet of the trail code, for Hall's horse had helped pull hers along in the doldrums as the evening turned to night. However, Hall was reluctant to ignore Ruprecht's challenge, given his second-place standing. "I knew Potato was over an hour ahead of us, but I didn't know his status. There was a slight chance he might have been pulled and then we would be riding for first. That was really the main reason why I kept up with her challenge." Despite Hall's misgivings, the pair raced to the finish, and although they finished with equal ride times, the official timer gave the nod to Hall as he crossed the finish just ahead of Ruprecht. As it turned out, Richardson had officially finished in first place. "Hal is an awesome competitor, and I learned a lot riding on his tail," said Ruprecht the next day.

At the Haggin Cup judging the next morning, Bogus Thunder trotted out boldly and carried good weight after covering so many miles. Hall beamed as the Haggin Cup was presented to him. This was Hall's third Haggin Cup. He won the other two with El Karbaj in 1972 and 1978.

"The Haggin Cup is the pinnacle of horsemanship. The Tevis Cup satisfies the competitive urge, but to think you can travel over such a route through the Sierra, meet the challenges, and then have a healthy, fit horse the next day is quite a feat. With all the hardship stories, sometimes it amazes me that we finish." The victory was even more sweet as his wife, Ann, had bred Bogus Thunder. Although Hall was asked to nominate his horse for the 2002 World Equestrian Games as a member of the U.S. team, Bogus did not have the miles needed in order to qualify, and Hall was not willing to push the horse for those miles. "I have ridden on U.S. teams, I have been a selector, I coached the Japanese team, and it has been an honor to represent the USA—but my first love is the Tevis."

Amidst all of the celebrating by the victors and their friends, Jon Stevens was also celebrating, but for vastly different reasons. He and his horse fell from the trail late at night and tumbled down a steep cliff toward the river. In fact, the 2002 ride turned out to be incredibly difficult from an organizational standpoint.

Merv Pyorre had been appointed as the 2002 ride director. Of his appointment Pyorre laughed and said, "I guess I didn't step back fast enough." However, the choice of Pyorre was no laughing matter. He has earned eleven Tevis Cup belt buckles, so he knows the intricacies of the ride well and has been involved with many different aspects. "This was a very hard ride to manage this year, and the volunteers did an excellent job. We had a high incidence of unusual incidents."

The first serious episode involved a helicopter rescue for an ailing rider. "A rider went into shock partway up Devil's Thumb. The Boy Scouts manning Deadwood and some of the other volunteers went in and packed out the rider." Fortunately the rider was all right and recovered fully. A horse on the ride was not as fortunate and, for the first time since 1983, a horse died during the ride. "It was dark and at the end of California Loop 1 by the Dardanelles—a horse slid down the cliff," explained Pyorre. "The rider bailed out up-slope and was relatively unhurt, but the horse was killed in the fall."

No one ever likes to see tragedies, but at an event with the level of difficulty presented by the Tevis Cup, occasional accidents do happen. "SOS [Sweep Riders of the Sierras] was involved in several serious incidents and they did a great job," added Pyorre of the volunteers who provide aid and deal with any kind of incident that may arise. Of the serious injuries and the horse's death, Pyorre commented, "These circumstances will affect ride planning." He then mused, "I wonder about horsemanship and conditioning. This is a very difficult ride and maybe some people don't take it seriously enough. I see in the completing riders that they have mentors, they are well-prepared, and they have good crews."

The third incident could have been the most tragic of the day, but fortunately it had a heroic ending. Jon Stevens and his riding buddy, Chris Martin, were heading into California Loop 2 and the start of the switchbacks into Francisco's. It was about 11:30 P.M. and they were less than twenty miles from the finish. A Japanese rider was accompanying them and he was nervous about riding the trail in the dark. "I told him to just put his horse's nose in Spider's tail and that we would lead him through since we had regularly ridden this part of the trail," laughed Stevens at the irony of his words.

Going along the trail, Spider stumbled, and as he reached forward to regain his footing, the trail took a turn to the right. Spider's left hoof connected with the ground and then it slipped away. "We went off the side together, but about thirty feet down I was thrown clear," said Stevens of the pair's harrowing fall. "I have hands so I can grab things, and I kept grabbing onto things until I stopped my fall. Spider wasn't so lucky." The gray horse crashed and tumbled down the hillside.

"He had glow lights on his breast collar and I could see him tumbling end over end. I was sure he was going to die," said Stevens of watching his horse crashing down the steep slope. Spider fell past the two remaining switchbacks and actually sailed over the head of a rider traversing a lower switchback.

"And then everything went completely quiet," said Stevens. "There were no more sounds, no more glow lights, and I realized he had gone over the edge. I was sure my horse was dead." Stevens paused. "Chris gave up his hard-earned Tevis position to help me out. I was just shouting and shouting for Spider, trying to hear something. I told Chris to keep going to Auburn and to tell the officials at Francisco's about the accident. I told him he had to make it to Auburn. There was nothing more he could do for me." Martin ultimately made it to the finish line with only fifteen minutes to spare, but it was a bittersweet accomplishment because of the worry he carried for his riding partner.

"I decided I was going to stay on the trail until daylight. I was exhausted, but I had to find out about my horse," continued Stevens. It was too dark for Stevens to attempt to go down the steep canyon side. "I couldn't leave him. I was worried about mountain lions too. I hiked to the bottom of the switchbacks, but I didn't dare go any further down because I couldn't tell where the vertical drop started." The trail heads off west toward Francisco's, and the river is another five hundred feet below the trail at this point.

SOS drag riders came by around 2:30 A.M. and told Stevens they couldn't leave him there. After much protesting and begging, Stevens reluctantly hiked back up the canyon with the riders. "I couldn't believe it, but Dick Nogelberg, WSTF President, was there to meet me and help me out." Nogelberg had heard about the terrible accident and came to lend assistance. He ferried Stevens back to the fairgrounds, and when they arrived, chief veterinarian Jamie Kerr was loading up his truck preparing to head out to help Spider. "I couldn't believe that after [working] all day they were so ready to help me," said Stevens. Dawn was just breaking as they hiked into the canyon where Spider fell. "All the way there Jamie kept preparing me for the worst. I've had animals my whole life, so I understood." They found where Spider had fallen off the cliff and they began to make their way down. They followed broken manzanita bushes and snapped twigs, indicative of Spider's tumbling descent to the bottom of the canyon.

As they dropped down to an almost vertical slope, to their complete amazement they found Spider perched on a small flat ledge about two hundred feet above the river. "Jamie stabilized him and I got his tack off. It was so steep I didn't want anyone to get killed attempting to rescue my horse," recounted Stevens. Kerr took Spider's rope and started making his way down the almost vertical cliff, while Stevens and the other volunteers held on to Spider's tail to help slow his descent. "We crawled down that hill like mountain goats," said Stevens. "The horror hours had passed and I felt hopeful we were actually going to save Spider. It was amazing how our hearts changed when we saw that horse standing there. There aren't words to describe the group who helped Spider." Once at the river, they decided to walk out as the horse was responding positively. They stood him in the cold mountain water and washed off a layer of dust and grime, and superficially cleaned his wounds.

They crisscrossed the river several times before they could make their way up to a road and a horse trailer. Spider finally arrived in Auburn about 4:00 P.M. with scrapes, contusions, and one serious laceration. He was in good spirits and Kerr was amazed by the horse. "I took his rope when we began to first move him off the ledge, and I never let go of him. I felt so responsible for that horse and I think we bonded. He is very special." Kerr reiterated that the incident was very unfortunate, but simply an accident. Stevens has not given up on his Tevis dreams, and would return in 2003 for another Tevis Cup attempt. Kerr's one regret was that he didn't get to see the top ten horses for the Haggin Cup, as he was helping rescue Spider during the judging. "I just love looking at the Haggin Cup horses."

❧ 28 ❧

SAVED FROM SLAUGHTER

Heather Bergantz came to the 1999 Tevis Cup with the goal of a top-ten finish. She had completed the ride in 1996 and knew what to expect of the trail. Bergantz grew up around horses and fell in love with endurance riding. She met up with Skip Lightfoot, an avid ride-and-tie competitor, and he asked her to start riding some of his horses to keep them in shape. One day he received a phone call from a friend who knew of three Arabian geldings sent to a local slaughterhouse. "I didn't need any more horses," explained Lightfoot. "I had a couple already that I was doing ride-and-ties on, but she wouldn't stop calling me." Lightfoot went to the slaughterhouse and bought all three horses, all brothers. They were underweight and pathetic, but with care, training, and lots of attention, each one bloomed.

The oldest of the three geldings he called Major Motion, or "Red" around the barn. Lightfoot planned to make Red his new ride-and-tie mount. "At my first ride I realized he was way more than a ride-and-tie horse. I thought he was international caliber." Lightfoot asked Bergantz to ride the gelding and the two clicked. With a single one-hundred-mile ride as preparation, Bergantz entered Major Motion in the Tevis Cup. "He was very consistent," said Bergantz of their day. "I just put him on his pace. He is very conditioned, and he is a great horse with a great future." They came in seventh, and at the awards ceremony Bergantz was presented with the Haggin Cup. This helped launch their international career as they went on to represent the United States at a number of international rides and the World Championships, taking top honors in many of the rides.

Bergantz (now married, and known as Heather Reynolds), returned to the Tevis Cup in 2003 with Red's younger brother, Split, named for the split in his left ear. "He won the Washoe 100 by over an hour with Tom Johnson," said Reynolds of the gelding's endurance resume. "He has about seven hundred career miles and he thinks rather than explodes. He is easy on himself and I think he has international caliber."

The year 2003 saw a significant change in the ride. For the first time in history, riders had to qualify to enter. Head veterinarian Jamie Kerr was a chief proponent of this change, based on recent lower-than-average completion rates. "This year riders had to have completed a total of 150 miles," explained Kerr of the criteria. "The lower number of horses had a dramatic effect on the whole ride," continued Kerr. "The [reduced] stress level for everyone, from riders to crews to vets to ride officials, was noticeable. Everything was smoother and I think the riders appreciated it." Many riders did comment that the overall tone of this year's ride was much less hectic and stressful. "I am going to push to keep the lower number of starters and the Board of Governors will do what's right for the horses," concluded Kerr. "The qualification criteria removed the element of novice riders," added WSTF secretary Shannon Weil, who has two Tevis Cup finishes. "This is not the ride to cut your teeth on; the Tevis honors those with experience, and experience showed through this year." Instead of the normal two-hundred-plus horses starting the ride, only 152 left the starting line at Robie Park.

Despite rigorous planning before the ride, Mother Nature was most uncooperative. Huge snowstorms hit the Sierra Nevada in the late spring, resulting in a much later snowmelt. In fact, there were still snow fields in some of the higher elevations traversed in the first third of the route. The late snowmelt also delayed the necessary trail repair and maintenance dedicated volunteers attend to each spring. Riders had a tough time getting ready for the ride as the date was early (July 12), and the late snows and rains delayed serious conditioning preparation for many riders. They simply could not get out on the trails as Northern California was deluged with rain.

Despite the rainy spring months, Reynolds managed to prepare her horse well. Heading out from Robie Park the morning of the ride, Reynolds rode among the front-runners. She had a strong horse and was aiming for a top finish. Throughout the day they vetted easily through the checks, and Split steadily ate up the miles. As the day wore on, Michel Bloch, originally from France, caught up with Reynolds after clearing Foresthill, the second mandatory one-hour hold checkpoint. They stayed together for the remainder of the ride.

The finish of the Tevis Cup could have been a duel, but Bloch yielded the finish line to Reynolds. "It was an absolute example of sportsmanship," said Reynolds of the moment. Following his finish, the tall Frenchman explained his actions simply, "She deserves it. She was ahead of me all day and is a great woman with a great horse. They deserved to be the winners. There was no need to race the horses."

Bloch and Reynolds rode together for the final twenty-five miles. At Francisco's, Bloch brought up the subject of the finish in the course of their conversation. "I told her I was scared of the dark and if we could ride together I would make her a deal that I wouldn't race her to the finish," said Bloch with a twinkle in his eye. Reynolds laughed when presented with Bloch's story. "He was such a gentleman and it was very generous of him. He told me he thought my horse had more left, so why didn't we just ease up and ride together the rest of the way in. We took it so easy that at the last few miles, we heard the others coming up on us, so we had to pick up the pace," laughed Reynolds.

Bloch first visited the United States in 1972 and fell in love with the country. He had shown in lower-level dressage and show jumping competitions in France, and once settled in the United States, he competed at a few hunter/jumper shows. One day a friend was visiting and wanted to go for a ride in the Sierra Nevada. Once again Bloch fell in love—this time with the mountains and the wilderness. "I finished my first Tevis Cup in 1993," said Bloch with a grin. "It took me ten years to recover! I guess I'll get my thousand-mile buckle when I am 142." Of his horse, Monsieur Joseph, Bloch had nothing but praise. "This is his third one-hundred-mile ride this year and he is at his capacity. We even earned our FEI certification, but I am a man without a country. Perhaps I'll ride for Israel!" Bloch stumbled across his horse when he saw a classified ad in the paper for an Arab gelding for $1,000. "No one wanted him. He didn't even have a name, but then the owner found his papers. He has good American bloodlines. Finishing the Tevis Cup with him this year was exhilarating; a Zen-like experience."

Unlike past Tevis Cup rides, all of the top-ten riders came in within an hour of one another. Often the first one or two riders come in and then an hour will pass until the next rider or two arrives. Usually two hours separates the top riders, but this year they finished very close to one another at regular intervals. Third and fourth were Cassandra Schuler and Peter Toft. "Exhilarating," was one of many descriptive words Australian Peter Toft used in describing his Tevis experience. Although a number of international riders compete each year, they usually lease a locally based horse for the ride. Toft shipped his Arabian/Appaloosa cross, Electra BBP Murdoch, from Mirburg in Queensland, Australia. "On June 3 we finished the Quilty [Australia's famous one-hundred-mile ride] in third and got best condition, and he is only seven years old. Usually I like to give a horse at least six weeks' rest between rides. He only got five and we put him on a plane right after the Quilty." Toft found the Tasmanian-bred gelding two years ago as a green-broke five-year-old. "He had this way of going. He has amazing recoveries. In 2000 my wife, Penny, rode him on the Australian gold medal World Equestrian Games team, and the 2002 bronze team. Our eight-year-old daughter, Alexandra, rides him at home and does his training. We are lucky. Endurance is our passion, our love, and our business."

Toft had heard of the Tevis and many U.S. riders had gone to contest the Quilty, including Wendell Robie and Dr. Barsaleau. "The Tevis Cup has been my interest and goal for thirty years," explained Toft. "The Quilty was formed off the Tevis, but it has no fixed course. This ride lived up to its name. I had no concept. I watched a video two nights ago and it scared me. You have mountains; in Australia we have hills." Not only was the terrain much harder than anything Toft had ever faced, but he and his horse were coming from winter to summer. In the high country Toft suffered from altitude sickness, but as they descended, he recovered. "I spent a lot of my time out there on the trail sightseeing. I loved every minute. There wasn't a moment I didn't think I was the luckiest person."

At the Haggin Cup judging the next morning, seven of the ten horses were presented to the waiting veterinarians and the Cup Committee. Dr. Barsaleau provided introductions and explanations. People eagerly watched each horse as it was trotted on the large circle and the straight-away. Reynolds's horse, Split, looked ready for another hundred miles with his bouncy trot and perky disposition. Toft's horse was equally solid and looked quite refreshed after his journey through the Sierras. The committee retired to discuss the horses.

All of the horses and riders were invited into the presentation area for the awards, and head vet Jamie Kerr proudly announced the fourth-ever dual winner of both the Tevis Cup and Haggin Cup in the same year. Reynolds and Split joined only three other riders who have ever won both awards in the same year: Sam Arnold, in 1976; Marcia Smith, in 1992; and Erin McChesney, in both 1991 and 1996. "Wow," was all Reynolds could utter. However, Skip Lightfoot was not at a loss for words. "This is it!" he exclaimed after their dual victory. "This is like Seabiscuit! The underdogs won! Heather told me she was going to come here to win. That is a big, bold statement," continued Lightfoot. "I wanted to win the Haggin more than anything," added Reynolds with a shy smile. "We out-P & R'd [pulse and respiration] everyone. Others have to ride hard to catch up." Reynolds qualified two horses for the 2003 Pan Am Games, and at press time was not sure which horse she'd take. "The Tevis is more of an adventure than a race," stated Reynolds. "It is really fun and exciting. This is a very special event and it means a lot to me. I can win major international races, and all people want to know is how I've done in the Tevis Cup!"

The veterinarians were impressed with the caliber of horses, especially the top ten. "The first couple of horses rode right all day," said Dr. Kerr. "I was impressed. The Haggin Cup was a unanimous decision among the vets. There is always lots of discussion and the top ten all looked good."

Since its inception, the Tevis Cup veterinary team reviews each of the top ten horses carefully, and then presents their recommendation to the Cup Committee, of which the head vet is a member. Until recently, the Haggin Cup judging was always held in a small, out-of-the-way arena on the Auburn Fairgrounds, with no place for spectators to sit and watch the proceedings. No explanation was provided as to what was going on, or what the vets were doing. This resulted in the mistaken perception that the judging was secretive and closed. People did not clearly understand that the vets used comprehensive and objective criteria, combined with their general perceptions of each of the horses in question, gleaned throughout the previous day's ride at each of the various rest stops and vet checks. Once the award was presented, except for a few cursory remarks about the winning horse, no one officially discussed the veterinary review. With a lack of official information, spectators' opinions were open to conjecture and speculation.

During the 1991 ride, Dr. Benson invited an equine journalist to accompany the vets during the Haggin Cup judging. Some people, including some ride officials, were upset by this and the journalist was asked to leave the grounds. This proved to be the final catalyst Benson needed for a push to make a change. Benson knew that the Haggin Cup judging was performed using comprehensive, quantitative methods, and that the veterinary panel evaluated many criteria pertaining to each horse, but he was disturbed by this perception of the judging methods and sought change.

He headed home, determined to influence changes for the following year's judging. Benson was proud of the Tevis Cup and his involvement in it and wanted to ensure the ride's eminence, nationally and internationally.

During the post-ride review and subsequent meeting, and after much discussion, the Western States Trail Foundation Board of Governors completely restructured the judging. The criteria and process remained the same, but the presentation was vastly different. In the following year after the 1992 ride, the top ten horses gathered at the opening of the main stadium where they had all taken their victory lap upon completion of the ride the night before. Word had spread about the change in the judging presentation, and several hundred spectators eagerly assembled in the bleachers. Dr. Barsaleau welcomed everyone, and then served as the master of ceremonies for the judging process.

As the top ten horses finish, the crews work all night to help their horses recover and to stave off stiffness in order to present them for the next morning's Haggin Cup judging. At this point, every minute of rest can be precious before the judging takes place. Crew members will take over for the rider, walking the horse every hour or so to keep lactic acid from settling in its muscles and causing soreness, due to the strenuous effort it has just put forth. In some cases, masseuses might also work on the animal throughout the night. Often the horses nap, munch on hay, and sip on water, all the while slowly replenishing what the trail took out of them.

If a rider decides his horse is not in condition for the judging due to significant post-ride muscle soreness or some slight lameness, the rider may choose not to present the horse to the veterinarians and the Cup Committee. Only the top ten finishers are invited, and riders choosing to decline to present their horses are respected for their decision.

At least ten vets review the horse according to the specific tasks assigned to them. Some check for gut sounds to make sure the digestive system is functioning normally. One vet draws blood to check for illegal substances and to submit the data to the U.C. Davis researchers. Other vets check the horse's legs for cuts, scratches, or swellings. Still others check the horse's eyes and gums, and another runs his hands along the horse's back, loins, and haunches to check for unusual sensitivity or soreness.

As each horse is presented, based on the order of their finish the previous night, the veterinarians each have their own specific tasks. Each horse's resting pulse rate is taken, and they are then trotted three hundred feet up and back on a chalked line, with the horse's pulse taken a second time to determine recovery rates. To determine soundness and willingness, the horses are each trotted in a fifty-foot circle in both directions. The vets evaluate the way the horses move, their soundness, and their overall body carriage and attitude. Throughout the entire process, Dr. Steve Leonard videotapes each animal for the purpose of ongoing research, and to provide reference information should any questions arise.

The vets do not expect the horses to be blemish-free, but they do not like to see significant cuts, swelling, or muscle soreness. Per the conditions set forth by Dr. Barsaleau, Wendell Robie, and those involved with the creation of the Haggin Cup, the chosen horse must best represent the ability to continue working. Like equine predecessors of over one hundred and fifty years ago, the Haggin Cup winner is the horse the Cup Committee feels is in the best condition to continue down the trail, as if he was carrying the most important mail in history.

That first year the Haggin judging was done publicly was particularly special. Before the judging began, Dr. Benson gave the audience a review of what the veterinarians were looking for, then each horse and rider was presented to enthusiastic applause. During the physical exam of the horse, which can take up to ten minutes, Dr. Barsaleau spoke about elements of horsemanship, the biomechanics of the horse and how they affect its gait, and other relevant information. Several key ride officials spoke about the ride, related high points from the previous day, and acknowledged all those who dedicated their time and skills to the ride. However, as each horse got ready to trot out, all talk ceased. Audible *ahhs* trickled across the stadium if a horse was slightly lame, or showed a reluctance to move forward willingly. Wild applause and cheers erupted for a horse that trotted in a sprightly manner, or even gave a small, frisky buck. No matter what rider someone may have crewed for, or what horse the crowd hoped would win, any horse that demonstrated liveliness and excellent condition was rewarded with unrestricted cheering.

Benson's efforts to elicit change and his insistence on making the Haggin Cup judging a more open and informal procedure has only resulted in making the award itself that much more prestigious.

"For They Had Crossed the Mountains"

Forty-nine years ago when Wendell Robie saw his vision become a reality, even he probably did not imagine the breadth and scope of his creation. Almost eight thousand riders have started the Tevis Cup and over four thousand have finished the journey. Along the way Robie's vision evolved into a defined sport that spread throughout the country, then the world. His idea also gave birth to the sport of ultramarathons, with the Western States 100 the original such event. Over three thousand men and women have made the arduous journey on foot along this historic trail.

Growth has not come without its challenges and difficulties. Today the sport of endurance is divided along two camps: those who see the sport as a long-distance ride, and those who see it as a long-distance race. As Middle Eastern countries, like Dubai and the United Arab Emirates, have grown increasingly interested in endurance riding, this division has grown. These countries have infused huge amounts of prize money into a sport where there once was none. Top endurance racers can earn tens of thousands of dollars of prize money at major international events, many of which are either sponsored or produced in the Middle East.

Many of these competitions are held over relatively flat ground, and riders push to maintain as fast a pace as possible for as long as possible. Few of these high-speed rides present such extreme challenges of elevation and terrain as does the Western States trail.

[Arabs kept hearing word of of the Tevis Cup, and Musallem Al Amri and Ali Khalfan Al Jahouri of the Al Watha Stables in the United Arab Emirates tried the 2001 ride. They leased horses and obtained assistance from Robert Ribley, a well-known competitor who has six Tevis finishes to his name. "We want to gain experience on a very famous ride," said Al Amri of their journey to the ride. They were overwhelmed by the Tevis's many challenges. "We did this to make us better. We will be in the top ten next year," said Al Amri. However, when entries were being accepted for the 2002 ride, Shannon Weil, who runs the WSTF office, noticed the Al Wathba Stables entries were missing. She notified them and a few days later received a short fax: "Ride too hard. Not coming."]

Ann Hall presenting Bogus Thunder for the 2002 Haggin Cup judging. [Marnye Langer photo]

Although the Western States Trail Foundation Board of Governors has been approached about making the ride an official international ride sanctioned by the FEI, they have thus far declined. "FEI rides are very different from the Tevis," explained WSTF vice-president Chuck Mather. "The Tevis has established traditions that don't lend themselves to the FEI. We have repeatedly been asked to get involved, but the Tevis is too unique and we would have to make sacrifices to meet the FEI's requirements. We can't increase participation in part because of the limitations regarding the Granite Chief Wilderness, and the Board of Governors are adamant that we don't offer prize money. That goes against the vision of Wendell Robie. Besides, we are afraid that prize money would draw people just looking for the money, and we don't want the horses unnecessarily pressured. The ride is very hard and we don't need to lure those who are just pot-hunting."

Marcia Smith echoed many of Mather's thoughts. "FEI events tend to be fast and flat. The Tevis is very strategic. Both types of rides require intense focus, and mental and physical preparation. However, the focus at FEI rides is on speed. Unless that changes I don't see the Tevis Cup becoming an FEI event. Besides, it was great getting to go to Qatar for the 2001 President's Cup. There I was galloping along in the desert in the birthplace of the Arabian horse, but the Tevis will always be very special to me."

Denny Emerson represented the United States at the 1976 Olympics as a member of the three-day eventing team. He was also part of the gold medal–winning team at the 1974 World Championships, and has twice been a national eventing champion in the United States. Emerson came to the Tevis Cup in 2003 with his horse Rhett Butler. "The Tevis Cup has raised my own standards of what is possible with a horse." Three-day eventing requires riders and horses of enormous courage, as they are asked to jump huge, challenging obstacles from a gallop. Most riders look at top international eventing riders and just shake their heads in wonder.

However, Emerson, a brave, aggressive rider, was amazed at the Western States Trail. "This is way, way tougher terrain than I have ever ridden. I couldn't imagine it. First there was the snow field, and then when we got through that, there was the rock field," he explained of his high-country experience. "Then there were the incredible long, downhill terrains. If there is a hole anywhere in you or your horse, the Tevis Cup will find it. You need a horse with absolutely no holes. It takes a hell of a horse to do the Tevis Cup."

As a boy Emerson rode in the Green Mountain Horse Association three-day rides that covered one hundred miles. "My parents had a farm in Vermont near the GMHA and I started riding in the three-day ride in 1956." Emerson turned to three-day eventing in 1962, but came back to endurance riding in the late 1990s. "A friend, Alana Wright, asked me to ride one of her horses in a hundred-mile ride in South Carolina. I had a cold, I felt miserable, but I had a great time on the ride. Endurance riders must love to suffer all the way to the end."

After that ride Emerson was hooked and found a nice Arabian horse to begin competing. He had heard of the Tevis Cup and always wanted to do it. A broken leg and hip replacement in 2002 slowed him down, so he set 2003 as his goal. Unfortunately his horse, Rhett Butler, suffered from a stone bruise several weeks before the Tevis Cup, and although they began the ride, the rocky terrain of the high country took its toll. At Dusty Corners Emerson decided to pull his horse, as he was not traveling right. The vets concurred, but Emerson remains committed to attaining a Tevis Cup belt buckle to add to his Olympic gold medal. "Seeing people cantering their horses up Squaw Peak changed my perception of what a horse can do," said Emerson.

The Tevis Cup continues to attract people to its wonders and challenges, and most remain fascinated the rest of their lives. "The Tevis for me is an addiction," said Liz Henry, who earned her first buckle in 2001. "I thought finishing one time and getting the highly coveted buckle would be enough . . . but no, I had to do it a second time. And guess what? I am already signed up for a third Tevis. Why, I ask? Several reasons come to mind. One, it is where it all started. Two, it is the toughest ride on the planet. Three, like the mountain explorer said, 'Because it is there.'"

Barbara White, Julie Suhr's daughter, tried to retire from the Tevis Cup. In 2001 when she won her twenty-fifth buckle, she was almost tearful as she said, "This is my last Tevis. I will be back as crew and a volunteer, but this is my last Tevis." The lure of the ride proved too much and she finished her twenty-sixth Tevis in 2002, and plans for a twenty-seventh in honor of the ride's fiftieth anniversary in 2004. "I meant it when I said it," said White in 2002 of her previous year's remarks, "but most of my friends didn't believe me. I found out it is easier to ride the Ride than quit the Ride." White and Suhr have both competed in the ride since the 1960s, the longest actively competing participants of the ride, and proof of its magical allure. Both women acknowledge that the Tevis Cup has had a profound impact on their lives. In fact, Suhr recently wrote and self-published a book entitled *Ten Feet Tall, Still,* with all the proceeds going to benefit trail preservation. "When you reach the top of Squaw Valley it is an incredible emotional experience. You look back over your right shoulder and you see Lake Tahoe in the morning light, and then you look forward over your left shoulder and you see range after range of purple mountains, and you know that somewhere beyond that is Auburn."

The Western States Endurance Run has its own aura, and it is as highly regarded in the running community as the Tevis is in the endurance community. "One-hundred-mile events are the goal of many ultramarathoners," explained Stan Jensen, an active participant in the sport. "The Western States 100 is the most prestigious for a few reasons. First, it is the oldest. Second, it was featured on ABC's *Wide World of Sports*. Third, it has a lottery in order to enter, and fourth, over three thousand individuals have finished it, so most ultramarathoners know someone who has done the run." David Blaikie echoed Jensen's statements. "The Western States was the original trail one-hundred-miler, and it is the best known of all of them, as Boston is to the marathon." *Runner's World* magazine equates the Western States Run to the "Holy Grail of endurance trail running."

In 2003, through the efforts of the Western States Trail Foundation and its sister organization, the Western States Run (led by Shannon Weil), Auburn was designated the Endurance Capital of the World. "This proclamation for Auburn was long overdue," stated Mayor Kathy Sands. "These events have worldwide attendance and participation. It is wonderful and we are so proud to show off."

Dr. Barsaleau has seen many horses and riders come through the Tevis Cup over the years. "Over the years I realized the very best riders shared two traits. In them, persistence and determination are omnipotent." With so many riders coming to seek their personal Tevis Cup experience, Barsaleau holds up Marcia Smith and Erin McChesney as shining examples of what a Tevis Cup rider should aspire to. "They are great examples I have admired. They have the right kind of attitude, and both ride with a nice feel. They are representative of professionalism, and horsemanship."

The Western States Trail Foundation's Board of Governors is constantly evaluating the ride and seeking to make it better. Chief veterinarian Jamie Kerr takes that role very seriously. "This particular ride, over this particular trail, is the granddaddy of modern-day endurance riding," explained Kerr. "This is about the most you can ask a horse to do in twenty-four hours. This is a difficult trail, and there is so much history to the trail because of the pioneer routes. This really is the ultimate."

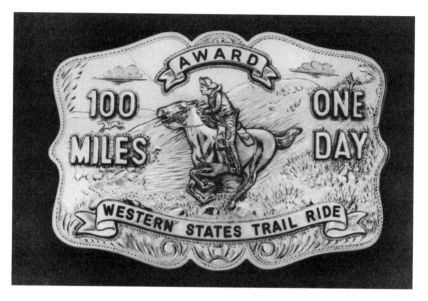

Tevis Cup belt buckle.

The Tevis Cup is a special fraternity of people who come together one weekend a year for an experience few can understand who haven't been there. A little more than half of them make it all the way to Auburn in their quest, and during the journey they will make discoveries and have experiences that will stay with them for the rest of their lives. The Tevis Cup truly is the test of an individual, and only those with the fortitude necessary to guide themselves and their horses over a difficult trail under demanding conditions will succeed. Many riders describe facing situations and emotions they've never experienced before, and are likely never to experience again. Once they head out on the trail, on their quest, they are ultimately alone—fatigue, and their remarkable horses, as their only companions. Like the early explorers and immigrants who came west in search of a new life, the chance of wealth, or simply to quench an adventuresome spirit, these riders embark on their journey accompanied only by their noble horse, and a nearly impossible goal. The Tevis Cup is a journey of the self, testing the mind, the body, and the spirit.

∾   ∾   ∾

As Bernard De Voto wrote:

> What they had done, what they had seen, heard, felt, feared—
> the places, the sounds, the colors, the cold, the darkness, the
> emptiness, the bleakness, the beauty. 'Til they died, this stream
> of memory would set them apart, if imperceptibly from any-
> one but themselves, from everyone else. For they had crossed
> the mountains.

⇶ Appendix ⇜

Roster of Tevis Cup
Participants (1955 to 2003)

Name of Finisher	Year(s) of Finishing	Name of Finisher	Year(s) of Finishing
Kim Abbott	1998, '00, '02	Tony Amadio	1986
Mary C. Abbott	1999, '00	Gaetmo Ambrosio	1987
Lila Abdul-Rahim	1997, '99, '00, '03	Bruce Amesbury	1959
		Claire Amm	1994
Lyn Abrams	1989	Jackie Amos	1988
Glen Ackerman	1958	Stan Amos	1986
Pearl Ackerman	1958	Dick Amundson	1985
Linda Ackers	1989	Bill Anderberg	1988, '94
Steve Acres	1966	Berrian Anderson	1958
Colin Adams	1973	Bruce Anderson	1982, '84, '86, '88, '90, '91, '93, '98, '99
Linda Adams	1983		
Ariel Adjiman	1996		
Leslie Adler	1986	Doris Anderson	1975, '78
Heidi Agler	1979, '80, '81, '82	Eloise Anderson	1968
Allison Aiello	1978, '80, '81, '83, '85, '88, '89, '90	Laurie Anderson	1991, '94
		Leslie Anderson	1997
		Marcia Anderson	1958
Harriet Aiken	1997	Terri Anderson	1984, '86, '90, '91, '92, '93, '94, '98, '99, '00, '02
H. Gordon Ainsleigh	1971, '72, '73 (on foot!)		
Musallem Al Amri	2001	Jack Andrews	1981, '82
Ali Khalfan Al Jahouri	2001	Charlane Anthony	1973
Osama Al Shafar	2001	Corbelletta Antonio	1995
Brenda Alderman	1991	Frederick Antonio	1976
Maryl Aldrich	1976, '80	Richard Ardito	1988
Ann Alexander	1967	Sharon Ardito	1981, '82, '84, '86, '88
Susan S. Allison	1986, '87		

NAME OF FINISHER	YEAR(S) OF FINISHING	NAME OF FINISHER	YEAR(S) OF FINISHING
Tony Ardito	1981, '84	Shelley Barling	1992, '94
Bud Arenz	1970	Drucilla Barner	1958, '60, '61T,
Marion Robie Arnold	1958, '61, '64, '67,		'62, '63, '65, '66,
	'68, '69T, '70, '71,		'70, '71, '74
	'74, '75, '94	Carol Barnes	1980
Natalie Arnold	1987, '88, '99	Joellen Barnett	1985
Phyllis Arnold	1993, '01	Kathy Barnett	1978
Sam Arnold	1972, '73, '76TH	Julie Barnfather	2000
Wendell Arnold	1994	L. C. Barone	1966
Elizabeth Arthur	1981	Kari Barrett	1979
John Arthur	1986	Nancy Barrett	1973
Suzanne Arthur	1976	Mary Grace Barsaleau	1998
Stephany Ashley	1997	R. B. Barsaleau, DVM	1964, '67, '68,
Roy Atkin	1991		'69, '73, '74, '75,
Margo Atwood	1971		'76, '77, '78, '80,
Theresa Auker	1985		'81, '86, '87
Susan Austin	1974	Norm Barstad	1970, '85
George Austin, MD	1975, '76, '78,	Phyllis Bartholomew	1995
	'79, '80	Jim Bartlett	1986
Enrique Aveleyra	2002, '03	Jim Bartneck	1989
Jamie Averille	1987	Lea Bartneck	1987, '89
Carl Avery	1986	Cindy Barton	1998
Douglas Avery	1983	Whitney Bass	1991, '97
Jeri Avila	1988	Sandy Bass-Bolinger	1991
Chuck Ayres	1984, '85, '87	Chrisie Bayuk	2000
Keith Azevedo	1993	Karen Bean	1981, '82
Leigh Bacco	2002, '03	Merle Bean	1984, '86
Barbara Bacon	1980	Paul Beasley	1978
John Bacon	1966	Al Beaupre	1976, '78, '79,'80,
C. E. Andy Bailey	1993		'81, '87, '92, '97
Ed Bailey	1966, '68	Jackie Beaupre	1978
Rho Bailey	1969, '72, '74, '75	Carolyn Beck	1967
Susan Bain	1995	Bruce Becker	1986, '90
Annette Baines	1975	Gloria Becker	1981
Betty Baird	1991, '97	Chuck Beebe	1991, '93
Gayle Baldwin	1971	Bob Beeler	1997
Jim Baldwin	1995	Karen Beeler	1996
John Ballereau	1979	Helen Beffa	1976
Judi Bank	1965, '66, '69, '70	Karlene Beffa	1974
Peter Bank	1965, '70	Scott Behrens	1981
Chere Bargar	1986	Robin Bell	1991
Dan Barger	1982, '87	Barbara Bellamak	1972, '73, '76,
Mary Barger	1982		'80, '82, '86, '87,
Kelly Barikmo	1983		'88, '89, '91

Name of Finisher	Year(s) of Finishing	Name of Finisher	Year(s) of Finishing
Robert Bellamak	1974, '75, '78	Kathy Bohannon	1982
Steven Bellevance	1986	Laurie Bohannon	1984, '89
Leisa Belser	2002	Linda Boisa	1995
Andrew Bender	1980	Carin Bokhof	1990, '92
Terry Finali Benedetti	1988	Amber Bolton	2001
Tony Benedetti	1991, '98, '99, '01, '02	Nina Bomar	1987, '99
		Jeanne Bonner	2000
Brenda Benkley	1992, '94, '01, '02, '03	Nina Bookbinder	1986
		Harley Boos Jr.	1990
Frank Bennett, DDS	1985	Lavone Booth	1980
Linda Creighton Benson	1972, '75, '76, '78, '79	Charles Booth, MD	1968, '70
		Scott Bordon	1996
Linda Gallagher Bentham	1980, '81H	France Borka	1970
W. H. Bentham, DVM	1972, '74, '76, '79, '80, '81	Linda Borka	1975
		John Boswell	1989
Nan Benzie	1961, '62, '63, '64, '65, '66, '70, '72, '73, '75	Karen Bottiani	2000, '01, '02, '03
		Michael Bourdat	1980
		Larry Bowers	1986
Connie Berto	1986	Renee Bowers	1993, '97
Dennis Berube	1986, '92	Vonita Bowers	1994, '96
Megan Berwick	1995	Shawn Bowling	1999
Margit Bessenyey	1970	Tom Bowling	1971, '81
Jerry Bevans	1992	Wendy Bowling	1984
Sylvia Beverly	1995, '96, '98, '00	Johnathon Bowman	2001
Andrea Bianchi	1998	Peter Bowman	1965
Stephanie Biggs	1980	Mary Boykin	1987
Alexander Bigler	1963, '66, '67	Sally Boyle	1957
Sally Billingsley	2002	Nalisa Bradley	2002
Anita Bingeman	1992	Terry Bradley	2001, '02
Norma Birch	1996	Dave Braithwaite	1992, '93
Elizabeth Blackwelder	1975, '79	Linda Lee Branch	2000
George Blair	1959, '60, '61, '62, '63, '65, '66, '67, '69, '70, '72	Mary Branscomb	1979
		Paulette Brehob	1992
		Erich Breitenmoser	1995
Jane Blair	1999	Vi Brendl	1977
Pat Blair	1960, '63, '67	Claude Brewer	2000, '03
Vicki Blakslee	1972	Ray Brezina	1983
Roger Blalock	1998	Debra Brickel	1987, '88, '92
Jess Blankenship	1992	Tony Brickel	1985, '86, '87, '88, '90, '92, '94, '96, '98, '99
Michel Bloch	1993, '03		
Kelly Gardner Blue	1999		
Kathy Boesser	1975	Shelley Bridges	1998, '00
Bill Bohannon	1982, '84	Conrad Briggs	1996, '00
Bob Bohannon	1981, '84	Jeanette Briggs	1965

Name of Finisher	Year(s) of Finishing	Name of Finisher	Year(s) of Finishing
Linda Briggs	1983	Samuel Cabish	1964
Pamela Briles	1995	Kent Cadwalader	1970
Barbara Brinig	1992	Sherrie Calaway	1997, '98
Beth Brinkley	2001	Otis Calef	1996
Audrey Brooks	1981, '86	Karen Callan	1992, '94, '96
Robert Brooks	1968	Meichelle Callarman	1989
Rosemary Broome	1979, '84, '86, '88, '90	Sarah Callen	1993
		Sandra Camazzi	1985
Donna Brow	1999	Debbie Caminati	1974
Alan Lee Brown	1966	Bill Campbell	1983
Alexandra Brown	2001	Kathy Campbell	1991
Isabelle Brown	1975, '78, '79	Frank Cano	1994, '98
Jim Brown	1993	Cheryl Cape	1974
Julia Brown	1965, '67	John Cape	1977
Lanny Brown	1990	Mary Capistrant	1998
Sandy Brown	1998H, '00	Julie Caprino	1997
Dr. James Browne	1964	Martha Carey	1997, '98, '99, '02
Pat Browning	1985, '92, '98	Eugene Caringer	1961
Nadja Brozina	1973	John Carlson	1994
Carl Bruno	2001	Judy Carnazzo	2001
Lali Brunson	1975	Faith Carr	1983, '88
Jack Bryan	1965	Les Carr	1983, '88, '90, '93, '94, '95, '98
Hugh Bryson	1980H		
Terri Buckman	1995	Nancy Carroll	1981
Florence Buckner	1992	Susan Carson	1977
David Bullard	1984	Blair Carter	1984, '85
Kathleen Buman	1974	Richard Carter	1986, '87, '89
Jackie Bumgardner	1985, '86, '87, '88	Thomas Carter	1984, '85
Jim Bumgardner	1985, '88	Bill Cary	1960, '72
Daniel Bunn	1986, '90H	Bill Casey	1959, '61
Diane Bunnell	1970	Linda Cassarino	1970
Debby Burgess	1986	Meggan Cassorotti	2003
Kate Burgess	2000	Margaret Cassen	1994
Mary Burgess	2001	Robert Castle	1976
Moira Burke	1958	Sesi Catalano	1980, '82, '84, '85, '87, '88, '90, '91, '92, '93
Kathy Burling	1968		
Darcy Burns	1965		
Charlene Burt	1983	Genelle Cate	1982
Bruce Burton	1998	Julia Cate	1971, '79
Nancy Burton	1995	Henry Cate Sr.	1971
Darolyn Butler	1981, '99	Bridget Cavanaugh	1997
Julienne Buxton	1989, '92, '94, '99	Jose Cebrian	1963, '65
Mary Byergo	1988	Chuck Centers	2003
Tom Byrd	1978	Mariana Cesarino	1998

NAME OF FINISHER	YEAR(S) OF FINISHING	NAME OF FINISHER	YEAR(S) OF FINISHING
Laurence Chaffin	1971	James Clover	1995
Cydney Chambers	1972	Terry Cochran	1984
Jean-Luc Chambost	1980	Janice Cochrane	1979
Lise Chambost	1980	Ann Coefield	1987
Pierre Chambost	1980	Kenneth Coffman	1976
Ron Chandler	1967	Annette Colbert	1966
Tonjia Chandler	1987, '88, '89, '90, '91, '92, '95, '97	Linda Collier	1963
		JoDe Collins	1998, '99
Dianna Chapek	1986	Sandra Comazzi-Thompson	1985
Bob Chapman	1970, '71, '72, '73, '74, '77	Bob Combes	1972, '79
		Colleen Combes	1972
Pam Chapman	1978, '94	Patricia Combes	1981
Nicole Chappell	1992	Liana Comeaux	1995, '96, '97
Patricia Chappell	1980, '82, '84, '85, '86, '87, '88, '89, '90, '91, '92, '93, '94, '95, '96, '98	Celeste Comfort	1992
		Kassandra Conley	2003
		James Constanti	1978, '79
		Janet Constanzo	1982
Karen Chaton	1998, '99	Jan Cook	1984
George Chauvin	1992	Ken Cook	1999
Joe Chavez Jr.	1961	Marci Cook	1996, '98, '99, '01
Stephane Chazel	1984	Marie Cook	1993, '94, '97
Laura Chenel	1986	Mary Cook	1995
Elizabeth Cherry	1973, '74	Nora Cook	1979
Maggie Chevallier	2000	Richard Cook	1993, '94
Joe Chevreaux	1981	Sharon Cook	1986
Meredith Chevreaux	1978	Walter Cook	1981
Cathy Chiazzese	2001	James Cooke	1968
Heidi Chisholm	1974	Ron Cooley	1968
Susan Christ	2001	Valerie Cooney	1993
Peggy Christensen	1994	Deborah Cooper	1997
Julie Christiansen	1999	Gordon Cooper	1993, '94
Kathy Christiansen	1986, '88	Jack Cooper	1966
Robert Christiansen	1986	Mabel Cooper	1968
Sarah Christie	1997	Antonio Corbelletta	1995
Kim Christlieb	1998	Nancy Corbelletta	1992, '00, '01
Henry Christmas	1998	Douglas Cornell	1966
Thomas Christofk	1997, '98, '99, '02	Karyl Kay Corrigan	1987, '89
Dave Clagett	1975, '76, '78	Kathleen Corum	1981
Jillian Riggall Clark	1997, '00	Karen Coté	1985
William Clark	1972	Roberta Cotton	1978
Dale Clark, DVM	1987	Wesley Cotton	1978, '79
Rev. William G. Clarke	1979	Teresa Coughanour	1984
Lon Clearwaters	1987	Carol Couk	1977
Debbie Cleveland	1976	Kathleen Cox	1985

NAME OF FINISHER	YEAR(S) OF FINISHING	NAME OF FINISHER	YEAR(S) OF FINISHING
Linda Cox	1994, '95, '96	J. C. "Bud" Dardi	1964, '65, '66T, '67H, '68T, '75, '79, '81, '84, '95
Jim Cranmer	1987		
Linda Crandall	1981, '95		
Ann Crandell	1989		
John Crandell III	1989, '95	Mia Dardi	1976, '79, '82, '87, '94
John Crandell Jr.	1989		
Susan Crask	1988	Helen Dargie	1978
Patti Crawford	1998	Sally Dargie	1968, '69, '70, '73, '74, '75, '76, '77, '78, '79
Rhonda Poston Craythorn	1976, '77, '78, '81, '88		
Scott Craythorn	1990		
Connie Creech	1988, '95, '96, '97, '02	Charlotte Daugherty	1976
		Ivey Daughtridge	1995
Jan Creighton	1975, '77, '78, '81, '82, '86	John Davidson	1987
		Linda Davidson-Older	1980
Kathy Creighton	1975, '77, '81, '82	Parker Davies	1988
		Peter Davies	1989
Paul Creighton	1981	Bob Davis	1986
Maureen Crerar	1999	Carolyn Davis	1981, '97
Paul Critchfield	1979, '80, '81, '82, '84, '92	Heather Davis	1980, '81, '84, '85, '86, '88, '89, '92, '93, '95, '96, '99
Prue Critchley	1994	Jan Davis	1986, '87, '88
Penelope Crofts	1965	Katie Davis	1998, '00
Wayne Crook	1989	Leonard Davis	1981, '84, '85, '87, '89, '90, '92, '95, '96, '99
Jenni Cross	1971		
Teresa Cross	1971, '74, '91, '96		
		Poppy Davis	1982, '84
Myna Cryderman	2000	Rodger Davis	2000
Danica Cuckovich	1976	William Davis	1974
Natalie Cudney	1991	Noelle Dawe	1970
Kevin Cunningham	1975	Carolyn Dawson	1972, '78, '83, '99
LaVon Cunningham	1962	Dennis Dawson	1974
Marci Cunningham	1993	Mark Dawson	1974, '75
Bob Curtis	1970	Richard Dawson	1974, '78, '98, '99, '00, '01
Dave Curtis	1970		
John Curtis	1967, '69	Barbara Deadwiley	1979
Roy Cust	1986, '92, '96, '00	Larry Deakyne	1980, '81, '83, '86, '87, '89
Teri Dahl	1981		
Janice Daigh	1972	Susan Deakyne	1987
Charles Dake Jr.	1974	Brian Dean	1989, '90
Kathy Daley	1993, '97	Christi Dean	1995
James Dandy	1968	Danielle Dean	1993
Patty Danley	1984, '94	Dolly DeCair	1983, '86, '93, '96, '99, '00
Richard Darcy	1970	Richard Decker	1980, '82

NAME OF FINISHER	YEAR(S) OF FINISHING
James Dedini	1984
Lisa Dedini	1986
Alexandra Dees	1987
Mark Dees	1984
Pat Deeter	1979, '82
John Degenfelder	1970
Charles DeGuigne	1963
Ron Deiro	1992
Wayne Delbeke	1996
Shirley Delsart	1992, '94, '97
Melissa Demas	1996
George Demay	1989
Leslie Demay	1988, '90
Colleen Denison	1985, '93
Nadine Denney	1979
Philip Denney, MD	1979
Chuck Dent	1990, '91, '95, '99
Mary Dentinger	1994
Douglas Denton	1963
John DePietra	1998
Carl DePietro	1992
Sally DePietro	1992
Norman Depoy	1962
Carolee DeWitt	1995
Sharon Dickerson	2000
Nancy Dickey	1986, '87, '89
Sands Dickson	1995, '97, '99
William Dieper	1982
Alida Dierker	1988
Jamie Dieterich	2001
James Dietz	1984
Joanne Dietz	1982
Kiel Dinapoli	1973
John DiPietra	1991, '95
Anita Disparte	1979
Ellen Disparte	1979
Kathy Divito	1981
Dexter Dobberpuhl	1974, '75, '77, '78, '80, '82
Karen Dockendorf	1983
Earline Dodson	1981, '82, '83
Sylvia Dodson	1979, '80, '82, '83, '84, '85
Christine Doelger	1981

NAME OF FINISHER	YEAR(S) OF FINISHING
Sharon Dolan-Truax	2000
Glenn Dollar	1985
Linda Dollar	2003
Moira Donald	1971, '72, '74, '76, '79, '80
Nancy Donaldson	2003
Alejundro Donoso	2003
Elaine Dornton	1986, '87, '89
Elaine Dowdin	1976, '77, '78, '79, '80, '81
Richard Dowdin	1982, '83
Joan Dowis	1979, '82, '83, '84, '86, '87, '92, '97
Lissa Downer	1984, '85, '86, '87
Roger Downey	1999
Janet Drager	2003
Ina Drake	1956
Leslie Dravetsky	1983
Carol Driscoll	1994, '99
Uri Driscoll	1995
Loraine Duff	2001
Patrick Duffy	1976
Rebecca Duffy	1972
Shanna Duffy	1976
Sue DuHamel	1972
Wendy Dunbar	1993, '95
Theresa Duncan	1986, '88
Tania Dunlap	1983
Mark Dunlap, DVM	1982, '85
John Dunn	1957
Nancy Dunn	1986, '87
Pierre Dupont	1988
Tim Durante	1965
Dineen Dusenberry	1973
Karon Dutcher	2001
Diana Dye	1992
Terry Dye	1992
Darleen Dyer	1981
Skip Dyke	1978, '80, '81
Susan Dyke	1978, '79
Anne Dziadul	1998
Debbie Early	1972, '78, '81, '85
Harry Eastlake	1971, '73
Ellen Ebbett	1995, '96

Name of Finisher	Year(s) of Finishing	Name of Finisher	Year(s) of Finishing
James Edmiston	1975	Leslie Fairbanks	2001, '03
Sheila Edmondson	1990, '02	George Fairlee	1986
Patty Edward	1987	Mark Falcone	1994, '95, '96,
David Edwards	1966		'98, '99, '00
Joe Edwards	1995	Traci Falcone	1994, '95, '96
Patty Edwards	1963	Jan Falkenstein	1983, '84
Isabel Ehrenreich	1975	Chi Fallini	1964
Jerry Eischens	1984, '85	Johanna Fallis	1960
Carol Eiselt	1982, '83, '85, '86	Molly Farkas	1968
A.C. Ekker	1992	Frank Farmer	1989, '91
Cindy Eklund	1985	Roger Farmer	1978
Kathy Ellinghouse	1991	Bob Farrell	1975
Dawn Elliot	1998	Fran Farrell	1987
Linda Elliot	1979	Kenny Farrell	1957
Nancy Elliot, DVM	1999, '02	George Farrell, MD	1957
Steven Elliott	1995, '01	Barbara Fawcett	1970
Jerry Ellison	1983	Laszlo Felso	1996
Debbie Emery	1984, '85	Gary Fend	1997, '01, '02
John Emery, MD	1984, '85, '87, '89	Jamie Fend	2003
Elena Emich	1999, '01	Diane Fergus	2002
Mimi Emich	1995	Dave Ferguson	1995
Fred Emigh	1975, '76, '80,	Vivian Ferkin	1994
	'81, '82, '86, '88,	Roberto Fernandes	1995, '96
	'91, '93, '94, '95	Brenda Ferris	1978
Jack Enderle	1997	Rebecca Fiedler	1999T
Lorna Enever	1982, '83	Langdon Fielding	1994
Dixie Engelhaupt	1973	Joel Peter Fields	1973
Jim Enos	1966	Mary Fields	1998
Sue Eoff	1984	Claude Filleul	1989
Tracy Epping	1995	Dabney Finch	1996
M. E. Erickson	1966	Jordan Finley	2003
Mark Erickson	1977	Carolyn Finston	2001
Bart Eskander	1990	Sharon Finston	1999
Janine Esler	1996, '99, '00	Anita Fiondella	1997
Jerry Estebez	1971, '73, '74,	Jackie Fisher	1988
	'75, '77, '81, '82,	Linda Fisher	1998
	'85, '88, '89	Montgomery Fisher	1974
Judy Estebez	1972	Donna Fitzgerald	1960, '61, '63,
Judith Etheridge	1997		'65, '66, '69, '70T,
Lawrence Etter, MD	1956, '57		'71T, '72T, '73T,
Lorna Etzler	1980		'74, '75T, '76T,
Churstie Evans	1976		'81, '83
Jack Evers	1983, '86	Mike Fitzgerald	1976

Name of Finisher	Year(s) of Finishing	Name of Finisher	Year(s) of Finishing
Pat Fitzgerald	1958, '60, '62T, '63T, '70, '76, '77, '78, '79, '80, '81, '82, '83, '84, '86	Daniel Frenette	1984
		Ute Frey	1999, '02
		Jeff Frier	1970
		Phillip Frier, DVM	1968
Susan Flagg	2000	Jerry Fruth	2001
Teri Fletcher	2001	Harry Fryer	1980
Chris Flores	1978	Kim Fuess	1990, '91
M. E. Flores	1977	Richard Fuess	1992, '95
Kristan Flynn	1995	Bill Fulks	1970
Kurt Foell	1972	Lucille Fulks	1970
Allen E. Fogo, MD	1964	Kay Fullerton	1973
Peter Folley	1998	Charles Gabri	1997, '98, '00, '01, '03
Lisa Fonseca	1988		
Regina Fonseca	1986, '87	Nancy Gabri	1997, '98, '99, '00, '03
Richard Fonseca	1980, '84, '91		
Amy Ford	1986, '93	Patricia Gaglioti	1998, '03
Denis Ford	1985	Mark Gale	1981
Garrett Ford	1984, '85, '97, '99	Edward Gallano	1982
Rodger Ford	1982, '89, '91, '92, '93, '97, '98, '00	Linda Gallano	1982
		Jean Galloway	1968, '69
Tyler Ford	1995	John Gardner	1976, '88, '01
Inez Fort	1972	Phillip Gardner	1968, '69, '71, '74, '79, '81, '91, '98, '01
Karen Forte	1973		
Charlotte Foss	2001		
Dorothy Foster	1990	Susan Gardner	1986, '87, '98
Hal Fowler	1970	Kelley Gardner-Blue	1999
Jenny Fowler	1976	Jack Garnett	1974, '76, '79, '80, '82H, '83, '85, '86, '91, '95
Murray Fowler, DVM	1961		
Pat Fox	1967		
William Fox	1973, '77H	Kim Gastman	1984, '88, '89
Wilma Fox	1975, '77, '82	Jim Gault	1986
Rita Francis	1975	Pat Gavitt	1967
Stephen Francone	1985	Patricia Gayt	1998
Candace Frankhouser	1980	Jim George	1977
Marilyn Franks	1978	Andrew Gerhard	2003
Donald Franks, MD	1976	Judy Gerhard	1978
Bodil Frederiksen	1978	Nora Gerhardt	1990, '91, '96
Pat Fredrickson	1990	Gretchen Gerhart	1983, '88
John Freeman	1974, '76, '79, '84	Ruth Gerson	1992
Henry Freitas	1975, '78, '79, '80, '81, '82	Holly Gervais	1988
		Pat Gervais	1978
Pat French	1981	Elise Geske	2000H
Phillip French Jr.	1969	Cathy Gess	1975

NAME OF FINISHER	YEAR(S) OF FINISHING	NAME OF FINISHER	YEAR(S) OF FINISHING
Thomas Gey	1997, '99, '00	Craig Green	1972
Hank Gibbons	1965, '68, '69, '70, '71	Jeff Green	1979
		Jerry Green	1982, '83
Mandy Gibbons	1979	Jim Green	1978, '79, '81, '82, '83, '84, '85, '86, '87, '88, '92
Vicki Giles	2002		
Jerry Gillespie, DVM	1982, '91		
Gail Gilmer	1964	Susan Green	1969
Beth Gingold	1994, '96, '97, '99, '00	Cora Greene	1994
		Ernest Greene	1978, '79, '81, '82, '83, '84, '85, '86, '87, '88, '97
Marty Ginsburg	1975		
Joel Giroux	1962, '63, '64, '66, '72, '74, '75, '77, '79, '80, '84	Rebecca Erin Greene	1983, '84, '85, '86, '87, '88, '90, '91, '92, '93
Cindy Gish	1966	Roxanne Greene	1976, '77, '79, '81, '82, '83, '84, '86, '87, '88, '90, '91, '94, '95, '96, '97, '98, '99, '00, '01
Pat Gisvold	1991, '97		
Becky Glaser	1994		
Neel Glass	1975		
Gary Glazer	1997		
Linda Glazier	1988, '89, '90, '91, '95, '98, '99, '02		
		Bruce Greenwell	1972, '73
Don Glendhill	1981	Valerie Greenwell	1971, '72, '73
Cherisse Glenn	1999	Bill Greer	1961
Douglas Glover	1971	Jan Gregory	1990
Vicki Godward	1968	Quinn Gregory	1979
Ann Goldberg	1979	Shirley Gregory	1976
Richard Gomez	2001	William Gregory, DVM	1976
Don Gonzales	1957	Larry Griffith	1981
Monta Gonzales	1958, '70, '75, '76, '77, '78, '79, '80, '86, '87	Donald Griggs	1962
		Georgianne Gross	2003
		William Lee Guinn	1968
Randy Goodale	1994, '95	Linda Gurnee	1991, '92
John Goodrich	1988, '90	Earl Guyton	1956
Kristin Goodrich	1991	Peggy Murphy Hackley	1974, '77, '79, '81, '91
Sara Goodrich	1989, '90, '92, '93, '94, '95, '96	Walt Hagman	1990
Kristen Goodwin	2003	Neal Hagstrom	1977
Jennifer Goppert	1994	John Hale	1978
Ira Gordon	1976	Ann Hall	1982, '96, '99, '00, '01
Leila Graham	1993		
Susan Graham	1998, '00	Dianne Hall	1977
Fritz Granere	1966	Hal Hall	1970, '72H, '74T, '75, '77T, '78H, '79, '80, '81, '82, '83, '84, '85, '88,
Danny Grant	1993, '94, '95, '00		
David Grant	1986		
Beverly Gray	1992, '00, '01		

NAME OF FINISHER	YEAR(S) OF FINISHING	NAME OF FINISHER	YEAR(S) OF FINISHING
Hal Hall *(cont.)*	'89, '90T, '91, '93, '94, '96, '98, '00, '02H, '03	Florence Hart	1991
		John Hart	1970, '72, '75, '77, '78
Judy Hall	1991, '93	Virginia Hart	1973, '74
Sally Hall	1999	Jeff Harter	1997
Don Hallock	1984	Kristine Hartman	1997, '99, '02
Jerry Hamilton	1998	Seiichi Hasumi	2003
Gerald Hammer	1971	Clydea Hastie	1987, '88, '90
Joe Hampton	1968, '69, '70	Shellie Hatfield	1987, '91, '92T, '96, '01
Woody Hancock	1983		
Danny Handrich	1979	George Hatley	1974
Dave Handrich	1979	Jean Haugsten	1983
Roger Hanes	1984	Judy Haulman	1981
Don Haney	1977, '82, '85	Mary Havens	1973
Theresa Haney	1975, '76, '77, '80, '81, '84, '85, '86, '87, '89	Patricia Hawes	2000, '01
		Delbert Ray Hawkins	1965
		Suzanne Hayes	1972, '92, '96, '97, '98
Debbie Hansen	1981		
Robert Hansen	1980, '81	Mary Hays	1988, '90, '91, '92, '95, '97, '98
Tom Harbour	1973		
John Hardy	1982, '87	Dan Heath	1975
Sylvia Hardy	1983	Janeen Heath	1993
Gina Harkalis	1994	John Heath	1976
Marcia Harmon	1997	Casey Hecker	1989
Roberta Harms	2000	John Hecker	1973
Margarethe Harper	2002	Terry Hecker	1972
Paige Harper	1959, '60, '61, '62, '63, '64H, '65, '68H, '73, '77	Randy Heckley	1979
		Sue Hedgecock	2001, '02
		Bob Heffelfinger	1970, '71
		Tamara Heiland	1995
Marg Harrasymuk	1988	Chuck Heimsoth	1970, '71
Jenny Harries	1969	Cindi Hein	1997
Harold Harris	1983	Warren Hellman	1999, '00, '01
Jan Harris	1977	Hugh Helm	1994, '95H
Joanne Harris	1961	Emery Henderson	1978
Kenneth Harris	1963	Janet Henry	1974, '77
Lynn Harris	1986, '88	Liz Henry	2001, '02
Ralph Harris	1977, '79	Mary Henry	1974
Paul Harrison	1979	Margaret Hentges	1980
Raymond Harrison	1968	Frank Herald	1979, '80
Becky Hart	1976, '84T, '86, '88T	Danny Herlong	1982
		Heidi Herrmann	1975, '76
Don Hart	1969	Jeff Herten	1993, '94, '99, '00, '02
Dublin Hart	2000		

Name of Finisher	Year(s) of Finishing	Name of Finisher	Year(s) of Finishing
Susan Herthel	1984	Judy Houle	1983, '84, '85,
Douglas Herthel, DVM	1984, '87		'86, '88, '89, '90,
Adrienne Hewitt	1999, '00		'91, '93, '94, '95,
Catherine Hibbard	2002		'97, '98
Todd Hickerson	1986, '87, '88	Kenneth Houston	1971
Mary Jo Hicks	1985, '86	Marvin Houston	1970
Cookie Hickstein	1980	James Howard	1995
Jennifer Hillberg	1987	Linda Howard	1995
Elfta Hilzman	2001	David Howe	1989
Robin Hinrichs	2001, '02	Frank Howe	1966, '68, '72
Wayne Hinrichs	1988, '89, '93	E. Vincent Howes	1991, '92
Franklin Hoar	1968, '69	Ulla Howes	1994, '95, '96
Barbara Hobbs	1971, '83, '86, '87	Dean Hubbard	1968
Carolyn Hock	2001	Barbara Huddleston	1991
Linda Hodges	1987	Butch Huff	1979, '81
Steve Hoeft	2002	Susan McCrary Huff	1978, '79, '81
Cheryl Holbrook	1988, '89,	Suzanne Huff	1996, '00
	'90, '91	Brent Hughes	1990
James Holbrook III	1989, '94	Darlene Hughes	1972
Allen Holbrook Jr.	1972, '74, '76	Jack Hughes	1967, '68
Barbara Holland	1973	James Humphrey	1979
Clare Holland	1998, '01	Shirley Humphrey	1979, '80, '81,
Hannah Holland	1965		'83, '87
Hanne Hollander	1982, '83, '85	James Hunt	1970
Lew Hollander	1974, '83	Marilyn Hunter	1976
Lewis Hollander III	1985	Linda Hussa	1975
Cathy Hollenberg	1984	Andrea Hussey	2002
Gary Hollis	1983	William Hussey	1956
Walter Holst	1986, '92	Agnes Hutton	1963, '68
Cameron Holzer	2002	E. C. Hutton	1962, '63
Suzanne Honeyman	1965	Jon Hutton	1963, '65
Randolph Hooks	1989	Neil Hutton	1962, '63, '64T,
Ann Hopkins	1978		'65, '69
Kimberly Hopkins	1995	Jack Huyler	1975
John Hornbeck	1983	Brandon Hyers	1981
Susan Horne	1999	Buckley Hyers	1981
Jozsef Hornyeki	1996	William Ihde	1963, '64, '67
Judit Hornyeki	1996	Christian Indermauer	1979
Jennifer Horsman	1989, '91	Max Indermauer	1979
Laura Horst	1997, '98, '99,	Brian Irby	1986
	'02, '03	June Irwin	1966
Edward Hottell	1970	Karen Iverson	1968
Gail Hought	1999, '00, '01	Sue Iverson	1983, '86
Nancy Houlberg	1976	Beth Ivey	1987

Name of Finisher	Year(s) of Finishing	Name of Finisher	Year(s) of Finishing
S. Britt Ivey	1980	Joanne Johnson	1960
Barbara Jacinto	1983	Julianne Johnson	2001
Diane Jacinto	1980, '81, '85	Kay Johnson	1971, '82
Marvin Jacinto	1984, '85	Lee Johnson	1972
Patricia Jacinto	1981, '84	Mont Johnson	1967
Shirl Jackman	1972	Thula Johnson	1972
Dean Jackson	2000	Tom Johnson	1991, '00
Dory Jackson	1997	Jock Johnston	1988, '90, '92,
M. J. Jackson	1988, '02		'94, '95
Don Jacobs	1981	Kay Johnston	1997
John Jacobs	1975	Lawton Johnston	1995
Van Jacobsen	2000	Pamela Johnston	1972, '73, '88,
Ulla Jaeger	1967, '71, '79		'91, '94, '02, '03
Mike Jaffe	1997	Bill Johst	1991
Al James	1977	Cheryl Jones	1971
Pam James	1985	Fred Jones	1966
Susan James	1989	Noel Jones	1972
Patty Jamison	1969	Oliver Jones	1970
Christy Janzen	1992	Tom Jones	1992
Betty Jay	1960	Wayne Jones	1974, '75,
Harold Jay	1960		'78, '82
David Jay Jr.	1957	Yvonne Jones	1966
David Jay Sr.	1960, '62, '63	Birchall Jones Jr.	1972
Larry Jayko	1993	Albert Joplin	1960, '63
James Jeffers	1974	Joan Jordan	1966, '67, '68
Janis Jeffers	1974, '93, '94,	Janine Jorzik	1996
	'95, '96, '02	Barbara Juel	1985, '86
Kerry Jeffers-Morf	1986	Gene Juel	1987
Sandra Jenkins	1980	Thomas Jurgens	1994
Jeanne Jensen	1974	Laurie Jurs	1984, '94
Marcia Jeppson	1988	Jan Kahdeman	1987
Cynthia Jepsen	1990	Fred Kain	1960
Suzanne Jessen	1993	Bernice Kalland	1974, '75
Glenn Jobe	1975	Lawrence Kanavy	1978
Art Johnson	1997, '98	Valarie Kanavy	1978, '79
Barbara Johnson	1973, '76, '77,	Shinobu Katayama	1997
	'86, '87	Dyke Kauffmann	2001
Bill Johnson	1993	Bill Kauk	1967
Carolyn Johnson	1981, '82, '83,	Candy Kauk	1978
	'92, '93, '95	Nancy Kauk	1967
Christopher Johnson	1998	Pat Kavanaugh	1989
Doris Johnson	2003	Kelle Kearney	1999
Ed Johnson	1965T, '67T	Melissa Keeley	1984, '88
Jennifer Johnson	2001	E. J. "Jerry" Keithley	1979

NAME OF FINISHER	YEAR(S) OF FINISHING	NAME OF FINISHER	YEAR(S) OF FINISHING
Peggy Kellerman	1972	Arlene Kruse	1974
Ronald Kelley	1976	Beth Krusi	1970
Suzy Kelly	1981	George Krusi	1966, '67
Douglas Kemmerer	1979	LeRoy Krusi	1966
Howard Kent	2000	Leslie Kulchin	1981
Gilbert Ketcherside	1964	Douglas Kunze	1975
Lynn Kettell	1994	Wayne Kunze	1969, '70, '75, '81
Smokey Killen	1968, '70, '71, '73, '74, '75, '78, '79, '80, '81, '82, '83, '85	Kunjiro Kusuyama	1998
		Sheri Lacey	1999
		Linda Lacy	1983
		Murrel Lacy	1970
Greg Kimler	2000	Glenn Ladd	1969
Jim Kinder	1985, '86, '89	Dale Lake	1981
Rodney Kinder	1988	Deana Lake	1980
Floyd Kingsley	1977, '78	Jacqueline Lake	1980
Janet Kratt Kingsley	1979, '80	John Laken	1962
W. Kirchmier	1979	John Lakso	1991, '94, '95, '00
Jenny Kirk	2002	Jean Lamb	1986, '87
Kimberly Kirkpatrick	1992, '99	Roselyn Lambert	1988, '90
Sharon Kirkpatrick	2002	Dana Landale	1994, '95
Madeleine Kirsch	2002, '03	Janet Lande	1974
Dana Kirst	1963	Breann Larimer	1995, '96
Alex Klau	1990	Cena Larimer	1973, '75, '78, '80, '83, '86
Jennifer Klein	1999		
Paul Klentos	1990, '91	James Larimer	1970, '73, '74, '76, '78, '81, '82, '85
Sandy Klingler	1988		
Nina Knapitsch	1983		
Lynn Kneiff	1971	Zoie Larimer	1982, '85
Pam Knickerbocker	1975	Cynthia Larkin	1983, '84, '85, '86, '87, '88, '89, '90, '93, '94, '95, '01
Joanne Knight	1983, '84, '89		
Lollie Knight	1984, '87		
Chris Knoch	1993T, '94T, '95, '96	Robert "Joe" Larkin	1982, '85, '86, '92, '93, '96, '97, '98, '99, '00
Bettina Koehn	2000		
Jerry Koenig	1991		
Walt Koerner	1979	Shirley Larsen	1980, '81, '84, '87
Sarah Konst	2000	Theron Larsen	1966
Frank Kosek	1963	Louis Larsen, DVM	1979, '80, '81
Kurt Kosek	1963	James Larsh	1968, '70, '76
Norma Kover	1998, '00	Carolyn Latham-Finston	2003
Lynda Kovisto	1987	Emilie Laurencon	2000, '02, '03
Ann Kratochvil	1993	Judith Laursen	1987, '88, '89, '90, '93, '94, '97
Marcia Kreofsky	1993		
Sheri Krueger	1985	Judith LaVergne	1984
		Ona Lawrence	1997H

NAME OF FINISHER	YEAR(S) OF FINISHING	NAME OF FINISHER	YEAR(S) OF FINISHING
Carmela Laws	1977	Tom Lindsey	1961, '65
Skip Leahy	1995	Fred Lingley	1986
Cathy Leaver	1995	Jack Little	1983
Valerie Lebel	1978, '82, '88	James Little	1965, '75
Laurie Ledbetter	1988, '89, '90, '91, '97, '98, '99	Kenneth Little	1969
		Sonna Litton	1983, '85
Bruce Lee	1973	Marion Livermore	1972, '78, '80, '81, '97
Carolyn Lee	1973		
Charles Lee	1994	Dennis Lobenberg	1994, '95
Kevin Lee	1979, '81	Pamela Loftus	1997
Mary Lee	1980	Helen Logan	1984, '85, '86, '87, '88, '89, '90, '92, '93, '94, '95, '96
Robert Lee	1956		
Tom Lee	1956		
Elizabeth Lehmberg	1996, '98, '00, '01	Henry Logan	1984, '85, '88, '92, '93
Megan Leich	1991		
Sandra Leich	1991	Steven Lokken	1981
Jean Leininger	1962	Claxton Long	1980
John Lemke	1979	Judy Long	1993, '98
Peter Lemond	1983, '84, '85, '86	Garry Looney	1993
Steven Lenheim	1994, '95, '96, '00, '03	H. J. Lopez	1963
		Katherine Lovejoy	1982, '84, '85, '86
Ralph LePera	1991, '03	Ellen Lovett	1984, '85
Julie Leslie	1971	L. H. Lucas	1961
Allan Leslie, DVM	1967	Wendy Lumbert	1997, '98
James Lestor	1986	Hope Lundquist	1975, '78, '79, '80, '81, '82, '83, '86, '89, '92
Denis Letartre	1984, '92		
Marie Letartre	1984		
Kerstin Leuther	2002	Larry Luster	1969
Doris Levingston	1961	Diane Luternauer	1986
Cliff Lewis	1969	Gerald Luternauer	1980, '81, '86
L. D. Lewis	1981	Jeffrey Luternauer	1980, '86, '88
Larry Lewis	1977	Jill Lyle	1976
Sharon Lewis	1970	Mary Lyles	1967
Tom Lewis	1990	Debby Lyon	1989, '91, '92, '96, '98, '03
Charlene Lewis-Stueve	1998, '03		
Bill Leyden	1966	Bronc Lyons	1971
Frank Lieberman	2000	Paul Lyons	1972
Leonard Liesens	1997	Mary Macbeth	1995, '03
Skip Lightfoot	1987, '88, '92	Karlee MacDougal	1973, '76
Lorna Lincoln	1975, '76	Elena Macia	2002
Tom Lindgren	1995	Alexander Mackay-Smith	1962
Bett Lindsey	1972, '74	Elizabeth Mackay-Smith	1981
Rick Lindsey	1965	Matthew Mackay-Smith	1964, '65, '78, '81, '85, '95T
Sam Lindsey	1974		

NAME OF FINISHER	YEAR(S) OF FINISHING	NAME OF FINISHER	YEAR(S) OF FINISHING
Wingate Mackay-Smith	1965, '67, '78, '81	Cathy Mason	1980
Cheryl Madsen	1974	Dave Mason	1958
Douglas Madsen	1973	Gary Mason	1981
Gary Mahaffey	1977, '79, '81	Judy Mason	2003
Louise Mahoney	2000, '01	Mitsuko Masui	2001, '02
Pamela Maier	1966	Chuck Mather	1994, '96, '02, '03
Ronald Malone	1987	Cathy Mathews	1988
Patti Mameson	1974	Kay Mathews	1987
Dave Mandsfield	1980	Maureen Mathisen	1980
John Manhire	1959	Joan Diane Matlock	1973, '75, '76
Julie Maniord	1979	George Matsukas	1968
Robert Manley	1968, '78	Ursula Matsukas	1983, '86
Alan Mann	1979	Peter Mattei	1978, '79, '81
Gabrielle Mann	1999, '03	Jason Matthews	1998
Lisa Mann	1971	John Matthews	1998
Alan Mansfield	1960	Wendy Mattingley	2002
David Mansfield	1956, '57, '58, '60, '62, '63, '66, '67, '68, '69	Joe Mattos	1957
		Larry Matz	1983
		Michael Maul	1999
Lincoln "Nick" Mansfield	1955, '56, '57, '58, '59T, '60, '61, '62, '63, '64, '65, '67, '71, '72, '75, '80	Mary Anne Maynard	2003
		Michelle Maynard	1987
		L. A. Mayr	1978, '83
		Lois McAfee	1998
Nancy Mansfield	1956, '57, '58	Vicki McBride	1980
Richard Mansfield	1960	Nancy McCall	1970
William Tevis Mansfield	1974, '75	Dick McCallum	1987
Katie Mapes	1982	Larry McCallum	1983
Poppie Marinel, DVM	1978	Susie McCallum	1983, '85, '86
Kurt Markus	1981	Nancy McCarthy	1995
Diane Ripley Marquard	1967, '70, '78, '80, '81, '82, '83, '84, '85, '87, '91, '92, '94, '95	Erin McChesney	1980, '91TH, '96TH
		Kimberly McClain	2003
		Larry McClain	1983
Michael Marquard	1982	Brenda McClellan	1984, '85, '86, '88, '89
Chris Martin	1999, '02, '03		
Kathleen Martin	1988, '89, '90, '92	Roy McClimans	1981
Leah Martin	1968	Marilyn McCoy	1988, '94, '96, '98, '01
Lucy Martin	1986, '87		
Jan Martinez	1999	Barbara McCrary	1978, '79, '81
Georganna Martinson	1971	Ellen McCrary	1978, '81, '82
Wayne Martinson	1967, '68, '69	Frank McCrary	1976, '77, '79, '80, '82
Robert Marx	1994, '95, '97, '98, '99, '00		
		Janet McCrary	1979, '81, '82, '83

NAME OF FINISHER	YEAR(S) OF FINISHING
Carolyn McCullough	1970, '71
John McCullough	1967, '68, '70, '71, '74, '76, '78, '80, '81, '82, '83, '84, '85, '86, '87, '88, '89, '92, '93, '94
Blair McDonald	1979
George McDonald	1959
Marylyn McDonald	1976
Patrick McDonald	1987, '89, '90, '98, '99, '00
Reford McDougall	1976
Darryl McElroy	1976, '77, '78, '79
Jane McGrath	1985, '90
Joe Thom McGuff	1965
Donald McIntosh	1983, '86, '87
Gerald McIntosh	1983
Karen McIntosh	1982, '83
Kevin McIvain	1982
Jill McKee	1983
Patricia McKendry	1975, '76, '77, '78, '79, '80, '81, '84, '85
April McKenzie	2003
Brittany McKenzie	2001, '03
Jeffrey McKenzie	1993
Karen Jean McKenzie	1987
Jim McKibbin	2000, '01, '02
Lynn McKillp	1966
Bonnie McLane	1966, '68, '69, '70, '72, '73, '79, '81, '82, '83, '85
Dave McLane	1978
Ryan McLane	1987
Walter McLaren	1966, '68, '70, '71, '78
Chris Fanony McLemore	1981
Richard McManaman	1979, '81
William McMann	1964
Wayne McMinn	1982
Joy McVay	1989
Chester McWilliams	1972
Elena Macia	2002

NAME OF FINISHER	YEAR(S) OF FINISHING
Matt Medeiros	1986, '89, '00
Diane Medlock	1991
John Meeks	1976, '85, '87, '88
William Mein Jr.	1963, '64
Tami Mello	1981
Tony Mello	1972
Anita Mellott	1983
John Mellott	1980
Holly Meltesen	1999
John Melville	1989
Wilma Dasche Melville	1988, '89
Betty Meneffee	1967
Karl Mergenthaler	1998, '99, '01
Jim Mero	1968
Shirley Mero	1967, '68, '69
Martha Merriam	1969
Gene Merriman	1980
Harriet Merritt	1997
Marlene Merritt	1966
Richard Mesak	1989, '90
Marie Mestas	1966
Berit Meyer	1995
Terry Meyer	1976
Ed Meyers	2001
Laurie Meyers	1992
Phillip Meyers Jr.	1967, '69
William Miles	1977
Barbara Miller	1964
Carol Ann Miller	1994, '96, '97
Charles Miller	1995
Cherie Miller	1963
Douglas Miller	1971, '72, '74
Janet Miller	1975
Jeffrey Miller	1998
Nancy Miller	1983
Sharon Miller	1989, '90
Teri Miller	2000, '02
William Miller	1968
Jack Mills	1976
Carrie Miracle	1993
Alan Mitchell	1997
Alicia Mitchell	2000
Jamie Mitchell	2003

Name of Finisher	Year(s) of Finishing	Name of Finisher	Year(s) of Finishing
Jill Mitchell	1995	Nancy Moss	1983
Jim Mitchell	2000, '02	Rebecca Moss	1986
Frederick Mittleman	1987	Pam Mott	1990, '92, '94
Frank Moan	1964, '65, '66H, '76	Ruth Moxon	1978
Joyce Mocilan	2000	Barbara Moyle	1971
Michael Mocilan	2000	Dan Moyle	1963, '64
Lance Moffitt	1963	Jean Moyle	1963, '65, '70
Veronica Molloy	1983, '84	Marjorie Moyle	1965, '71, '72, '81
Marion Molthan, MD	1977, '78, '79, '80, '81, '82, '83, '84, '88, '89	Rex Moyle	1963, '64, '65
		Robyn Moyle	1970
		M. V. Mullenberg	1974, '75
Patricia Molyneaux	1967	Frank Mullens	1960, '61, '65
Pietro Moneta	1987	Babe Mullins	1961
Sheila Mongan	1983	Peter Mundschenk	2000
Charles Monroe	1984	Julie Munger	1977, '78
Jose Monsivais	1996	Maynard Munger Jr.	1971, '72, '73, '97, '99
Drusilla Montemayor	1993		
Cheryl Montgomery	1983, '87	Ginger Murphy	1992
Robert Moody	1971	Mike Murphy	1961
Wesley Moon	1984	Teresa Murphy	1978
Bill Mooney	1964, '65, '70	Carol Myers	2000
Loren Moorhead	1976, '77	Jerry Myers	1975, '79, '88
Liz Mooz	1976, '77, '78	Kathleen Myers	1993, '94, '97, '98, '00
Leonardo Morales	1996		
Rocco Moravito	1987	Linda Myers	1983, '86
Fred Morawcznski	1990	Ray Myers	1975
Judy Morawcznski	1987, '93, '94, '95	J. N. Myrick	1977, '79
John Morehart	1966	Robert Nail	1971
Maile Morehart	1994	Rusty Nail	1974
Matthew Morehart	1970	Abe Nance	1973
Roland Morehead	1969	Teresa Nash	1986
Jean Laris Morelle	1989	Lesley Navone	1970
Marie Claude Morelle	1988, '89	Gordon Neilson	1981
Linda Morelli	1998	Robert Nelms	1956
Kay Morgan	1996	Nancy Nelson	1977, '87, '88
Jeannette Morris	1981	Dominique Nettlingham	1994
Kathy Morris	1987	Niels Neustrup, MD	1967
Robert Morris	1980	Tuitti "Rose" Nichols	1999
Miki Morrison	1994	Diane Nicholson	1970, '72
Sidney Morse	1973	Dave Nicholson, DVM	1962, '63, '65, '70, '71, '72, '78, '79, '80, '81, '82, '83, '84
Terry Morstad	1974		
Suzanne Morstad, MD	1970H, '72		
Juliet Moss	1984, '86, '93	Jennifer Niehaus	2001

Name of Finisher	Year(s) of Finishing	Name of Finisher	Year(s) of Finishing
Darrel Nielsen	1977	April Ott	1996
Gloria Nightingale	1961	Mike Ottmann	1978
Katherine Nixon	1986	Robert Oury	1987, '93
Lynn Nogleberg	1985	James Oury, MD	1986, '88, '89, '93, '97
Richard Nogleberg	1984, '85, '87		
Neil Nordlander	1980	Downey Overton	1987, '89
Colleen Normanly	1984	Robert Padgett	1976, '78, '79
Michael Norrel	1977	George Pagan	1968
Alexandra North	2000	Caleb Palfreyman	1995
Cindy Northern-Gish	1966	Clark Palfreyman	1988, '91, '94, '98
Eleanor Norton	1978	Bill Palmer	1969, '70
Pierce Norton	1974	C. Dale Palmer	1968
Virl Norton	1973, '74, '75, '77, '78, '81, '83, '87	Gordon Palmer	1978, '79, '80, '81, '82, '83, '84, '85, '87, '89, '00
Renaud Nuel	1993		
Mary Nunn	1970	Kathy Palmer	1976, '77, '79, '80, '82, '83, '85
Tamara Nute	2001		
Steve Nybank	1986	Teri Palmer	1972
Barbara Oats	1986	Robert Palmeri	1998, '99, '00, '03
Sandy Obermeyer	1995	Cathleen Papa	1999
Edward O'Brien	1963	Cynthia Park	1981, '87
George O'Brien	1961	Bill Parker	1991, '94, '96
Karen Occhialini	1994, '96, '97	Molly Parker	1978
Pete Occhialini	1995	Noel Parker	1980
Courtney O'Connell	1983	Roxy Lynn Parker	1979
Robin O'Connell	1983	Sheila Parker	1972, '79
David Ogden	1960	Stacie Parker	1995
Donna Ogelvie	1985, '86, '87, '89	Karen Parli	1990
Judith Ogus	1996	Richard Parli	1990
Sharon O'Halloran	1976	Donna Parlier	1979, '83, '86
John O'Hanneson, MD	1965	Ed Parlier	1984
Lori Oleson	2002	Heather Parson	1992, '93, '94, '96, '97
Marilyn Pat Oliva	1986, '94		
Cindy Oliver	1984	Jackie Patriarca	1992, '93
Jennifer Oltmann	1991, '95, '98	Bill Patrick	1955
Teacia Opperman	1986, '87, '88	Doyle Patrick	1998
Robert Oram	2002	Darlene Patterson	1997
Jimmy Ornelas	1984	Elaine Patterson	1990, '92
Carol Orr	1975	Vickie Patterson	1994
Marilyne Orr	1973	Beverly Dale Paul	1981
Steven Orre	1956	Heidi Paul	1995, '96
Caroline Orrick	1997	Calvin Paulette	1971
Kathleen Osler	1979	Beth Paulson	1998
Cindy Oster	1986, '90, '95	Jimmie Pearce	1978

Name of Finisher	Year(s) of Finishing	Name of Finisher	Year(s) of Finishing
Alan Pease	1977	Kathy Pierroz	1977, '79, '82,
Donna Pedersen	1973, '74		'83, '87, '89, '91,
Marilyn Pedersen	1970, '71		'93, '94, '95
Michelle Pedersen	2001	Larry Pierroz	1987, '88
Trilby Pederson	1982, '84, '85,	Joe Piers	1973
	'86, '87, '89, '90,	Roger Piers	1966
	'93, '94, '95, '97,	Ann Marie Pinter	1987, '96
	'98	Melissa Plaggmier	1980
Larry Pedrett	1957	Patrick Plankers	1973, '75, '76, '79
Warren Pelton	1975	Frank Platt	1972, '73
Jeanne Pepper	1980	Roberta Pocan	1991, '92
Bonnie Peralez	1984	Dewayne Pohl	1968, '69
Michael Peralez	1979, '80, '83, '85	Catherine Pokorny	2002
Smokey Perisian	1987, '89	Diane Pokrajak	1988
Jimmie Perry	1976, '77, '80, '81	Glenn Polatty	1975, '81
Joyce Perry	1986	Clive Pollitt	2000, '01
Kathie Perry	1975, '76, '78T,	Rick Ponte	1960
	'81, '85, '86, '88,	Peter Pop	1998
	'92, '93, '94, '96,	Marinel Poppie, DVM	1978
	'98, '99, '01	Jim Porter	1986
Katherine Perry	2002	Tamera Porter	1989
Teresa Perry	1972	Barry Portman	1972, '74
Clydea Person	1972	Dave Poston	1976, '78, '81,
Patti Person	1984		'83, '84, '86, '87,
Roger Person	1974		'90
Jackie Peters	1971	Robert Poteet	1963, '66, '72, '75
Linda Peters	1972	Linda Potter	1989
Will Peters	1971, '74, '79	Loretta Potts	1992, '93, '94, '02
Christie Petersen	1972	Charlotte Poulsen	1995
Jesper Petersen	1966, '68, '71,	Gary Powell	1975
	'73, '76, '79, '81	Scott Powell	2000
June Petersen	1993	Sherode Powers, DVM	1971, '87H
Dale Peterson	1995, '97	David Pratt	1994
Kamile Peterson	2001	Lenita Prentiss	2002
Trudy Peterson	1966	Jon Priest	2002
Cynthia Peticolas-Stroud	1994, '96	William Prescott	1969
Teresa Petretti	1987	Gail Price	1976, '77, '78, '79
Scott Petty	1983	Lee Price	1970
Sue Petty	1978	Margaret Price	1979, '84, '86
Christine Phegley	1977	Meg Price	1979
Dorothy Sue Phillips	2001	Sue Price	1977
Leslie Phillips, DVM	1994	Joy Pritchard	1972
Michael Pickett	1995, '96, '99	Steve Proe	1990, '93
William Pieper	1987, '94, '95,	Robert Proper	1979
	'96, '99	Robbie Pruitt	1983, '89, '00

NAME OF FINISHER	YEAR(S) OF FINISHING	NAME OF FINISHER	YEAR(S) OF FINISHING
Valerie Pruitt	1970	Dana Reeder	1997
Hannah Pruss	2000	Judy Reens	1992, '00T
Marjorie Pryor	1976, '77, '78, '79, '81, '82T, '83T, '89	Marily Reese	1977
		Forrest Reeves	1978
		Beverly Reilly	1970
Janet Pucci	1983, '84, '86, '88, '90	Dennis Reilly	1975
		Susan Reilly	1969, '70
George Putnam	1986	Randy Reinholz	1983, '85
Jill Putnam	2002	Barbara Reinke	1985, '88
Delos Putz	1991	Jim Remillard	1980, '81, '91, '95
Judy Pyorre	1980	Suzanne Remillard	1990, '92, '95, '97
Judy Latham Pyorre	1989	Jacqueline Renaldo	1987
Mervin Pyorre	1978, '79, '81, '82, '84, '85, '86, '87, '88, '89, '90	Nadine Reser	1966
		Doug Reynaud	2003
		Heather Reynolds	1996, '99H, '03TH
Dale Qualls	1977		
Katie Qualls	1992	Jack Rhoades	1986, '90, '94, '96
Rick Qualls	1993	Melissa Ribley	1980, '96, '98, '02
Magali Quillerou	2000	Robert Ribley	1984, '86, '90, '95, '97, '01
Ervin Quinn	1992, '96		
James Quinn	1970	Joe Ricci	1961
Dave Rabe	1984, '85, '94, '95, '96, '00, '03	Rose Rice	1999
		Minette Rice-Edwards	1973H
Abby Radecki	1999	Peter Rich	1986, '88, '92, '93, '96
Jennifer Rader	2000, '02, '03		
Jean Ragland	1982	Julie Richard	1986
Chantal Rambosson	1980	Randy Richard	1986
Kayla Ramsdell	2000, '01, '02	Carmela Richards	1980
Troy Ramsdell	2001, '02	Mary Richards	1965, '67
Heidi Rankin	1980	Claudia Richardson	1986, '88, '91
John Rannenberg	1985	Cynthia Richardson	1996, '97
Robert Ranta	1975	Denise Richardson	1979
Linda Rapposelli	1998	Karen Richardson	1979
Michael Rapposelli	1995, '96, '99, '00	Potato Richardson	1975, '76, '77, '78, '79, '81, '82, '83, '84, '86, '88, '92, '93, '98T, '00, '01, '02T
Gus Raptos	1957		
Brenda Ratcliff	1956		
Gail Rauscher	1982		
Kathy Ray	1987T	Range Richardson	1997, '98, '00
Betty Lou Raymond	1971	Tricia Richardson	1983
Lauri Reed	1979	Wanda Richardson	1986, '88
Scott Reed	1981	Bob Richesin	1967, '69, '76, '77
Steve Reed	1999	Mark Richtman	1995, '97
Terry Reed	1970, '79, '81	Blake Ridgway	1974
Z. T. Reed	1979	Kirsten Ridgway	1985

Name of Finisher	Year(s) of Finishing	Name of Finisher	Year(s) of Finishing
Sally Ridgway	1971, '77, '83, '86, '87, '90	Angela Rose	1983
		Kathy Rose	1983
Kerry Ridgway, DVM	1970, '72, '75, '76, '77, '78, '81, '83, '84, '85, '86, '87	Regina Rose	1978
		Teri Rose	1998
		Ethel Rose, DVM	1984
Louise Riedel	1977	Leighsa Rosendaul	1997, '98
George Riedler	1984	Emmett Ross	1985H, '87, '88, '98
E. C. Riggs	1972, '73		
Linda Riley	1994	Kimberly Ross	1997
Eldon Rinehart	1978	Frank Rothschild	1998
Sharon Rinehart	1963, '67, '78, '81, '84	Tara Rothwell	2003
		Tom Rotkis	1988
Clint Ritchie	1978	William Routt, MD	1978, '79
Ben Roark Jr.	1960, '62	Sandra Rovane	1989, '93
Kathleen Robbins	1984	Cynthia Rowe	1982, '86, '87, '88, '89, '90, '92, '93, '94, '95
Bob Roberts	1973, '74		
Robin Robichaux	1982, '84		
John Robie	1962, '65	Chris Ruben	1980, '81, '83
Marcie Robie	1967, '72	Ann Rubenstein	1987, '88, '89, '90
Wendell Robie	1955, '56, '57, '58, '60, '62, '63, '65H, '67, '68, '70, '73, '74	Linda Rubio	1986, '87, '88, '89, '91, '92
		Barbara Ann Ruby	1966
		Ellis Ruby	1975
Patricia Robinett	1997	Brenda Ruedy	1985, '86, '91, '94
Dennis Robinson	1976	Carole Ruprecht	1999, '00, '02
Ina Robinson	1956	Marilyn N. Russell	1987, '89
Jessica Robinson	1998	Marilyn R. Russell	1981, '87, '88, '89, '90, '93
Lester Robinson	1976		
Neil Robinson	1974, '75, '76, '78, '79, '80, '81, '82, '83, '84	Lori Rutherford	1988
		Sharon Saare	1967, '68, '74
		Gary Donald Sabin	1966
Susan Robinson	1988	Richard Sabin	1990
Tammy Robinson	1995, '01, '02	Lance Sabo	1984
Linda Robocker	1981	Shauna Safford	2001
Diane Roedenbeck	1994	Denise Sager	1998
John C. Rogers	1962	Patricia Sager	1978, '89, '98
John M. Rogers	1962, '65	Ernie Sanchez	1960T, '61, '68
Norma Rogers	1975	Tony Sanchez	1983
Susan Rogers	1992	Harold Sanders	1975
Cathy Rohm	2001H	Sarah Sanders	2001
Stephen Rojec	1979	Anne Sands	1990, '91, '96, '97, '98, '99, '02
Patricia Rolf	1965		
Rosie Rollins	2000	Nancy Sandy	1986, '87, '89, '90, '93, '94, '95
Linda Romander	1990		
Cheyenne Romanini	1998	Raymond Santana	1989

Name of Finisher	Year(s) of Finishing	Name of Finisher	Year(s) of Finishing
Becky Santucci	1997	Matt Scribner	1994
Rebecca Sarro	1986	Penny Scribner	1980, '84, '85, '86, '97, '99
Aloha June Saunders	1965, '66		
Jon Saunders	1987	Sheila Scroggins	1992
Teri Saunders	1966	Cheryl Searer	1999
Carol Savidge	2003	Sheri Sedam	1992, '93, '94
Nancy Scanlon, DVM	1974	Winifred Della Sehm	1965
Paul Scannell	1975	Judy Selzler	1973
Sue Scantlebury	1970	Maureen Selzler	2000
Roberta Schaeffer	1981	Larry Semm	1983, '84, '86
Angela Schaffer	1969	Toni Semple	1995
Tony Schaurer	1982, '83	Ralph Sessa	1980
Mark Scheberies	1980, '81	Pat Sewell	1955
Mae Schlegel	1974, '81	Samuel Sewell	1967, '71
Marion Schlinger	1998, '99	Jerome Sexton, DVM	1974
Fred Schmidt	1979	Shelli Sexton, DVM	2003
Sharon Schmidt	1997, '98, '99, '00	Mohammed Shafar	1998
T. E. Schmidt	1971, '72	Scot Shafer	1999
Florian Schmidthus	1982, '83	Ingrid Shattuck	1987
R. D. Schmitz, DVM	1972	Phil Shattuck	1981, '86
Lisa Schneider	2002	Michele Shaw	2000, '02
Jean Schrieber	1986	Stephen Shaw	1983, '89, '95, '97, '98
Melissa Schuler	1982, '84, '03		
Cassandra Schuler, DVM	1979, '80, '81, '82, '84, '85, '87, '88, '90, '93H, '94H, '96, '97, '98, '00, '01, '02, '03	Jim Shea	1976, '77
		Lari Shea	1983, '84, '86, '89T, '91
		Janice Sheets	1965
Connie Schulte	1959	Jane Sheppard	1992
Alvin Schultz	1968	Melodi Sherman	1999
Joy Schumacher	1970	Ray Sherman	1979, '86, '88
Heather Schur	1986, '97	Vernon Sherman	1980
Karen Schwartz	1983, '90	Sala Sherwood	2003
Audrey Scott	1987, '88	Tom Sherwood	1974, '76, '81, '82, '83, '84, '85, '86, '87, '88
Don Scott	1978, '79, '80		
Gary Scott	1994		
James Scott	1982	Vicki Anderson Sherwood	1970, '71H, '74, '76, '79, '82
Jeri Scott	1980		
Marcelyn Scott	1999	Mary Shimmick	1972, '74, '76, '95
Ray Scott	1967	Ken "Cowman" Shirk	1982, '83
Sandra Scott	1999	Marcy Shone	1990
Ann Scribner	1963	Daniel "Bro" Shontz	1967
Daniel Scribner	1966, '76, '77	Herbert Shuler	1959
Druscilla Scribner	1991	Heidi Siegel	1983, '86
Jean Scribner	1987	Kay Silver	1982, '85, '86, '89, '90

NAME OF FINISHER	YEAR(S) OF FINISHING	NAME OF FINISHER	YEAR(S) OF FINISHING
Chester Simoni	2002	S. Taylor Smith	1983
Lynge Simoni	1989	Theresa Smith	1997
Carol Simpson	1988	Valerie Smith	1967
Leslie Simpson	1976, '77, '78	William Smith	1961
Elayne Sims	1963	Peggy Smyth	1996
Carla Singleton	1980	Loren Snider	1996
Hatden Singleton	1975, '79	Gayle Snow	1993
Karen Singleton	1978	Major Don Snow	1968
Kelly Singleton	1976, '78	Marvin Snowbarger	1990, '91, '92, '93, '95
Mark Singleton	1979, '81	Cory Soltau, DVM	1969, '76, '80, '82, '84, '85, '86, '88, '91, '92, '95, '99, '02, '03
H. R. Sites	1966, '70		
Jean Skeggs	1979, '81		
Leonard Skeggs	1979, '81		
Bob Slater	1976		
Kenneth Sly	1972	Lisa Somerville	2000
Maxine Sly	1967	Pascale Soumoy	2002
Marilyn Smart	1983	Jim Sours	1992, '94, '97, '99
Nancy Smart	1997	Joyce Sousa	1996, '00, '01
Bergen Smeding	2000	Joby Souza	1991, '92, '94
Lettie Smeding	1999, '00	Alison Spackman	1995, '01, '02
Jacquelyn Smeltzer	1995	Linda Spaletta	1987
Ali Smith	1978, '80	Joyce Spearman	1975
Barbara Smith	1958	Becky Spencer	2003
Beth Smith	1984	Dick Spencer III	1980
Dean Smith	1979, '80, '81, '83, '84, '86	Bob Spoor	1987, '88, '96, '97, '98, '00, '02, '03
Donna Smith	1966	Gary Spring	1968, '70
Eugene Smith	1979	Margaret Spring	1970
Frank Smith	1996, '97, '98, '99, '01, '03	G. W. Spring Jr.	1968
		Ron Sproat	1991
Gwen Smith	1957	Cara May Sproul	1971
Jenni Smith	2002, '03	Curtis Sproul	1972, '79, '86
Joannie Smith	1998, '03	David St. Charles	1993
Lorraine Smith	1975, '78, '80	Mickie Stacy	1979, '92
Louise Smith	2001, '02	Nancy Carol Stafford	1983, '86
Luci Smith	1980	Maxine Stahl	1983
Marcia Smith	1992TH, '97T, '98, '01T	Alyssa Stalley	2002, '03
		Charles Stalley	1978, '81, '02
Milton Smith	1958, '59	Jennifer Stalley	1999, '03
Molly Smith	1999	Pamela Stalley	1976, '78, '81, '82, '89, '99, '01, '02
Nancy Smith	1961, '64, '65, '76	Dale Stapp	1975
Ralph Smith	1978, '79	Roscoe Stark	1972
Richard Smith	1998	R. W. Stauffer	1967
Ruth Smith	1976	Lorna Steele	1986

NAME OF FINISHER	YEAR(S) OF FINISHING	NAME OF FINISHER	YEAR(S) OF FINISHING
Andy Steen	1962	Juliette Suhr *(cont.)*	'86H, '87, '88,
D'Ann Steere	1980, '81, '82,		'89, '90, '97, '00
	'84, '86	Robert Suhr	1976, '79
Leslie Steere	1968, '70	Godfrey Sullivan	1999, '00, '01, '03
Kim Steffen	1987	Hayley Sullivan	2003
Margaret Steinberg	1987	Sandra Sullivan	1985
Leo Steinbruch	1996	Suzanne Sullivan	1991, '94, '96,
Robert Stern	1967		'97, '99
Bob Stevens	1988, '89	Dennis Summers	1995
Elaine Steward	1999	Gary Summers	1980
Loreley Stewart	1977, '78, '79,	Susan Summers	1995
	'80T, '84,	Jeanne Sumrall	1984
	'86T, '87, '90,	Mary Sundwell	1968
	'91, '92, '94,	Sheldon Sussman	1984, '85
	'97, '98	Bob Suter	1984, '87, '93
Richard Stewart, DVM	1978, '80, '81	Don Sutton	1984
Eilge "Buster" Stillwell	1961	Richard Sutton	1977, '78
Darleen Stimson	1983, '84	Bronwyn Swan	1999, '00, '01, '02
Kenneth Stinson	1976, '79	Grant Swanson	1998
Jane Stipovich	1995	Wendy Swanson	2000
Cherry Stockton	1988, '00, '02	Lona Sweet	1968, '69
Bradley Stolfi	1987	Philip Sweet	1964
Bill Stone	1964, '65, '69	Eric Swenson	1979
Royce Stone	1967	Kathleen Swenson	1979
Tish Stoots	1991	Diane Swett	1964
Arnold Stoutamyre	1961	Leland Swett	1964
Lif Cory Strand	1982, '89	Beth Swier	2002
Paul Strand	1983	Stanley Swift	1968, '70
Marianne Strange	1984	Mary Sydnor	1977
Bobbie Maniord Stroud	1979	Carol Syer	1969
Ray Stroud	1978, '79	Toby Tackitt	1990
William K. Stuckey	1978	Masafumi Tanaka	2002
William N. Stuckey	1979, '80	Forrest Tancer	1985
Antoinette Stueve	1976	Kate Tancer	1988, '90
Duane Stueve	1976	Penny Tanner	1994, '98
Karen Stueve	1976	Lorna Tansey	1979
Mary Stueve	1976	Linda Tarnoff	1980
Michael Stueve	2000	Marcial Tavene	2003
Laurie Sturgess	1996	Bob Taylor	1970, '71
Larry Suddjian	1985	Eva Taylor	1970, '72, '73,
Juliette Suhr	1965, '66, '68, '69,		'74H, '81
	'72, '73, '74, '75,	Stephanie Teeter	1997
	'78, '79, '81, '82,	Linda Tellington-Jones	1961, '63, '68,
	'83H, '84H, '85,		'70, '72

Name of Finisher	Year(s) of Finishing	Name of Finisher	Year(s) of Finishing
Pat Teman	1977	William Towle	1962
Masaji Terasawa	1976	Jeff Townsend	2002
Jean Terry	1986	Sally Toye	1995, '98
Vivian Terwilliger	1995	Mike Tracy	1992, '95, '96,
Vicki Testa	1989, '91, '94,		'97, '00, '01
	'95, '96, '98	Nancie Traud	1973, '86, '87
Sandra Tevis	1960	Darleen Travis	1986
Ramona Thacker	1981	Michaele Tristram	1994, '97
Ann Theodore	1974	Tracy Tromp	2002
Eileen Theodore	1982	Joann Trosi	1980
Elizabeth Theodore	1974, '79, '82, '84	Cornelia Trousdale	1972
R. H. Theodore	1973, '74	Nancy Trussell	1987
Richard Theodore	1974	Judy Tudsbury	1987, '88
Ronald Theodore	1974	Tiffany Tudsbury	1988
Jutta Thoerner	1992	Earl Turner	1980, '81
Cheryl Thompson	1981	Mary Lou Turner	1983
Eric Thompson	1980	Barry Turner, DVM	1987
Kathy Thompson	1971, '83, '97	B. Twardowski	1981
Sandra Thompson	1977, '79	Nancy Twight	1996, '99, '00, '01
J. Ward Thompson, DVM	1978, '80	George Twiss	1969
Callie Thornburgh	1970	Joe Twiss	1971
Tracy Thornburgh	1976	Mickey Twiss	1969, '71, '72
William Thornburgh	1969, '70, '77	Naomi Tyler	1988, '90, '91
Dick Threlfall	1972	Ruth Tyree	1969
Denise Throgmorton	1973	Robert Ubry	1986, '87
Linda Throgmorton	1978	Holly Ulyate	1975, '94, '97
Bill Throgmorton, DVM	1970, '71, '73, '74	Jack Underwood	1974, '75, '83,
Beverly Tibbitts	1967, '72, '80, '81		'84, '91
Walter Tibbitts	1967, '68, '69H,	Mary Dale Underwood	1971
	'71, '72, '73, '88,	Yvonne Underwood	1984, '89, '90, '91
	'90, '91, '96	Linda Upton	2002, '03
Matthew Tillis	2000	Mari Ural	2001
Joannie Timms	1998	Clydea Vaca	1978
Mary Tiscornia	1968, '70, '74,	Dennis Vaca	1978
	'76, '79H	Marilyn Van Ackerman	1983
Peter Toft	2003	Robert Van Buskirk	1962
Rita Toikka	1992	Hettie Van Sickle	1975
Steve Tomac	1978	Lucian Vandegrift	1990
Joseph Tomaselli	1986	Adrian "Ed" Vandenhoogen	1978, '82, '84,
Lynne Tomovick	2000		'85, '86, '87, '88,
Claire Toomey	1996		'89, '90, '91
Bob Toothill	2000	Desiree Vandenhoogen	1982, '84, '87, '89
Cindy Tough	1981, '82, '84	Margo Vandenhoogen	1981, '83, '84, '85
Ola Mae Towle	1962	Mieke Vandenhoogen	1984

Name of Finisher	Year(s) of Finishing	Name of Finisher	Year(s) of Finishing
Tom Vandenhoogen	1989	James Walker	1981
Heidi Vanderbilt	2001, '03	Jeannie Walker	1976
Gloria Vanderford	1987, '90, '91, '94, '97, '98, '02, '03	Joan Walker	1966
		Lynda Walker	1976, '78, '79, '80, '81, '84, '85
Hugh Vanderford	1987, '88, '89, '91	Jeffrey Wall	1990, '00
Gaetmo Varriale	1987	Carol Walpole	1965
Katie Vaughn	2000	Lynda Waltenspiel	1975, '78
Betty Veal	1959	Ron Waltenspiel	1979, '84, '87, '88
Jack Veal	1956, '59	Ruth Waltenspiel	1975, '78, '82, '83
Fran Veon	1986	Robert Walz	1976, '84, '85, '86, '87
Arden Verbeck	1973		
Scott VerHagen	1996	Elaine Wang	1986, '87
Patricia Verheul	1999	Jocele Wang	1989
Debra Vietor	1990, '94	Don Ward	1968
Warren Vietor	1971, '72	Jane Ward	1985
Margle Villaneal	1977	Nick Warhol	1998, '99
M. L. Vincilone	1971	Linda Warnekros	1975, '78, '79, '80, '84, '87
P. H. Vincilone	1969		
Raymond Visco	1988H, '01	Ed Warner	1958
Robin Vitti	1990	Kathie Warren	1987
Barbara Vohland	1999	Trevor Warren	1988
Micheline Voight	1980	David Wasden	1956
Frederick Von Lederbur	1960	Jill Wasden	1982
Karen Voyles	1989	Patricia Wasmund	1993, '97
Marjorie Vulk	1988, '89	Sharon Watson	1972
Beth Wachenheim	1988, '90, '95	Bob Waugh	1987
Scott Wachenheim	1995	Karel Waugh	1983, '86, '87
Janette Wackerly	1995	Bonnie Way	1989, '94, '95, '00
Teresa Wackerly	1993		
Ellen Waddell	1978	Robert Webb	1965
Reed Waddell	1986	Tracy Webb-Hoskins	1998
Carol Wadey	1990	Koylynn Webdell	2000
Con Wadsworth	1991	Shannon Yewell Weil	1977, '79
Ralph Wadsworth	1982, '86	Lucille Weiland	1975
Tod Wadsworth	1988, '91	Meggan Weinke	1998, '99
Ty Wadsworth	1986, '89	Nancy Weinzinger	1979
David Wagner	1985	Carolyn Wells	1979
Debbie Wagner	1985	Leslie Ann Wells	1978
Barry Waitte	2001, '02	Jerry Wendland	1967
Bonnie Waldron	1998	David Wendler	1977
Jeannie Waldron	1998, '00	R. Craig Wesson	1973, '74
Charles Walker	1976	Bob West	1986
Gertrud Walker	1996	Buzzie West	1976, '79

Name of Finisher	Year(s) of Finishing	Name of Finisher	Year(s) of Finishing
Gene West	1973, '74, '75, '76, '77, '78, '79	Terry Williams	1965
		W. J. Williams	1968
Niels West, MD	1965, '66, '67	Blake Wilson	1978
Sharon Westergard	1996	Charles Wilson	1964
Darla Westlake	1991	Debora Wilson	1998
Debbie Wheeler	1970, '71, '72	George Wilson	1995
Shirley Wheeler	1971, '72	Jane Wilson	1983, '99
Charles Wheeler Jr.	1963	Keith Wilson	1970, '71
Raymond Wherry	1968	Robert Wilson	1981
Ross Whetten	1979	Sandee Wilson	1970
Barbara White	1968, '69, '72, '73, '74, '75, '78, '80, '82, '83, '84, '85, '86, '87, '88, '89, '90, '92, '93, '94, '96, '97, '98, '00, '01, '02, '03	Jeff Windeshausen	1985, '86, '92
		Jenine Windeshausen	1992
		Lori Windows	2002
		Elwin Wines	1970, '71, '72
		Lela Wines	1974
		Jim Winston	1983
		Cheryl Winter	2000
Clinton White	1972	Wiggy Wisdom	1974, '75H
Landon White	1971	Ernest Wiseley, DVM	1972, '73
Margaret White	1973	Juanice Wiseley	1973
Marta White	1987	Larry Witherow	1976
Sally White	1978, '02	Andy Witmer	1984
E. D. White Jr.	1978	Katy Woelfel	1992
Charlene Whitfield	1969, '70	Dineen Wold	1979
Marilyn Whitney	1986	Torgils Wold Jr.	1972, '78
Ronald Whitney, MD	1986	Dede Green Wolf	1980, '81, '82, '83, '84, '85, '86, '87, '88, '91
Kirsten Whitsett	1997, '99		
Jeanne Whittington	1970		
Susan Wiley	1980	Jacqueline Wolf	1959
Cinda Wilford	2000	Anna Wolfe	1999, '00
Ruth Will	1987	Jazon Wonders	1996, '99, '02
Anthony Williams	1996	Becky Wood	1977
Damaris Williams	1960	Denise Wood	1998
Donna Williams	1988, '89, '90	Sonya Wood	1986, '88, '91, '93, '94, '96, '98, '99, '00, '02, '03
Jaclane Williams	1980		
Jan Williams	1986		
Jim Williams	1986	Tom Woodall	1975
Kevin Williams	1982, '84	Laurie Wood-Gundlach	1992, '93, '94, '95, '96, '97
Linda Williams	1986		
Margaret Williams	1960	Douglas Woods	1960
R. M. Williams	1968	Nicole Jean Woodson	1999, '00
Sandra Knox Williams	1972, '73, '79, '81, '82, '83	Rick Woodson	2000
		Gordon Woolley	1961, '69
Sean Williams	1996	Terry Woolley	1989, '90

Name of Finisher	Year(s) of Finishing	Name of Finisher	Year(s) of Finishing
Marcia Worden	1984, '85, '86, '87	Janet Young	1967
Marsha Workman	1979	Jerry Young	1984, '95
Stephen Workman	1978, '79, '94	Lori Young	1978, '81, '82, '87
Sandy Worth	1978, '79	Robert Young, DVM	1976, '79, '80,
Anne Wren	1990		'81, '82, '84,
Henry Wright	1981		'85, '86
Kris Wright	2003	Sarah Zegers	1990
Carolyn Wurtz	1977, '78, '80	Joan Zeleny	1987
Diane Wyatt	1990	Greg Zelmar	1983
Cheryl Wylie	1977	Inta Ziedens	1987
James Wyllie	1979	John Zimmerman, DVM	1971, '72
Terry Yates	1993	Debbie Zinkl	1987
Dannan Yeagley	2002	Boyd Zontelli	1978, '79T, '81T,
Roger Yohe	1983, '84, '88,		'84, '85T, '98,
	'99, '01, '03		'99, '00
Betty Young	1990	Cheyenne Zontelli	1984, '86
Bonita Young	1978	Karyne Zontelli	1980, '83
David Young	1992	Shawn ZumBrunnen	1992
Don Young	1977	Robin Zuniga	1985

LEGEND

T = Tevis Cup winner
H = Haggin Cup winner
TH = winner of both

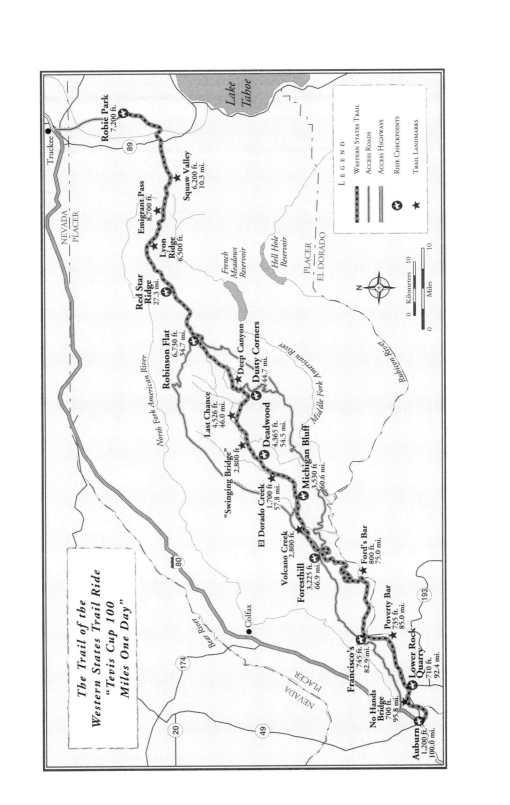

The Trail of the
Western States Trail Ride
"Tevis Cup 100
Miles One Day"

LEGEND

Western States Trail
Access Roads
Access Highways
Ride Checkpoints
Trail Landmarks

Kilometers
Miles

N

Lake Tahoe

Truckee

NEVADA
PLACER

Robie Park
7,200 ft.

89

Emigrant Pass
8,700 ft.

Squaw Valley
6,200 ft.
10.3 mi.

Lyon Ridge
6,500 ft.

Red Star Ridge
27.3 mi.

French Meadows Reservoir

Hell Hole Reservoir

PLACER
EL DORADO

Robinson Flat
6,730 ft.
34.7 mi.

Deep Canyon

Dusty Corners
44.7 mi.

Last Chance
4,526 ft.
46.0 mi.

Deadwood
4,365 ft.
54.5 mi.

Michigan Bluff
3,530 ft
60.6 mi.

North Fork American River

Middle Fork American River

Rubicon River

"Swinging Bridge"
2,800 ft.

El Dorado Creek
1,700 ft
57.8 mi.

Volcano Creek
2,800 ft.

Ford's Bar
800 ft.
75.0 mi.

Foresthill
3,225 ft.
66.9 mi.

Poverty Bar
735 ft.
85.0 mi.

193

Francisco's
745 ft.
82.9 mi.

Lower Rock Quarry
710 ft.
92.4 mi.

No Hands Bridge
700 ft.
95.8 mi.

Auburn
1,200 ft.
100.0 mi.

Colfax

Bear River

174

NEVADA
PLACER

20

49

80

❧ BIBLIOGRAPHY ❧

BOOKS:

California Department of Food & Agriculture Resource Directory 2002. "Agricultural Statistical Review." Sacramento: California Department of Food & Agriculture, 2002.

Genini, Ronald and Richard Hitchman. *Romualdo Pacheco: A Californio in Two Eras.* San Francisco: The Book Club of California, 1985.

Gilbert, Bil. *Westering Man: The Life of Joseph Walker.* New York: Atheneum, 1983.

Hall, Hal. *The Western States Trail Guide.* Self-published, 1992.

Hill, Mary. *Geology of the Sierra Nevada.* Berkeley: University of California Press, 1975.

Johnson, Allen and Dumas Malone, eds. *Dictionary of American Biography.* New York: Charles Scribner's Sons (1933, 1967): 384.

Scott, Edward B. *Squaw Valley: Pictorial History of the Squaw Valley-Sierra Nevada Region.* Lake Tahoe: Sierra-Tahoe Publishing Co., 1960.

Suhr, Julie. *Ten Feet Tall, Still: The Very Personal 70-Year Odyssey of a Woman Who Still Pursues Her Childhood Passion.* Scotts Valley, CA: Marinera Publishing, 2002.

Wilson, Bill. *Challenging the Mountains: The Life and Times of Wendell T. Robie.* Newcastle, CA: Arrowhead Classics, Inc., 1998.

Publications:

Benbow, Judy. "A History of Innovation: The Auburn Ski Club." *Sierra Heritage*, Winter 1982.

Brant, John. "Mountain Man." *Runner's World*, July 2003.

Carter, Dave. "Pioneers of Winter Sports: The Auburn Ski Club." *Sierra Heritage*, February 1999.

Chandler, Robert. "Wells Fargo Medals." *The Journal of the Pacific Coast Numismatic Society*, No. 37, October 1993.

Christie, Sarah. "The Arabians of Rush Creek Ranch." *Western Horse*, March 1998.

"Dashing Young Rider Covers 200 Miles in Less Than Half a Day." *San Francisco Chronicle*, July 10, 1923.

Elliott, Marnye. "McChesney Wins the Tevis Cup." *The Chronicle of the Horse,* August 10, 1991.

———. "Smith and Harry Score Double Tevis Cup Wins." *The Chronicle of the Horse*, September 25, 1992.

———. "Saxx Proves His Mettle at the Tevis Cup." *The Chronicle of the Horse*, September 3, 1993.

———. "Knoch Wins Second Straight Tevis Cup." *The Chronicle of the Horse*, August 19, 1994.

———. "Mackay-Smith and Knoch Share Memorable Tevis Cup Experience." *The Chronicle of the Horse*, September 8, 1995.

———. "No Hands Bridge Will Be Opened for Tevis Cup." *The Chronicle of the Horse*, June 28, 1996.

———. "McChesney Sweeps the Tevis Cup's Awards for the Second Time." *The Chronicle of the Horse*, August 30, 1996.

———. "Tevis Cup Makes a Perfect Birthday Present for Marcia Smith." *The Chronicle of the Horse*, August 8, 1997.

———. " 'Potato' Harvests His First Tevis Cup Victory." *The Chronicle of the Horse*, September 4, 1998.

———. "Reens Earns Win of a Lifetime in Tevis Cup." *The Chronicle of the Horse*, August 4, 2000.

———. "The Third Tevis Cup's a Charm for Smith." *The Chronicle of the Horse*, August 24, 2001.

———. "Richardson Charges to Contentious Tevis Cup Victory." *The Chronicle of the Horse*, August 9, 2002.

———. "Reynolds Joins Elite Company With Tevis Cup Scores." *The Chronicle of the Horse*, August 8, 2003.

Federal Wilderness Areas in Sierra Nevada: www.wilderness.net/index.cfm?fuse=NWPS

Graetzer, Dan. "History of the Marathon." http://ctc.coin.org/marathon.html

Hughey, Richard. "Jedediah Smith Blazed Trail Across Sierra" and "Explorer Joseph Walker Discovers Yosemite Valley." www.mtdemocrat.com

Livingston, Robert D. "Lloyd Tevis: Corporate Raider." *Sacramento History Journal*, Vol. II, No. 3, Summer 2002.

"Lloyd Tevis Passes Away After a Brief Illness." *San Francisco Chronicle*, No. 10, July 25, 1899.

Mackay-Smith, Alexander. "Trail Ride at Olympic Level." *The Chronicle of the Horse*, August 24, 1962.

Peck, Linda H. "James Ben Ali Haggin" from the "History of Kentucky." Louisville, KY: J. S. Clarke Publishing Company, 1928.

Phelps, Alonza A. M. "California's Representative Men," "James Ben Ali Haggin; Lloyd Tevis," San Francisco: A.L. Bancroft and Company, Publishers (1881): 325–328.

"Pony Express Rider Will Tevis: Iron Man of the Age." Sonora, CA: *Union Democrat*, Vol. XXVI, No. 2, No. 302, July 1959.

Runner's World Web site. Brief profile on Tim Twietmeyer and 2003 Western States Run. www.runnersworld.com

Spilsbury, Duane. "The Tevis Cup Ride." *California Horse Review*, June 1984.

Stewart, Bill and Wendell Robie, letters to the editor. *Western Horseman,* February 1950, March 1950, October 1950, date unknown 1951.

Suhr, Julie. "The Weight is Over." *Ride! Magazine,* April 1999.

Western States Trail Foundation. *Tevis Forum* (newsletter) and annual "State of the Ride and Trail Report," 1967, November 1998, 1999, Spring 2000, 2001, Spring 2002, 2003.

INTERVIEWS:

Interview with Gordon Ainsleigh.

Interview with Richard Barsaleau.

Interview with David Blaikie.

Interview with Gary Carlson, DVM.

Interview with Jim Edwards, DVM.

Interview with Denny Emerson.

Interview with Pat Fox.

Interview with Roxanne Greene.

Interview with Hal Hall.

Interview with Stan Jensen.

Interview with Scott Jurek.

Interview with Erin McChesney Klentos.

Interview with Debbie Lyons.

Interview with Patricia Fox Nuccio.

Interview with Kathie Perry.

Interview with Ken "Cowman" Shirk.

Interview with Marcia Smith.

Interview with Larry Suddjian.

Interview with Betty Veal.

Interview with Jack Veal.

Interview with Shannon Weil.

Interview with Boyd Zontelli.